The Critics and the Ballad

THE CRITICS

&

THE BALLAD

READINGS

SELECTED and EDITED by

MacEdward Leach

AND

Tristram P. Coffin

SOUTHERN ILLINOIS UNIVERSITY PRESS

CARBONDALE

PREFACE

WHILE books such as William J. Entwistle's *European Balladry,* Gordon Gerould's *The Ballad of Tradition,* and M. J. C. Hodgart's *The Ballads* are essential handbooks for any study of folksong, there has long remained a need for a book of readings to supplement the many collections of ballads on the market. The present volume is designed to satisfy that need. The essays have been carefully selected to make available in one spot some of the basic studies that previously lay scattered through inconvenient-to-use journals. They offer the reader a clear view into the major areas of ballad scholarship, introduce him to the latest ideas in the field of folksong, and give him an insight into ballads that goes far beyond amateur enthusiasm and entertainment. They are written by internationally recognized authorities and in each case have become standard statements of the particular thesis they argue.

All the essays deal with theory, that is, with ballad origins, variation, transmission, and artistic atmosphere, and for the most part concentrate on Anglo-American tradition. Each essay, in the opinion of the editors, is important and at the same time difficult for students and seriously interested amateurs to locate at a moment's notice. No effort has been made to include materials that are presently in wide distribution or deal with the more technical aspects of ballad work, such as collecting, ways of annotating music, the mores of informants. Nor has it seemed necessary to reprint chapters from successful books such as Louise Pound's *Poetic Origins and the Ballad* or Gordon Gerould's *The Ballad of Tradition.*

The readings advocate no one point of view. Rather they bring forth in a sort of "symposium" conflicting ideas, theses the editors don't support, and even remarks that are inconclusive. In this way, it is hoped that *The Critics and the Ballad* will introduce its readers to the intellectual ferment in a subject that is frequently dismissed as mere entertainment. It is hoped too that the volume may inspire the authors as well as their colleagues to further insights and investigations.

MacE. L.

T. P. C.

ACKNOWLEDGMENTS

PERMISSION to reprint the essays in this book has been kindly granted by the following journals and publishers: The English Association, *Harvard Studies and Notes in Philology,* the *Journal of American Folklore, The Journal of the English Folk Dance and Song Society, Publications of the Modern Language Association, Southern Folklore Quarterly,* and *Western Folklore.* The editors are particularly grateful to Nancy Leach for her efforts at the typewriter.

JOSEPH W. HENDRON came to prominence as a ballad authority in 1936 with the publication of *A Study of Ballad Rhythm* (Princeton, 1936). He has continued to be active as a scholar and collector, and at present teaches English literature at Western Maryland College. "The Scholar and the Ballad Singer" first appeared in *The CEA Critic,* XIII (1951), 1 f., and is published here as it was reprinted in part in the *Southern Folklore Quarterly,* XVIII (1954), 139–46.

THELMA G. JAMES is a former President of the American Folklore Society and an ardent collector of the mass of foreign folklore that exists in her native Detroit. As a teacher of folksong at Wayne State University, however, she has maintained a scholarly interest in the ballad. Her article, condensed here from the *Journal of American Folklore,* XLVI (1933), 51–68, has become a classic in that it is the first soundly documented American refutation of "Child Worship."

FRANCIS B. GUMMERE (1855–1919) is still one of the truly controversial figures in ballad scholarship. A student of F. J. Child at Harvard, he developed the now famous "communal theory" of ballad scholarship and presented it in a number of articles and books, the most famous of which are *Old English Ballads* (Boston, 1894) and *The Popular Ballad* (Boston, 1907). Although his theories are generally discredited today, there are still scholars who believe one of his main tenets, that folk groups can compose narrative material spontaneously. The following essay, which first appeared in 1897 in the "Child Memorial Volume" of *Harvard Studies and Notes in Philology*, V, 40–56, is a pretty good summary of Gummere's ideas.

GEORGE MCKNIGHT (1871–1951) was for many years a prominent medievalist at Ohio State University. His writings on the Middle English romances, on Middle English humorous tales, and on Teutonic grammar are still widely read. In the article printed here, he is taking issue with an essay written by Louise Pound in the *Publications of the Modern Language Association*, XXXIV (1919), 360–400. Dr. Pound (1872–1958) had gained fame as a vigorous opponent of the Gummere communalists. In a series of articles, later developed into the book *Poetic Origins and the Ballad* (New York, 1921), she demonstrated convincingly that the ballad is a late medieval form, that it is too urbane to have been developed spontaneously by ignorant groups, and that its origins were undoubtedly with individual composers. Her remarks on the relationship of the ballad to the dance argue that narrative song has seldom, if ever, been used as an accompaniment for dancing. McKnight's comments on this thesis appeared originally in *Modern Language Notes*, XXXV (1920), 464–73.

ALEXANDER KEITH is best known in America for his editing of Gavin Greig's *Last Leaves of Traditional Ballads and Ballad Airs* (Aberdeen, 1925). He is also distinguished, however, by his work on Burns and folksong. At one time a newspaperman with the *Aberdeen Daily Journal*, he has devoted his efforts in recent years to a study of Aberdeen Angus cattle and in 1958 published a history, *The Aberdeen Angus Breed*, with James R. Barclay. He is currently President of the Aberdeen Chamber of Commerce. The article printed here first appeared in *Essays and Studies by Members of the English Association*, XII, 100–119 (Oxford, 1926).

PHILLIPS BARRY (1880–1937) collected folk songs avidly from about 1903 until his death. His energy and enthusiasm and that of such devoted followers as Helen Hartness Flanders and Fannie Eckstrom, made New England one of the most thoroughly collected of all areas. His articles in the *Bulletin of the Folk Song Society of the Northeast*, which he produced almost single-handed, made that journal invaluable, while his notes and remarks in the *New Green Mountain Songster* (New Haven, 1939) and in *British Ballads from Maine* (New Haven, 1929) are models for the anthologists. The essay published here has never before appeared in print. It was given by Dr.

Barry to Annabel Morris Buchanan and is reprinted here with her kind permission.

BERTRAND H. BRONSON of the University of California (Berkeley) is one of the very best of a fine group of American folk musicologists. His monumental study of *The Traditional Tunes of the Child Ballads,* now being published by the Princeton University Press, is perhaps the most significant folklore study of this century. Dr. Bronson is also noted for a series of penetrating articles on folk music that have been appearing in folklore and musical journals during the last twenty years. The present article first appeared in the old *California Folklore Quarterly* (now *Western Folklore*), III (1944), 185–207.

SAMUEL P. BAYARD, a professor at Pennsylvania State University, is considered to be one of the top folk musicologists in the world. Author of a number of significant articles and the book *Hill Country Tunes* (Philadelphia, 1944), he has made a steady effort to educate his colleagues to the fact that the music of the ballads exists, wanders, and varies independently of the texts. The essay reprinted here is from the *Journal of American Folklore,* LXIII (1950), 1–44.

CHARLES L. SEEGER, who has held prominent positions in musicology ranging from a professorship at the University of California (Berkeley) to Chief of the Division of Music and Visual Arts of the Pan American Union, is the author of *Harmonic Structure and Elementary Composition* (with E. G. Strickler, Berkeley, 1916) and *Folk Song U. S. A.* (with the Lomaxes and Ruth Seeger, New York, 1947). He is also a musician and composer of note. In the following article from the *Journal of American Folklore,* LXII (1949), 107–13, he outlines the situation in the study of folk music in America and then suggests the norms in the relationship between the amateur and the professional approaches to the subject.

GEORGE R. STEWART, JR., who is Professor of English at the University of California (Berkeley), is well known for his works on Western Americana and English versification. On his bibliography are such well-known titles as *Names on the Land* and *American Ways of Life.* He is also the author of a study of Bret Harte. The article included here appeared in *Publications of the Modern Language Association,* XL (1925), 933–62. More detailed developments of Professor Stewart's ideas can be found in his *Modern Metrical Technique as Illustrated by Ballad Meter* (New York, 1922) and *The Technique of English Verse* (New York, 1930).

HOLGER OLOF NYGARD is at present Associate Professor of English at Duke University. He is a recognized authority on the Scandinavian ballads and their Anglo-American counterparts and has published a group of significant articles in this general area. The article printed here first appeared in the *Journal of American Folklore*, LXV (1952), 1–12, and has since been incorporated into Dr. Nygard's extensive treatment of textual variation, *The Ballad of Heer Halewijn* (Knoxville, 1958).

ANNE G. GILCHRIST (1864–1954) built an international reputation as a folklorist and musicologist without ever publishing a book. Scholars from all over the world sought her advice on problems in folksong or called on her amazing memory to help them locate tunes. In addition, her work on classification of pentatonic and hexatonic tunes and on American revival music blazed trails that Cecil Sharp and George Pullen Jackson were to travel to fame. The study of "Lambkin" was originally published in the *Journal of the English Folk Dance and Song Society*, I (1932), 1–17.

W. EDSON RICHMOND, the Editor of *Midwest Folklore* and the compiler of the American Folklore Society's *Annual Bibliography*, is known here and abroad as a ballad authority. Recently, much of his attention has been concentrated on Norwegian folksong and its international relationships. However, the article below deals with Anglo-American matter. It first appeared in *Southern Folklore Quarterly*, XV (1951), 159–70 and treats the effects of print on oral tradition, indicating the steady influence the transcribers have had on the ballad texts.

Scotsman JOHN SPEIRS has built an international reputation as a medievalist. He has been on the faculty of the University of Riga in Latvia, at the University of Cairo in Egypt, and is at present at the University of Exeter in England. His books, *The Scots Literary Tradition* (Toronto, 1940), *Chaucer the Maker* (London, 1951), and *Medieval English Poetry* (London and New York, 1957), are widely used in this country and in Britain. His essay first appeared in *Scrutiny*, IV (1935), 35–45.

TRISTRAM P. COFFIN teaches at the University of Pennsylvania and is the author of two reference works, *The British Traditional Ballad in North America* (Philadelphia, 1950) and *An Analytical Index to the "Journal of American Folklore"* (Philadelphia, 1958). He published the article printed here in the *Journal of American Folklore*, LXX (1957), 208–14.

CONTENTS

i

****

BALLAD ORIGINS

&

BALLAD DEFINITIONS

———

✳✳✳✳✳✳✳✳✳✳✳✳✳✳✳✳✳✳✳✳✳

The Scholar and the Ballad Singer

JOSEPH W. HENDRON

CENTURIES ago Sir Philip Sidney made the famous observation: "I never heard the olde song of Percy and Douglas that I found not my heart mooved more then with a trumpet." Not so long ago a Georgia mountain farmer remarked to Alan Lomax, "Every time I hear 'Barbara Allen' it makes the hair rise on my head."

Notice that the emotional responses are roughly identical, though the two men stand worlds asunder in time, space, social position, and cultural environment. There is no doubt, from these and many other recorded observations, that the charm of a great ballad is human rather than fashional. Scholar and mountaineer both love a ballad when they hear one.

Yet they have seldom thought about them in the same way. Through the centuries scholars have had a typical habit of looking at ballads from a literary, if not a downright bookish point of view, an attitude unknown among the people from whose singing voices all traditional ballad texts have been learned or recorded. What a ballad is "supposed to be" has never been an easy question to answer categorically. And it has not grown easier. Nowadays students of the subject are finding it necessary to revise their ideas concerning the position of balladry in American culture. Things have been happening. The old picture puzzle has been recut and shuffled. Let us try to piece together a few of the easier-looking combinations.

The fashion of regarding *ballad* and *poem* as interchangeable terms was established in eighteenth-century England by such men as Addison, Percy, and Scott, who (like Selden and Pepys before them) worked mostly from manuscripts and were interested in collecting literary antiquities. The characteristic attitude of these early collectors was quickly caught by the learned world and has been typical of it ever since.

Bishop Percy expressed the attitude neatly in his 1794 preface: "In a polished age like the present I am sensible that many of these reliques of antiquity will require great allowance to be made for them. Yet they have, for the most part, a pleasing simplicity and many other graces, which, in the opinion of no mean critics, have been thought to compensate for the want of higher beauties, and if they do not dazzle the imagination are frequently found to interest the heart." Addison was less apologetic. Said *The Spectator:* "An ordinary song or ballad that is the delight of the common people cannot fail to please all such readers as are not unqualified for the entertainment by their affectation or ignorance." Notice the word *readers*. As a rule, early collectors thought it advisable to "correct" or "improve" their texts in passages where they looked too outrageously inelegant. The irascible Joseph Ritson was a century ahead of his time in protesting against such creative archaeology.

During these early times published collections of much doctored-up "ancient British music" also appeared in considerable number. On first thought it seems strange that this music has made so little impression on posterity in comparison with the great influence of the poetic texts. It becomes less puzzling if we remember that this folk material came to the educated classes by way of books, and that only a minute fraction of the people who can read language have ever been able to read musical scores.

It seems likely too that the great Romantic poets indirectly aided and abetted the literary slant by welcoming balladry into the belletristic drawing room. Their adaptations were notably successful and contagious. No one who has enjoyed the magic of the "Ancient Mariner" (and who hasn't?) would look down his nose at a ballad poem. Add to this the work of Scott, Burns, and Wordsworth in assimilating ballad structure and idiom into the mainstream of learned literary tradition. Consider the number of well-known poems all the way from Scott to Masefield, in America as well as England, that are based on ballad conceptions. It would be strange if the combined impact of this work on the popular imagination would not produce an unconscious turn toward the poetic, or nonmusical orientation.

The effect of Child's great compilation must not be left out of account. Its prestige ran so high that for decades the "Child ballads" were virtually synonymous in learned circles with balladry itself and in some academic quarters still are. Child worked in a scientific spirit. What he might have done with the tunes if he had had access to more of them we can't be sure. As it happened, though, he printed very few of them and the effect of his great work was to popularize and perpetuate the poetic interest in balladry which the great scholar had legitimately inherited.

Despite heavy attacks the literary attitude has shown great vitality in our century. Even today the word ballad calls to many educated minds not a folksong but a printed poetic text, not meant to be sung or read as music but meant to be recited or read as verse, in the same manner as one would read "The Charge of the Light Brigade." Robert W. Gordon's *Folksongs of America*, published in 1938, contains no tunes. In a recently published college dictionary, *ballad* is still defined as primarily a poem, though adapted for singing. The typical college anthology of today gives scant attention to the melodic significance of its ballad material.

Musically-minded scholars of our generation have tried hard to combat this view, and with considerable success. They argue that the mere verbal text is by no means the true ballad, being analogous rather to a fossil relic; that the native beauty and peculiar charm of traditional balladry can never be appreciated apart from its music. They are, of course, right. No one familiar with balladry in its varied aspects could reasonably disagree with their contention.

Yet, despite the obvious validity of such a claim, the venerable fossils are clearly defensible on their own ground. Certainly it would be a cultural loss if the reading of folk poetry, old style, were to be generally abandoned as obsolete. Verse abolitionists and depreciators should be reminded, for one thing, that a large and well preserved corpus of ballad verse exists whose music is irrecoverably lost. Some of Child's paragons have not been equalled in quality among later-recorded variants. "Geordie," "Lord Thomas and Fair Annet," and dozens like them, are strong and handsome poems, as mellow and hard as seasoned oak wood. And their value is, and must continue to be, strictly poetic.

There is no doubt that editors and critics of the past have worked a sore injustice upon ballad music. Its relative merits have not been adequately understood. The genuine tunes until recently have not been made accessible, so that for generations readers of musical inclination were not accorded the privilege of exercising an intelligent choice between ballad song and poetry, or better yet of enjoying both forms. It was time for a new deal; but the preference for the musical performance is by no means universal, and the bare texts have abundantly earned the right to be regarded as an artistically respectable and thoroughly legitimate, though derivative, form of the ballad.

The resources of ballad poetry, it might be added, have not yet generously been tapped. In Child's thesaurus alone, the range of highgrade texts is actually much larger than anyone would suppose from the anthological repetition of a restricted favorite group well represented by such undeniably beautiful specimens as "Edward," "Sir Patrick Spens," and "Lord Randal." Few seem to realize that the pages of more recent British and American collections, too, hold an attractive inventory of texts, many of them comparable to Child's in poetic worth, and likely to offer in addition an easier vocabulary along with more accurate authenticity. Some excellent British ones, like "Bruton Town" and "Early, Early in the Spring," are not represented in the Child volumes.

It is well understood that scholars are primarily responsible for making the poetic ballad what it is today in popular esteem. Not so well known is the extent of their responsibility likewise for the current popularity of musical presentation, and on all levels from the graduate seminar to the juke-box. The availability of this music as well as the recognition of its value must largely be regarded as the result of learned enterprise in which, strange as it may seem, English teachers of all ranks and descriptions have played an indispensable role. Professors Kittredge and Wendell of Harvard, Gordon Gerould of Princeton, Alphonso Smith and A. K. Davis of Virginia, J. H. Cox of West Virginia, Reed Smith of South Carolina, Frank Dobie and John Lomax of Texas—this is a partial list even among prominent names, but it will serve as a rough indication of the scale on which this effort has been moving forward. A great deal has been accomplished, needless to say, by inconspicuous teachers who love folk music and are willing to share their experiences with students.

Ballads are folk songs, but who are the folk singers? In old England the recognized status of the peasant reduced the difficulties of answering this question. Prior to the eighteenth century the British educated classes seem to have been virtually ignorant of folksong, or else almost totally indifferent to it. Perhaps rigid social barriers prevented cultural exchange of this kind. At all events, the survival of British ballads practically everywhere in the United States seems a fair indication that a high proportion of the early settlers knew them and cherished them. Wherever these British and Scotch and Scotch-Irish settlers have been allowed, or obliged by environment, to continue their traditional modes of life, we also find the old ballads flourishing in the purity of their ancient idiom, both of language and melody. The Southern mountaineers are the most famous and publicized group of this sort. The early collector Cecil Sharp, a Britisher himself, immediately noticed that "their speech is English, not American, and from the number of expressions that they use which have long been obsolete elsewhere, and the old-fashioned way in which they pronounce many of their words, it is clear that they are talking the language of a past day . . ." Back-country New England is another region in which English songs are very well preserved. In America we must go to singers of this type to find English ballads in their more archaic state of survival. Wherever the settlers were subjected to radical linguistic or environmental change, their ballads tend to be modified or forgotten. For example, one version of "Early, Early in the Spring," which I collected from an islander off the coast of Maine, shows the setting, speech, and modality of old English folksong; another variant of the song which I got from a Nevada cowhand shows Western setting and melody and cowboy characters—a beautiful example of extreme regional variation. Even the title is changed to "Mexico Trail."

In the United States, where social democracy allows considerable intermingling of population ingredients, the status of the folk singer cannot rigidly be defined. But we can roughly summarize his generic characteristics. (1) He lives in a rural or isolated region which (2) shuts him off from prolonged schooling and contact with industrialized urban civilization, so that (3) his cultural training is oral rather than visual. If you want a good psychological explanation of ballad origins, imagine yourself living in a community stripped of theater, motion pictures, orchestras, night clubs, radio, television, books, magazines, newspapers, big-time athletics, and mechanical transportation; where for recreation you and your neighbors would have to turn to whatever resources you had in your own memories and imagination. Such was the lot of the Old World rustic; and such, with certain modifications, has been the condition of American pioneers, lumbermen, sailors, cowboys, miners, share-croppers, mountaineers, and dirt farmers. Such people have been, and still are, the folk singers par excellence.

But their sons and daughters have been drawn by thousands into the towns and cities, into the armed forces, and into schools and colleges. These people, for one or two generations, are likely to remember their parents' or grandparents' songs and perhaps sing them as well. Educated persons in towns, cities, and on college campuses have furnished modern collectors with considerable material. Here is a secondary fringe of folk singers, or at least quasi folk-singers, to which the reader may himself belong. Anyone who has ever sung from memory "Frog Went a-Courtin' " or "London Bridge Is Falling Down" is a folksinger to that extent. A common professional experience is to be greeted, following a lecture, by a smiling lady who says: "I thought I didn't know any folksongs, but Grandma McClintic used to sing 'Barbara Allen.' I still remember two or three verses of it. And our colored maid used to sing 'Roll, Jordan, Roll' in the kitchen. I still know that one by heart." The tradition in our country has tended to follow family lines. The songs may be cherished heirlooms, and to judge from the records of collectors the womenfolk have been more interested, or at least more articulate, custodians of these heirlooms than their husbands and brothers.

It is evident, in a word, that the term folk singer has become more indefinite in application. We may safely discount the picturesque hallucination of screen and radio, that ballads are a monopoly of "hillbillies," a race of gaunt, bearded primitives, drinking whiskey out of tin dippers and singing ballads when they ain't feudin'.

Tin Pan Alley, by all indications, has fallen into something of a creative decline; even the juke-boxes are far gone in nostalgic and Western repertories. Meanwhile across the land has swept a great popular interest in traditional music. Square dance and folksong are reaching a currency undreamed of by students and advocates of these ancient arts two decades ago. The double reversal of trends probably adds up to the most significant phenomenon in popular music of our generation. Dozens of authentic collections from various regions of the country have been published, many equipped with excellent critical introductions. Many hundreds of phonographic recordings are available. Ballad singers like Burl Ives have become famous in radio and motion pictures. Well informed articles have appeared in popular magazines like the *Country Gentleman* and *Holiday*. The concert stage (including austere Carnegie Hall) has become hospitable to the tunes of the sailor and the mountaineer. Folksong themes are being utilized in Broadway shows and have inspired contemporary fine-art music such as Kurt Weill's opera *Down in the Valley*. As a result of exposure to genuine folk music via stage and mechanical dispersion, people everywhere, on all cultural levels, are acquiring a conception of balladry roughly similar to that held by collectors or by the folk singers themselves.

The impetus behind the present folksong movement seems to converge from several directions. Folklore societies, often with university connections, have contributed a dynamic share, and academic interest has also been generated by objective studies. The work of field collectors during the past thirty or forty years has, of course, been a paramount factor. It was Cecil Sharp who in 1917 opened up the abundant resources of the Southern Appalachian mountaineers. Following Sharp's pioneering labors the 1920's yielded a bumper crop of splendid collections. Barry's *British Ballads from Maine*, Cox's *Folksongs of the South*, Davis' *Traditional Ballads of Virginia*, Mackenzie's *Ballads and Sea Songs from Nova Scotia*, Scarborough's *On the Trail of Negro Folksong*, Smith's *South Carolina Ballads*, Sandburg's *The American Songbag*, Randolph's *Ozark Folksongs*, Belden's *Folksongs of Missouri*, and the Frank C. Brown *Collection of North Carolina Folklore* (Volumes II and III) are fair samples of this vintage, and numerous books of comparable quality have appeared since. To John and Alan Lomax must go our gratitude not only for discovering the cowboy songs but for their large share in acquainting the American public with the range and beauty of other indigenous material. These indefatigable collectors have placed thousands of field recordings in the Library of Congress, whose Division of Music has been rendering an exemplary service. Many people today collect folk music just as a personal hobby. The folksong movement is great and still growing. Scholars have not furnished seed or soil, but the rich harvest could not have matured without the stimulus of scholarly pollination. Our contemporary situation, gradual and continuous in building up, does not show the earmarks of a passing fad. It looks like an important cultural movement, one in which scholar and ballad singer have been collaborating in a healthy and significant fashion.

Of course there is more to the story. It was not accidental that town-folk were first attracted to folk music about the time of World War I, or that the present flowering has been coincident with another war and the stormy days that have followed. Evidently our response has been, in one sense, a natural product of heightened national and folk consciousness. North Americans have been struggling to preserve their cultural heritage, and what was more natural than to turn to their own cultural inner core. Folksong is the voice of the people in the deepest sense in which that phrase can have meaning. It is not class-conscious or élite or obsequious or partisan—just basically and honestly human, an example of a civilized use of language. It was natural, too, in times of stress, that preference should somewhat diminish for the relative shallowness of the hit-parade bag of tricks.

Such a climate of feeling plus a recently deepened sense of national maturity must also largely account for the current swing toward native American tradition and away from the old emphasis on the British. Earlier in the century few learned people took cowboy songs and such native products seriously. All this is changed now. Recent general folksong publications are revealing: *Singing America* (1940), *A Treasury of American Song* (1940), and *Folksong, U. S. A.* (1947) have gone native almost completely. Record albums and radio programs, sensitive to audience reaction, reflect less extreme but significant ratios. The American community has lived long enough and successfully enough to have grown into an authentic veneration for its own legends. Chanties, spirituals, work songs, once a natural part of occupational life, have attained a stature in the imagination that only the passing of time could bring about.

The learned world first got acquainted with folksong through balladry, a fact that provides one explanation of the familiar scholar's dichotomy of ballads, on one side, and other types of folksong on the other. But a further accounting should also be considered. There is some justice in Robert Gordon's reference to ballads as the "aristocrats of the folksong world." To the educated mind the ballad doubtless carries a stronger appeal because of its superior dramatic power, its more intellectualized content, and its wider variety of subject matter. "Deep River" is just as moving a performance as "Lord Randal," but it lacks "Lord Randal's" strangely modern-looking trick of telling a story by implication, so that the hearer is allowed the pleasure of discovering the meaning for himself. Curious, how the ballad makers, following their native avoidance of abstraction, have hit upon devices of narrative techniques which in our generation are reckoned as highly sophisticated.

As late as 1922 a prominent critic saw fit to write that "American folksong as a whole, has been imported from the Old World." Today such a statement seems grotesque. Thanks to an adventurous past and a heterogeneous population, America is probably richer in folksong than any other nation. Think of the variety. Pioneer songs of the Western trek. Chanties from the seven seas. Musical adventure yarns from lumberjacks, canal men, and railroad builders. Negro work chants whose hypnotic rhythm and powerful expressiveness can never be understood from printed words on a sheet of paper. Love lyrics, some with the delicate charm of "Pretty Saro," others ironical or whimsical like "Old Smokey." Songs of sorrow and passion from the jet-black Negroes of the Mississippi delta and the Brazos River Bottom. Ballads in abundance, some still redolent of Old-World atmosphere, some transformed by the new environment almost beyond recognition. Dance tunes, prison and outlaw songs. French Canadian and Mexican melodies with hemispheric popularity. And consider the quality of these songs: the tremendous gusto and vitality of the chanties, the narrative artistry of a great ballad, the passionate intensity of both White and Negro spirituals. The catalog could go on. I list some of the important types only to locate the ballad more visibly in the setting where it belongs. In contemporary America, balladry, both British and native, appears as one surpassingly brilliant strand, but one only, in a rich and highly varied texture of traditional music.

✳✳✳✳✳✳✳✳✳✳✳✳✳✳✳✳✳✳✳✳✳

The English and Scottish Popular Ballads of Francis J. Child

THELMA G. JAMES

THE third edition of *The English and Scottish Popular Ballads* edited by Professor Francis James Child in 1882–98 suggests two interesting problems: first, was Professor Child adhering to a fixed principle in selecting ballads for inclusion? Second, is it possible to derive a definition of the ballad from a study of this collection? Whether he followed a fixed notion is a matter of uncertainty among critics. Miss Louise Pound in her *Poetic Origins and the Ballad* declares that he fluctuated in his decisions: "The similarity in style of the pieces he included was the chief guide of Professor Francis James Child in his selection for his collection of English and Scottish Ballads . . . He would not have altered his decision concerning so many pieces had the test of style been so dependable as is usually assumed." [1] Dean Walter Morris Hart, on the contrary, feels that "the significant fact is that for at least forty years Professor Child retained without essential change his conception of the traditional ballad as a distinct literary type." [2] Professor Gummere thought: "It is clear that the notion of a traditional ballad existed in a very exact shape for Professor Child when one thinks of the hosts he rejected." [3]

A re-examination of the material included in the first and third editions [4] should resolve these differing opinions. In this study, the method was: first, to determine what was omitted from the first edition in compiling the third; second, to examine the new material added to the third edition, particularly those ballads available to Professor Child in 1858 (first edition) which were not utilized until 1882; third, to examine, as far as possible by means of Professor Child's own comments, his reasons for these exclusions and inclusions; and finally, to attempt to reach some conclusion concerning the principles governing the selection. The task was complicated by the fact that in the third edition Professor Child completely ignored the two earlier editions. Further, the inconvenient numbering of the pieces in the first edition makes cross reference possible only through titles, which are more trouble than help. For example, one finds "The Enchanted Ring" under "Bonny Bee Home," and the "Birth of Robin Hood" under "Willie and Earl Richard's Daughter." Nor is it always easy to say whether a ballad has been included or excluded; for instance, "Waly, Waly, gin Love be Bonny" is given in an appendix to "Lord Jamie Douglas"; "The Gaberlunzie Man" is in an appendix to "The Jolly Beggar"; the "Playe of Robin Hood" in an appendix to "Robin Hood and the Potter." Does the assignment of such pieces to an appendix signify their inclusion, exclusion, or merely a dubious compromise bringing into question Professor Gummere's belief in the "very exact shape" of Professor Child's conception of a ballad?

In the Preface to his first edition, Professor Child says of it: "It contains nearly all that is known to be left to us of the ancient ballads of England and Scotland, with a liberal selection of those which are of a later date. Of traditional ballads preserved in a variety of forms, all the important versions are given, and no genuine relic of olden minstrelsy, however mutilated or debased in its descent to our times, has been on that account excluded, if it was thought to be of value to the student of prose fiction . . . [The purpose was] to adhere to the originals as they stand in the *printed* collections" (italics supplied). In the Preface to the first volume of this third edition he wrote: "It was my wish not to begin to print *The English and Scottish Ballads* until this unrestricted title should be justified by my having at my command *every* valuable copy of every known ballad." In 1880, when the second edition was printed, some change in the general plan was already in Mr. Child's mind (although his definition of the ballad was not necessarily concerned), for he says in that Preface: ". . . the popular ballad deserves much more liberal treatment. Many of the older ones are mutilated, many more are miserably corrupted, but as long as any traces of their originals are left, they are worthy of attention and have received it."

In his article, Dean Hart says that 115 ballads were omitted from the first edition and my figures agree with his. On the basis of Professor Child's comments, these 115 ballads fall into the following divisions: 9 (numbers 1–9) were rejected as having been unduly "edited" by modern editors; 16 (10–25) as romances; 41 (26–66) as of nonpopular origin from broadsides, stalls, minstrels, rerhymed literary plots; 10 (67–76) as translations of foreign parallels rather than native ballads; 4 (77–80) as types of ballads on nonpopular subjects; 16 (81–96) as lyric types lacking a narrative element; 18 (97–115) as simple narrative poetry lacking ballad style.[5] Dean Hart summarizes: "It is not difficult to see why the 115 ballads are excluded from the later collection, and one gets the impression that, had Professor Child chosen to enforce the conception of the ballad which he had already in mind, most of them would have been excluded from the earlier collection as well. This impression is deepened by an examination of the comments scattered through the ballads."

The ninety ballads included for the first time in the third edition fall into two groups: first, those 37 ballads which were not available in 1858; and second, those 53 ballads which were available, but which were withheld until the third edition. Obviously no change in Professor Child's definition of the ballad can be deduced from his inclusion in the third edition of the 37 ballads to which he had not previously had access. If any change is to be noted, we shall find it in the 53 ballads which Professor Child knew in 1858 and rejected, although he later included them in 1882. It is highly significant that 35 of these 53 ballads were available in 1858 only through Buchan, an editor of whose methods Professor Child had grave suspicion. Only 9 Buchan texts were added to the third edition without confirmation from other sources. Even in the preparation of his first edition, Professor Child had serious distrust of the Buchan texts, for he says in that Preface: "Some resolution has been exercised and much disgust suppressed, in retaining certain pieces from Buchan's collection, so strong is the suspicion, that, after having been procured from very inferior sources, they were tampered with by the editor."

In the head notes to the third edition Professor Child seldom has more than scathing comment on the style and substance of the Buchan ballad texts: of the "Bonny Lass of Anglesey" (220) he says: "Buchan quite frightens one by what he says of this version . . . 'It is altogether a political piece and I do not wish to interfere much with it' "; of "Auld Matrons" (249), "This piece was made by some one who had an acquaintance with the first fit of 'Adam Bell' . . . Stanzas 2–5 are hackneyed commonplaces"; of "Thomas of Yonderdale" (253), "This looks like a recent piece, fabricated with a certain amount of cheap mortar, from a recollection of 'Fair Annie,' etc."; of "Willie's Fatal Visit" (255), "Stanzas 15–17, wherever they came from, are too good for the setting; nothing so spirited, word or deed, could have come from a ghost, wan, weary, and smiling"; of "The New Slain Knight" (263), "A large portion of this piece is imitated or taken outright from very well known ballads . . . This particular ballad, so far as it is original, is of very ordinary quality. The ninth stanza is pretty but not quite artless"; of "The White Fisher" (264), "But we need not trouble ourselves to make these counterfeits reasonable. Those who utter them rely confidently upon our taking jargon and folly as the marks of genuineness. The 'White Fisher' is a frumpery fancy"; of "The Beggar Laddie" (280), ". . . it is inconceivable that any meddler should not have seen this [mistake]"; of "Child Owlet" (291), "The chain of gold in the first stanza and the penknife below the bed in the fourth have a false ring, and the story is of the tritest. The ballad seems at best to be a late one, and is perhaps a mere imitation, but, for an imitation the last two stanzas are unusually successful"; of "The Queen of Scotland" (301), "The insipid ballad may have been rhymed from some insipid tale"; of the "Holy Nunnery" (303), "The rest is wanting, and again we may doubt whether the balladist had not exhausted himself, whether a story so begun could be brought to any conclusion"; of "Brown Robin" (97), "The sequel to c is not at all beyond Buchan's blind beggar, and some other blind beggar may have contributed the cane, and the whale and the shooting and the hanging in B." The general comment on "The Bent sae Brown" (71) summarizes Professor Child's feeling clearly: "The introduction and conclusion of some incidental descriptions. . . . are the outcome of the invention and piecing together of that humble but enterprising rhapsodist who has left his trail over so large a part of Buchan's volumes. . . . The silliness and fulsome vulgarity of Buchan's versions are often enough to make one wince and sicken, and many of them come through bad hands or mouths; we have even positive proof in one instance of imposture, though not of Buchan's being a conscious party to the imposture." With all this in mind, it is not curious that Professor Child withheld so much Buchan material for later verification in manuscript and other sources.

The remaining 18 ballads, which Professor Child knew in 1858 but reserved until 1882, show a period of waiting on his part for fuller, older, or more widely known forms. In short, the treatment he accorded them testifies to his scholarly approach to his problem. His aims became more definite. In 1858 he intended to give a somewhat popular survey of balladry (a survey which I am strongly inclined to believe was modelled after Percy's *Reliques*); in 1882, he sought to print "every valuable copy of every known ballad." In 1858, he could find room for romances, translations, broadsides, and a variety of heterogeneous materials; in 1882, he excluded them. The rejections and inclusions in the first and third editions show no material change in Mr. Child's conception of the ballad; although, it may be granted, that they do show a marked change in his aims.

The demonstrated stability of Professor Child's ideas serves rather to confuse than to clarify the general problem of ballad definition, for his collection was made and printed without any pronouncement on this subject. The advertisement to the first volume of the edition shows that he realized the need of some formal statement: "It was the Editor's wish and intention to insert in the concluding volume an essay on the History of Ballad Poetry." Two other opportunities slipped by, for the article in the *Johnson Cyclopedia* is merely a résumé of ballad poetry in general; and the third edition of *The English and Scottish Popular Ballads* lacks the formal introduction promised by Professor Child. According to Mr. Gummere's note,[6] such an essay had not been even remotely formulated at the time of Professor Child's death, although Professor Kittredge suggests in the Introduction to the first volume of the third edition that it had at least been planned. Coming towards the completion of the work, such an essay would necessarily have been a defense, quite as much as an exposition, of the principles which dictated his selection. As it is, he nowhere seems to say anything more definite than this: "The word *ballad* in English signifies a narrative song, a short tale in lyric verse, which sense it has come to have, probably through the English, in some other languages. . . . The *popular* ballad, for which our language has no unequivocal name, is a distinct and very important species of poetry . . . The fundamental characteristic of popular ballads is . . . the absence of subjectivity and self-consciousness." [7]

In the absence, then, of a more specific definition from Professor Child's hand, later writers have sought to derive a definition from the ballads included in his collection. The endeavor has no doubt been stimulated by Gummere's description of the Child collection as "itself a definition of balladry." [8] Dean Hart does not attempt a formal definition, but rather seeks to give the positive and negative characteristics of the type as Professor Child presumably saw it: a ballad must tell a story, and that only partially; the transitions must be abrupt, although not incoherent; the introduction must be closely integrated with the story; there must be brevity; the action can seldom be carefully localized; description or exposition of the supernatural is omitted. The style must be artless, homely, without conceits or description of states of mind; it is marked by commonplaces which are retained in distorted form in several ballads on the same theme; it must be impressive, fine, spirited, pathetic, tender, and finally, lyrical. The subject matter must be of popular origin, the foreign parallels should exist; it may be pseudo-historical, must deal with heroic sentiment, occasionally it may be derived from other ballads. The ballad must not show extravagance or exaggeration; it must not be prosaic, over-refined, cynical, sophisticated, sentimental, moralizing; but a certain degree of probability is demanded of the plot, which must not be trite.[9]

Professor Kittredge, in the one volume edition of the Child ballads, says that the author must be of the folk, the material derived from popular sources, the structure moulded by inherited influences, the product early given to the folk, who subject it to the process of oral transmission. "That most of the 305 numbers in Mr. Child's collection satisfy these conditions is beyond question. In other words, most of these poems are genuine popular ballads within the limits of any reasonable definition of the term." This, too, is a definition derived from the actual study of the texts. In a somewhat different way, Miss Pound generalizes the so-called "true" ballad of "the Child type," as differentiated from "other types of ballads and songs," by examining the 305 ballads.[10] The ballad might, she says, "at times be fitted to well-known dance tunes, or be utilized as a dance song," although this is an unessential characteristic. She regards oral preservation as the test of inclusion, although its importance has been greatly exaggerated. Much more important are "anonymity of authorship or traces of a medieval style." Indeed, "the only dependable test elements in ballads are lyrical quality and a story element, and for traditional folk-ballads, anonymity of authorship." "The lowly as against the aristocratic, hardly plays any part in the *English and Scottish Popular Ballads*." The ballads are not so impersonal as is often assumed; "there is only the uniformity of simplicity to be expected of popular songs of all types." The ballads preserve in style and structure many archaic traits, use alliteration, some literary words, include occasionally a satirical legacy, shade off into literary verse or into some other type of folk verse or popular verse such as: the allegory, and epic *chanson*, romance, verse chronicle, dialogue, debate, aube, lyric, coronach, carol, theological discussion. (All these shadings are represented in the Child collection, but notwithstanding, Miss Pound and other scholars persistently use the phrase "the Child type.") The ballad is further marked by the presence of strophes, meter, the use of refrain (in the later texts), by repetition, and parallelism. In summary, Miss Pound arrives at the following definition: "It is enough to say that in English we mean by a ballad a certain type of lyrical or narrative song or song-tale, which appears rather late in literary history; and we may discard as unessential for defining this type reference to the origin of such pieces in the dance."

Another summary of the tests for inclusion is made by Professor Gordon Hall Gerould: "The tests by which it (the traditional ballad) must be judged, I take it, are three. The first is purely personal, the critical sense of the scholar who has learned by long continued and careful study to distinguish the false from the true, to separate the chaff from the wheat. The second is the external evidence with reference to the circumstances of discovery, whether the collector or collectors be trusted. The third is the source of the material, whether the narrative is the product of tradition or of some clever inventor." [11]

An examination of the 305 ballads as "constituting a definition of balladry" leaves one puzzled at their diversity. No single definition can include "The Carnal and the Crane" (55), "Dives and Lazarus" (156), "The Cherry Tree Carol" (54), "Sir Patrick Spens" (58), "Bonny Barbara Allen" (84), and "Thomas Rhymer" (37). There is scarcely the unity of style so frequently assumed, and certainly no unity of either spirit or subject. The individual pieces vary widely in worth.[12] If one were to use only those ballads upon which Professor Child commented favorably,[13] there would still be a tremendous diversity of materials. As Professor Gerould points out, "That ballads of very various degrees of worth may be regarded as valuable to the study of the type is evidenced by comparing the contents of the last two volumes of Child with the earlier ones." [14]

The definitions which have been quoted above do not inspire one to formulate another. These definitions fail for various reasons: Dean Hart aims at being descriptive and loses himself in details which are not properly integrated nor subordinated to one another; Professor Kittredge is discussing the problems of ultimate origins; Miss Pound frequently uses the phrase "the Child type" [15] at the same time that she demonstrates that, for all practical purposes, there is no such single clearly defined classification possible. In view of such vague definitions of a mass of materials so nearly indefinable, it is not difficult to see why the warm discussion of communal origins, or of any other ballad theory for that matter, cannot be resolved. Obviously, the debate turns upon a different subject with each interpreter: it deals now with the origins of primitive popular poetry and now with the modern folk ballad, subjects between which there could be no possible confusion were the terms precise and clearly understood.[16]

In some mysterious way, these 305 ballads have come to be canonized as superior to all other folk-songs of the English people. This in the face of such evaluations as Professor Child himself put upon some of them sufficient to indicate their widely divergent values and types. Even the number 305 has come to possess a curious magical connotation which has exerted sway for twenty-five years.[17] When Miss Pound says of ballad-making that "It is a closed account for ballads of the Child type," [18] there is much sound truth in the remark. It has been the purpose of this paper to show that a "Child ballad" means little more than one collected and approved by Professor Child.[19]

✳✳✳✳✳✳✳✳✳✳✳✳✳✳✳✳✳✳✳✳

3

The Ballad and Communal Poetry

FRANCIS B. GUMMERE

BALLAD critics of eighty years ago, with the conspicuous exception of A. W. Schlegel, were fain to welcome the doctrine of Jacob and Wilhelm Grimm that a song of the people is made by the people as a whole. The process, it was conceded, lay in mystery; but mystery had no terror for an age which delighted in abstractions and ideals. Critics of our own day, on the other hand, have closed accounts with the ideal and the abstract; they treat the vagaries of Grimm with an indulgent pity; and they are all of Schlegel's mind.[1] Grundtvig, it is true, still held with Grimm, and the last words of ten Brink were for a modified form of Grimm's doctrine; but the main body of scholars have turned from the theory in any shape.[2] The folk is out of favor, and democracy itself is put upon the defensive. Ballads for a while held out bravely; but now even ballads, like folklore in general, have been annexed to the domain of art.[3]

If I venture to regard as still open a question so vehemently determined by all sorts and conditions of scholars, it is with no idea that the communal theory can be upheld as it was stated by the Grimms. There is, however, a theory of ballad origins quite opposed to the modern notion, and yet far from finding expression in those fantastic catchwords about the folk that composes, and about the song that sings itself. If instead of such phrases as these, instead even of Steinthal's *dichtender Volksgeist*,[4] we think of a process such as Lachmann implies when he speaks of *gemeinsames Dichten*, is not a clearer question before us? [5] Does a single artist always make poetry, of whatever sort, or may one allow a concert of individuals in the act of composition? Is the folk song brought to the folk, or is it made by the folk? Is the chorus, the communal song, essentially one with the composed poem as we now know it—an individual, deliberate, and artistic work? Is there no real dualism in generative poetics,[6] in the literary section of that science which Renan put beside psychology and called the *embryogénie de l'esprit humain*—a dualism of chorus and solo, of throng and poet, of community and artist? If a folk song is brought to the folk, no matter how early the stage of composition, or how many additions and changes are afterwards made, then one must surrender the long-cherished and useful distinction of *Volkslied* and *volkstümliches Lied*, counting with the former as Mr. Jacobs explicitly concedes, any concert-hall jingle caught up by a crowd. If a folk song is made by the folk, the process must be clearly understood, and must be severed from those fantastic catchwords usually thought to express it.

It has been granted at the outset that a mere statement of this communal theory runs counter to the drift of modern thought. Nominalism is again in the lead; realism, the appeal to general ideas, to a species or a folk, is out of the running. Hence that open scorn expressed on all sides for the communal mind, and even for so respectable an abstraction as the spirit of the race. Professor Paul, in his excellent book on the *Principles of Language*,[7] condemns utterly the attempts of Steinthal and Lazarus to establish a psychology of the people as a whole, apart from the psychology of the single mind. "All psychical processes come to their fulfillment in individual minds, and nowhere else," he says; and again, "*it never happens that several individuals create anything in working together with united forced and divided functions.*" Paul is talking of language and its making, but this terse denial applies directly to the relations of verse and throng. To uphold it successfully is to overthrow the theory of communal verse,[8] however plausible and modern may be the argument for poetry that springs not from the artist, but from the mass of men; and we know that Paul elsewhere condemns in set terms the notion of gregarious composition.[9] Thus the master in philology; and with him, as quotations could readily prove, are such scholars as the late W. D. Whitney. Coming closer to our subject, we find Gerber, in his book on *Language as an Art*, taking a position similar to that of Paul;[10] the maker of words, the maker of connected speech, of poetry itself, must be perforce an artist. Poetry by its very terms of existence is an art; it implies an artist; and an artist is always individual and deliberate.

In short, the communal origin of song finds almost no recognition from modern scholars. To show how remarkably critics agree touching this matter, although their work lies in widely sundered fields, two writers may be quoted who essay a positive theory of the artist as final cause—one, an authority in sociology, M. Tarde; the other, a debutant in poetics, M. Kawczynski. Language, says the former,[11] is originally an invention of the single mind made lasting by imitation on the part of the throng.[12] This law of individual invention and communal imitation is true not only of speech but, if one will believe M. Tarde, of trades and arts, of literature, poetry, religion. We are all Dogberrians together if we dare to assert that anything came by nature. Even among the lower animals, it is not instinct common to a species, but imitation of the individual leader—and of the precedent invention—which explains alike the song of birds and the ingenious operations of bees.[13] Evolution itself is not radical enough to suit the views of M. Tarde. The evolution of the arts is not, as Mr. Herbert Spencer would have us believe, a progress from exterior and general to interior and particular.[14] In the amazing words of Tarde, poetry, for example, "begins always with a book, an epic, some poetical work for a remarkably great relative perfection—the *Iliad*, the *Bible*, Dante—some high initial source."

This is startling enough; one feels that one is losing old landmarks, and is swept by strange currents into a chartless and unsound ocean; but the lead sinks lower yet in M. Kawczynski's essay on the origin and history of rhythms.[15] Here one learns definitely that verse is never spontaneous. It is an art—not as John Fletcher called it one of the "improper" or universal arts, "such as nature is said to bestow, as singing and poetry," [16] but an art is always imitated, borrowed.[17] European poetry has been borrowed partly from the East, partly from Rome; and there are no exceptions to the rule, not even ballads, which the writer hopes to treat, as Cosquin treated popular tales, by drawing them into daylight out of "the night of spontaneity."

Now, to put the ballad, by its very name product and property of a dancing throng, into one class with the popular tale, by its very name a thing told or recited with sharp distinction of teller and hearers, is a task to be accomplished only by a suppression of those communal elements which went to the making of ballads, and by constant harping upon imitation and upon that far more difficult matter of invention. The people, of course, must be swept from popular poetry precisely as Mr. Jacobs sweeps away the folk from folklore. The "bucolic wit" of Mr. Jacobs does not appear in M. Kawczynski's list; but organists, "sacristans of the parish," and inevitable beggars and blind men, "who always went through an apprenticeship, a sort of schooling," are responsible for that mysterious "secondary invention" of the ballad which follows upon the primary imitation. Whence this imitation is derived, M. Kawczynski fails to inform us, save that we are never to look to the people. His pet aversion is "the false principle of spontaneity." To banish spontaneity from every phase of poetry is a lively task, and leads the writer into such vivacities as his statements about early German poetry in particular, and Germanic verse in general. Otfried, for example, founded German literature because he first put it upon the sacred path of imitation.[18] The Nibelungen Lay—thanks, we suppose, to Otfried—is a palpable imitation of the classics, and Siegfried merely a disguised Jason, with some dash of Achilles and Perseus thrown in! "Historic influences," the writer explains, "are stronger than the natural and proper gifts of any people." [19] Or, take the matter of beginning-rime, the "alliteration" of Germanic verse. Since the Germanic brain was notoriously unfit to invent this, or even to transmit it from Aryan origins, one must therefore fall back upon imitation. It is easy to see that "alliteration was developed in the classical languages, and was handed over from the Latin to the Irish; Irish gave it to Anglo-Saxon, and Anglo-Saxon artists taught it to the Germans and the Scandinavians." And Germanic verse itself? An imitation of the hexameter.[20]

Evidently it is going to be a bagatelle for M. Kawczynski to dispose of the general fact of poetry, and of its fundamental element of rhythm and harmony. Spontaneity, of course, is to be dismissed altogether from the reckoning. Rhythm, we are told, was a discovery, an invention made like any other invention; and it is to be considered without reference to instinct or natural impulse. Dancing, for example, was no instinctive matter, no inborn sense of rhythm expressing itself in outward movement, and thus timing spontaneously the voice of joy or sorrow that was fain to go with it; dancing was invented.[21] One is thus led to think gratefully, too, of whatever *sauvage de génie* first hit upon laughter, or upon tears, as an outlet for that rash humor, itself invented—who knows?—by some earlier anthropoid.

To this favor, then, we must come in poetics if we reject spontaneity—the only possible basis for any assumption of communal authorship—and hold that the formula of invention and imitation explains all progress in the arts of life. The thorough-going nominalist is bold to affirm that singing, shouting, laughing, even erect walking and jumping, were inventions of the artist. It is not too much to say that man thus invented himself, and has since filled history with a series of imitations and "secondary inventions." But must "the false principle of spontaneity" be banished? Is it a false principle? Renan held with Schlegel and the moderns that "poetry of the people, which is so thoroughly anonymous, always has an author"; but Renan saw spontaneity writ large over the entire life of primitive man.[22] Few critics, indeed, have had the hardihood to deny a fact about which so much evidence lies at hand; and when one considers further into what mazes one is led by such a denial, there seems to be every reason for adhering to the belief in certain spontaneous movements of the human mind, particularly as regards rhythmical expression. But this rhythmical spontaneity furnishes the chief argument for the assumption of early communal song; and it seems even to make difficulties for those who look upon poetry from the artistic point of view alone.

Aristotle is justly regarded as a fountain of common sense, if not as a final authority, in matters poetic; it is worth noting that he indirectly and briefly touched upon the question of communal verse. Poetry and music, he remarks,[23] are imitation by means of rhythm, language, and harmony; dancing is rhythm alone. "Imitation, then, is one instinct of our nature. Next there is the instinct for harmony and rhythm, metre being manifestly a species of rhythm. Persons, therefore, with this natural gift little by little improved upon their early efforts till their rude improvisations gave birth to poetry. Poetry now branched off in two directions, according to the individual character of the writers." Again: "Tragedy, as also comedy, was at first mere improvisation"—that is, was not poetry at all, but, as we learn elsewhere, mere communal excitement of the throng, breaking into rhythmic utterance and dances.[24] Presently comes the often-quoted statement that "Aeschylus . . . *diminished the importance of the chorus*," while "the iambic measure replaced the trochaic tetrameter, which was originally employed when the poetry was of the satyric order, *and had greater affinities with dancing*."

Waiving all question about the meaning of "nature and of imitation" one must admit that Aristotle sets up an antithesis between artistic and communal poetry. True, it is only the work of an artist that he will recognize as poetry at all; but he opposes to this the vast range of impoverished festal and choral verse, that communal song which we regard as still lingering, though crossed and disguised by manifold strains of art, in the ballads of Europe. Restore to the ballad its ancient rights. Give it again the dance as its source and condition; consider the jubilant throng, with its refrain steadily encroaching, as we retrace the course of development, upon the domain of the artist and his stanzas; take into account the constant repetition of words, phrases, verses; and, above all, note the fact of improvisation joined with a universal facility in rhythmic utterance—here is something which Aristotle did well to sever from the category of art.[25] It will be remembered that Gerber makes a dangerous concession to the spontaneity of primitive song. In point of fact, he is forced to exclude spontaneous verse, or what he calls improvisation, from his definition of poetry; for he defines poetry as "deliberation" added to "enthusiasm"[26] and remarks that "the improvisator cannot be a poet." To explain this improvised verse, Gerber makes shifty sentences about "natural art" and what not; ballads, he declares,[27] when they are improvised, belong merely to the art of language, not to the art of poetry, because the makers have a certain command of language, can juggle with words, and astonish us, as Archias astonished Cicero, with feats of mere diction.[28]

But we do not care for Archias; our eyes are fixed on the dancing, singing, improvising multitude; and Gerber's explanation breaks down utterly, because he does not recognize this dualism of the artist and the throng. Spontaneous composition in a dancing multitude—all singing, all dancing, and all able on occasion to improvise—is a fact of primitive poetry about which we may be certain as such questions allow us to be certain. Behind individuals stands the human horde. Preceding the beginnings of artistic drama, and in some fashion a foundation for it, Aristotle evidently saw such a horde or throng. An insistent echo of this throng greets us from the ballads. The deliberation of artistry excluded, it simply remains to ask how verse was made in, or even by, this mass of "enthusiastic" men. It remains, in other words, to study the rhythmic and emotional expression of a throng.

It is by no means certain that psychology must be a matter of the single soul. Crowds, communities, races,[29] have an individuality of their own, and this is a legitimate object of study. While Paul denies the fact of "demopsychology," Wundt, in a long article,[30] justifies it, and names, as its fundamental problems, speech, myth, custom—the three products of the communal mind. To these we must certainly add communal poetry, giving it a domain which Wundt divides between speech and myth. For the present day, communal poetry is merely a trace, a hint, a survival from the misty past analogous, in its logical and chronological relations to artistic poetry, with the relations of those faint traces of the ancient village community to the modern individual ownership of land. For primitive times we are to reverse all this. Communal poetry was doubtless the rule, with here and there a hint of artistry. We face, for the true study of our problem, a horde of primitive men; and we must remember that, contrary to old notions, the individual was not the father of society, but, as Reclus puts it, society was the mother of the individual.[31] It is only fair to carry this distinction into our idea of primitive institutions. Primitive religion was collective, a thing of rites and ceremonies, communal even in the sentiment which began, perhaps in earliest times, to cover the hard rock of cult with that moss of poetry and myth which so many critics have mistaken for the real basis of religion. By all evidence, poetry must also be regarded for those times as collective and communal. If civilization, which has spent its main energies to accent the individual, still finds its way barred by communal oppositions, and vainly applies to them the solvent which acts so readily upon the individual mind—if M. Le Bon [32] still sees in the throng of our own day "a single being, governed by the law of communal mental unity," a "sort of collective mind"—what shall one think of this collective mind, its inceptive and productive power, under primitive conditions, with the individual at his feeblest, thought immeasurably subordinated to emotion, and spontaneity almost absolute? If enthusiasm and deliberation—enthusiasm as of a throng, deliberation as of the artist, the solitary maker—are ultimate factors of poetry as we know it, shall we not assume, and does not Aristotle bid us assume, for earliest poetry a maximum of enthusiasm with a minimum of deliberation, or, in other words, communal spontaneity in such force as almost to exclude every trace of individual artistry?

To use Matthew Arnold's figure about Celt and German, are we not to think of modern poetry as a vast obscure communal basis with a vast visible artistic superstructure? To make poetry first and last a matter of the artist, to insist with Scherer upon poet and public, from the anthropoid's tree platform down to Browning societies, is tempting enough, simple enough, plausible enough, until one considers instead of aesthetic principles the stubborn facts of historical and generative poetics. Universality of the poetic gift among inferior races,[33] spontaneity or improvisation under communal conditions, the history of refrain and chorus, the early relation of narrative songs to the dance—these, I believe, are not to be referred to that offhand explanation of artistry about which Mr. Jacobs feels so confident. Grimm erred in asserting a communal origin for poems of comparatively modern date—in calling that a wild flower which, although sprung from wild stock, is nevertheless dependent on a certain measure of cultivation. But it is no absurdity to insist upon *the origin of poetry under communal and not under artistic conditions.*

For poetry began in a human throng, in the horde. The hard saying is not here, but in the assertion of simultaneous composition, of human beings working together "with united forces and divided functions" and creating something. Yet this difficulty is more apparent than real; for while nobody thinks it possible for a crowd to compose offhand and simultaneously a ballad [34] like Sir Patrick Spens—and a deal of scorn has been wasted over this pretty feat—it is quite another question when one reflects upon two facts which may be assumed as fundamental in primitive culture. The first of these relates to human speech. The sentence, the proposition, was the unit of speech,[35] just as the verse was and is the unit of poetry; and speech in the first instance was an immediate assertion of contemporary action. The second fact, proved by specimens of savage song the world over, is that repetition, endless repetition, was the chief element in primitive verse. To repeat a sentence was poetry, for the very foundation of harmony or rhythm is secured simply by saying a given sentence, and then saying it again. Add to these facts the lack of individuality, the homogeneous mental state of any primitive throng, the absence of deliberation and thought, the immediate relation of emotion to expression, the accompanying leap or step of the dance under conditions of communal exhilaration—surely the communal making of verse is no greater mystery than many another undoubted feat of primitive man. The wail of sorrow expressed spontaneously by the throng in a word or phrase, and repeated indefinitely to the motions of a funeral dance,[36] is poetry for the student of primitive culture, if not for the young lions of the Browning cult. Add the great fact of reproduction, upon which ten Brink laid such stress,[37] as vital in ancient poetry as original production is vital in our own, and the case is yet stronger.

Language itself, strenuously claimed by Professor Paul for artistic origins, has been referred directly to this mentally homogeneous throng. A suggestive article by Donovan on "The Festal Origin of Human Speech"[38] asserts that the earliest expressions of communal interest were in bodily play, in the excitement "found in all grades of development from that of the lowest Australian or American aborigines *up to the choral dance out of which the first glorifying songs of the race and its heroes are found growing.*" This "play excitement," added to communal elation following success in some tribal enterprises, has its natural result in rhythmic motions, in excited cries, out of which come music and speech—sounds connected with the origin and purpose of the excitement. Here, then, was the birth of poetry.[39]

Communal in its origin, poetry must have felt betimes the influence of artistry. An instructive essay by Dr. Krejci[40] contrasts the involuntary or mechanical element of poetry with the opposite element of logical or voluntary creation. The course of poetry runs steadily, he asserts, from a preponderance of the involuntary or mechanical, that is, of spontaneity, to a preponderance of the voluntary, logical, deliberate. The note of popular poetry, of course, is this element of spontaneity and lack of deliberation; if we could catch a glimpse of primitive conditions, we should find poetry entirely ruled by the mechanical, the spontaneous, the unreflecting element.[41] We may go further and carry the antithesis to its proper expression, the dualism of artist and throng. Individuality is the result of reflection; only when he combats spontaneity, curbs his communal impulse, and deliberates upon it, mingles emotion with thought, and separates himself from the shouting, swaying, dancing mass, does the communal singer begin as a poet. Evidently, then, the history of poetic development is not a course of artistry with some savage or anthropoid artist, which is as unscientific, unwarranted an assumption[42] as the communal creative power which Grimm defended for comparatively modern times. The formula to be applied to all poetry is the measure of communal element and the measure of artistic element. Taken as a whole, the ballads of Europe show far more of the communal than of the artistic element; but it is clear that a new classification is needed, and should be based upon the character and weight in any given ballad of those elements which are distinctly of communal origin.

Modern emotion, then, is of the individual, and poetic emotion is now almost wholly artistic and therefore saturated with thought.[43]

The prevailing sense of individuality, even under the most elaborately objective mask and the prevailing intellectual bias in emotion, are the chief marks of poetry today. Other poetry is regarded as childish, a fad, and the lover of ballads is often drawn by this contempt into an admiration of his own ware which he can hardly justify, while critics go on rebuking him as for "the love of little maids and berries," for a go-cart passion, and feel a sincere concern for the stunting of his better faculties. But the docile bairns of knowledge, as King James called sensible scholars in his day, are of kinder heart. They know that to assert the communal origins of poetry is not to degrade the poet, but rather to dignify him. To follow poetry back to that aboriginal wildness, that ecstasy of the horde, first utterance of unaccommodated man, is not a study that need deafen its student to the charm and melody of art. We search for poetry before the poet, somewhat in the spirit of Donne's fine conceit:

> I long to talk with some old lover's ghost,
> Who died before the god of love was born.

We find it in the throng. From this dancing throng came emotion and rhythm, the raw material of poetry. The poet added thought.[44] When Schopenhauer [45] complains of modern poetry that thought is too often subservient to rime, he says in other words that even now the artist cannot free himself from that haunting cadence of the throng. Mr. Spencer says [46] that "cadence is the commentary of the emotions upon the propositions of the intellect"—surely an inversion! Our modern poetry is the commentary of the intellect upon the cadence of the emotions. Primitive man had emotions, and emotions tend to converge; his poetry was communal. Modern men have thought, and thought tends to divergence of paths. We see the poet

πολλὰζ δ'ὀδοὺζ ἐλθόντα φροντίδοζ πλάνουζ

but behind this vividly lighted I or Thou or He of modern poetry lurks in shadow the We of that early throng. In the ballads one comes closer to this presence; one feels it, but one cannot clearly see it.

4

✳✳✳✳✳✳✳✳✳✳✳✳✳✳✳✳✳✳✳✳✳✳

Ballad and Dance

GEORGE McKNIGHT

THE last decade has done much toward clearing up hazy notions regarding the origins of the popular ballad. In this work an important part has been played by Professor Louise Pound, who in a series of able articles dispersed among various American philological journals, has contributed greatly toward bringing the subject out into clear daylight. In her latest contribution to the subject, however, that in the September [1919] issue of the *PMLA*, in questioning the relation of the ballad form to dancing custom, Miss Pound takes a position which, in my opinion, is not defensible. The views presented in her paper challenge full discussion, and I should like to offer, from the notes that I have been able to assemble on this subject in the last few years, a few arguments in support of the prevalent opinion that the distinctive features of the popular ballad reflect features of medieval dancing.

Regarding the history of the word "ballad" as evidence in point, Miss Pound makes a clear case. Let me add that the history of the word "carol" offers an interesting analogy. Originally the name of a circle dance, the name "carol" became shifted to the song connected with the dance, and then, by generalization, to joyous songs in general, and then, by specialization in turn, to the joyous songs of the Christmas season. Although in one or two instances the form of popular Christmas carols seems to be connected with older dancing custom, it would be obviously impossible to connect the Christmas carol in general, more usually of hymnal or pagan festival origin, with the medieval *carole*-dance. In the same way the word "ballad," originally meaning a song for dance accompaniment, by the sixteenth century, while still [1] some-times used in its earlier meaning, had become generalized so as to apply to songs of most varied type. Only in the eighteenth century, as Miss Pound has pointed out, did it become, somewhat arbitrarily, re-stricted to use as the name for one form of traditional narrative song.

In her consideration of the songs used as accompaniment to the medieval ring-dance in England called the *carole,* Miss Pound has shown that these were prevailingly lyrical rather than narrative in character. To the evidence cited by Miss Pound may well be added that of the "foolish song" sung for Touchstone by the two pages in *As You Like It,* for which the popular type of carol songs used for dance accompaniment seem to have offered a pattern. The "ditty" "It Was a Lover and His Lass," with its refrains, its reference to "the only pretty ring time," and its application to itself of the name "carol" may then be cited as evidence regarding the nature of the popular songs accompanying the carol dance in the latest stage, and indicates a lyrical form. Not only the songs of the medieval ring-dances, but those ac-companying children's ring-games surviving in our times, in which, rather than in the Child ballads, Miss Pound sees the relics of the older dances with song accompaniment, she points out, have in them, in gen-eral, little of the narrative element.

Thus far one can hardly dissent from the views expressed by Miss Pound. It should be noted, however, that the conclusions reached are negative in character. The usually accepted explanation of ballad crea-tion is discarded, but there is offered no alternative. Let us see, then, if something cannot be said in support of the prevalent theory.

In the first place, to dissociate the popular ballad in its origin from the old dancing custom, is to do away with the most plausible explana-tion for those qualities that distinguish the ballads of the Child canon from other forms of popular song. The objectivity, so marked a quality of the Child ballad, finds a satisfactory explanation in the con-ditions of choral origin. The elemental quality of the emotions dealt with, likewise, is of the kind suited for expression in choral dance. The ballad commonplaces also, the well-worn phraseology, the oft-used or-namental details of opening verses and of conclusions, indicate choral improvisation rather than more deliberate invention. The "incremental repetition" so much stressed by Professor Gummere, although by no means an exclusive property of the popular ballad, nevertheless afford-ing as it does, opportunity for lingering over certain situations, suits the character of the dancing ring. Above all, the refrains, persisting in so many ballad versions, even in versions recorded from the singing of soloists, afford indication which may not be disregarded, that at one time a chorus had its share in the song.

Such a priori considerations, briefly stated, afford sufficient reason for not lightly discarding the only plausible explanation available for the much-discussed features of the popular ballad. Let us now review the known facts regarding the use of narrative in the medieval choral dance. Did narrative form no part of the choral songs? Granted the prevalence of lyric themes, are there no instances where the subject matter was narrative?

The widely-circulated story of the Dancers of Kolbigk may be cited as evidence in point. To this diverting tale of the twelve young people who by curse were condemned to dance perpetually because of their sacrilege in disturbing the service in the churchyard on Christmas night, we are indebted by many concrete details which help form a picture of the *carole* dance. Most important for the present purpose is the Latin version of one of the stanzas of the song accompaniment and of the refrain:

> Equitabat Bevo per silvam,
> Ducebat secum Merswyndam formosam.
> Quid stamus, cur non imus?

There is to be noted not only the refrain and the use of a stanza form typical of the popular ballad, but the narrative character of the subject-matter. The story setting, to be sure, is not English, but it is told by Robert of Brunne, an English writer, who finds in the details nothing to comment on as other than typical use.

Unmistakable references to the use of narrative as theme for dance song in England are none too numerous. The exploits of Hereward, we are told, "were sung by the women and maidens in their dance," [2] and from the twelfth century has been recorded what is probably the burden or chorus of a song of Cnut "sung in these days by people in their dances." [3] Much later, in the sixteenth-century "Complaynt of Scotland," we have an account of the merrymaking of shepherds with tales and songs and ring dancing. The subjects of the dance songs are prevailingly lyrical, but at least one, *Ihonne ermistrangis dance,* and possibly a second, the dance of *Robene hude,* may have handled narrative subjects in ballad fashion.

Furthermore in the art poetry of the fifteenth and sixteenth centuries we have indirect evidence of the existence of popular models in the form of narrative song with refrain. Just as in Shakespeare's "It Was a Lover and His Lass," we have reflected the form and spirit of the lyrical accompaniment to the popular carol-dance, have we not a reflection of the popular narrative dance form in that art carol of mystical beauty with the refrain, "The faucon hath borne my make away"? Is not a traditional popular narrative choral song, also, to be assumed as the pattern for the art song by William Cornish in two-line stanzas beginning:

> The knight knocked at the castle gate;
> The lady marvelled who was thereat.

with the lyrical refain:

> You and I and Amyas
> Amyas and you and I,
> To the greenwood must we go, alas!
> You and I, my life, and Amyas?

The early evidence of narrative dance songs in England, it must be admitted, is none too abundant. In France so far as present knowledge goes, songs of this type did not exist before the end of the fifteenth century. It is to Scandinavian countries that one must turn for most convincing evidence. In most Scandinavian countries the prevalent use of narrative songs for dance accompaniment in the later Middle Ages is admitted by everyone, Miss Pound included. A not unlikely hypothesis is that the *carole*-dance custom was imported from France, possibly by the way of England, into Scandinavian countries and there connected with narrative themes. The marked similarity between the Danish *Folkeviser*, admittedly once used as dance accompaniment, and the English Child ballads, both in narrative themes and in metrical form, is such that it is hard to see how one can hesitate to accept the known explanations of the one as applicable to the other.

One may be disposed to agree with Miss Pound that "As to origins, the Danish ballads do not help the communalists," but for the association of the ballad form with the dance, the evidence of the Danish ballads is incontrovertible. The statement that the dancing to these Danish ballads was that of "the high born" is misleading. According to Olrik "the producers of these songs were the Danish nobility, *but* not a small number of noble families who later built the lordly castles;

rather a nobility distributed over thousands of farmsteads, who later sank back into the rank of peasants." [4]

Once prevalent, not only in Denmark but also in Norway, these dances to narrative songs went out of fashion in Denmark in the sixteenth century.[5] Among the isolated Scandinavian population of the Faroe Islands, however, they have persisted down to our own time. Miss Pound, in a footnote, quotes the remark of Gummere that "the ballad genesis is more plainly proved for the Faroes than any other modern people." In spite of the importance evidently to be attached to the evidence of the Faroe dances, her handling here is entirely inadequate. In a footnote appears the statement that: "The whole matter of Faroe folk song was cleared satisfactorily by Thuren in his book on this subject. In spite of this reference, she makes no use of the invaluable information offered by this remarkable book. In fact, she states that "the Faroe fisherman pieces are sung to hymn tunes or to familiar airs, not to invented melodies, or to traditional melodies—not at least to melodies traditional from ancient times," whereas in fact about one half of Thuren's book is devoted to the recording and discussion of the native music of the Faroe Island songs. One of his conclusions is that "it is not unreasonable to suppose that the Faroe system of melody developed on the islands." [6] He traces the development from "Recitativ" to the gapped five-tone, or Pentatonic scales and remarks that the transition from Recitativ to the Pentatonic forms is so natural, and the tone groups used are so simple, that one may well consider himself in the presence of the same phase of development that is frequently met with in the history of primitive song.

Thuren, in his book, establishes the identity between the Faroe dances, with their dance leader, their sinuous curves, and their distinctive dance movement, and the medieval *carole*-dance as we know it from detailed description of it under its later name, *branle*, in sixteenth-century books on dancing. Here then, transported, to be sure, to a new environment, but as so often in the case of transported customs, preserving its original character better than in the home of its creation, we have surviving the popular dancing custom which is believed to have given its impress to the form of the popular ballad.

The contrast between Faroe and Danish versions of the same ballad is interesting. In the Danish songs, which have been divorced from dancing, Thuren points out the shortening of the refrain. He also points out the development of the verse melodies since the form of the verse is no longer held in fixed rhythm by the accompanying dance. This comparison offers interesting suggestions regarding what we must assume to have taken place in England when the songs were separated from the dance.

In the Faroe dances the narrative subjects are not usually new stories, but well-known stories of great variety. Among them are included the old story of Sigurd Fafnersbane, that of the Faroe national hero, Sigmund Bretteson, tales of Roland, of Tristram, of Olufa, the daughter of Pippin, a great variety of isolated romantic tales, songs imported from Denmark and stories of church celebrities, of St. James, of St. Nicholas, even of the Virgin Mary. The dancers enter into the entertainment with zest. They show their interest in the subject of the narrative by accompanying gestures, and in the refrain give full expression to the feelings, joyous or sad, aroused by the story. Contrary to what one might suppose, the stories handled in this way are not short ones. Here, if one will reflect, are the conditions under which an active person would best enjoy a story. To the island fisherman, the enjoyment of the narrative would be enhanced because of the opportunity afforded for active expression of the feeling aroused by the story.

Tending at the present time to die out in the Faroe Islands, these dances are receiving artificial support and recently have been reintroduced into Norway, a work for which credit is due to the zealous effort of Hulda Garborg. In the summer of 1913 I personally had the pleasure of seeing some of these dances as performed by the young people of Ulvik in Norway. From the experience dates my first vivid realization of the connection between the song-dance and the ballad form. Frau Garborg has been also active in introducing these narrative song dances into Sweden and Denmark and reports that Fräulein Gertrud Meyer has recently introduced these dances into Germany and an American woman (unnamed) has introduced them into America.[7]

If the medieval ring-dance was once accompanied by narrative songs, it is remarkable if among the ring-games of the children, the song accompaniments of which, as has been shown above, are prevailingly lyrical, there are to be found no traces of narrative songs. As a matter of fact such traces do exist. Miss Pound herself cites from W. W. Newell a reference to the use of "Barbara Allen" in "play party" games in the early part of the nineteenth century in New England. Professor Child, as well as Gilchrist and Broadwood, are cited by her in evidence that "The Maid Freed From the Gallows" "has known game-song usage." Further she cites from Nebraska a version of "The Two Sisters" "that has been used as dance-song." To these instances of ballad words combined with dance, let me add other instances of a similar kind. Professor C. A. Smith cites an account of a highly diverting dramatic version of "The Maid Freed From the Gallows" among southern negroes. S. Baring-Gould says of a Cornish version of "The Elfin Knight," "This used to be sung as a sort of game in farmhouses between a young man who went outside the room and a girl who sat on the settle or a chair and a sort of chorus of farm lads and lasses." "Andrew Lammie" "used in former times to be presented in dramatic shape at rustic weddings in Aberdeenshire." [8] The Swedish version of "Willie's Lyke-Wake" is said to be often represented as a drama by young people in country-places.[9] Of the story of "Our Goodman" we are told that it is sung in several parts of France as a little drama. "Dugald Quin" as Professor Gummere has pointed out,[10] is very near to choral song. Another little ballad drama is the little Orkney Island "Play of the Lathie Odivere" of which the ballad original has not survived.

Among ballads outside the Child collection, ballads for which no connection with the choral dance can be claimed, there are a number that were presented in the form of song-plays, e.g., "Rowland's Godsonne" and "Attowel's jigge" in the Shirburn collection. This type of play in the sixteenth century was known as a "jig." "Attowel's jigge," it is interesting to know, was one of the operettas, or *Singspiele*, that formed an important element in the repertory of the Elizabethan player companies that travelled in Germany. Is it not likely that in artificial creations of this sort we have reflected features of the song dance of popular origin?

Miss Pound, commenting on the instances that she cites, says— "There is evidence from recent times that in a few cases well-known Child pieces have been vitalized into dance songs." She admits also that in the case of Mrs. Brown's "The Bonnie Birdie" or "The Maid and the Palmer" the refrains "might connect them with the dance." Is it not more plausible to suppose that in the case of ballads in our times associated with dance or play-game we have to do with older ballad qualities, which in versions of solitary singers have lain dormant, but which come again to life when the ballad is restored to choral associations?

It must be admitted that among the ballads of the Child collection are represented quite different degrees of closeness of relations to the dance. Whereas in ballads like "Babylon" and "The Maid Freed From the Gallows" one feels the choral band not far away, in other instances, as in the case of the border ballads, we probably have to do with songs of another tradition, which have only been modified in external form under the influence of the songs used by the dancing ring. The continuity in tradition of heroic songs of days antedating the *carole* dance may be shown in many countries. In Germany Heusler cites the younger *Hildebrandslied* and the *Ermanrich's Tod* in comparison with the OHG *Hildebrandslied* and the Eddic *Hamðismal* as showing "how alliterative heroic songs of the eighth century have been preserved in the late Middle Ages with fundamental change in style and in versification but with so little change in outline and such agreement in details, that they may be said in the course of the intervening six or eight centuries, never to have ceased to exist as poems." [11] Evidence of a similar kind is supplied by A. Olrik who shows how the concluding scene of the Danish heroic poem, the *Bjarkemål*, appears with modified form but unchanged content, in Faroe folk-song.[12] In the same way in England there was evidently a continuous tradition in heroic poetry. The ballads of "Otterburn" and "Chevy Chase," while dealing with events of later times, yet present not only situations and ideals, but even alliterative formulas surviving from the days before the Conquest. To quote a single instance, the Northumberland squire in "Chevy Chase" says:

> But whylle I may my weppone welde,
> I wylle not fayle both hart and hande,

just as four hundred years earlier, in the "Battle of Maldon," the Old English poet tells us that the English warriors—"faestlice wið ða fynd weredon þa hwile þe hi waepna wealdan moston."

The influence of the ballad form, however, may be seen by a comparison of different versions of these ballads. Take for instance the different versions of "The Battle of Otterburn." In the manuscript version, A, features of older heroic songs are abundant, notably the alliterative lines. In the versions recorded later from Scotch oral tradition, the alliterative lines have been almost entirely superseded by lines in the well-known ballad style. If, as is probably the case, these ballads never served as song accompaniment to a dancing ring, or to put it another way, if these songs never found dramatic interpretation in the gestures and attitudes of a dancing chorus, in any event their external form has been modified under the influence of songs which, if prevailing opinion is correct, have taken the impress of the dancing ring.

This brief paper, it is hoped, offers good reasons for dissenting from the conclusion reached by Miss Pound in her latest contribution to ballad literature. In attempting to dissociate the popular ballad from dance origins, she is not only doing away with the one available plausible explanation of ballad form, but she is disregarding evidence of a most definite kind.

5

✳✳✳✳✳✳✳✳✳✳✳✳✳✳✳✳✳✳✳✳✳

Scottish Ballads:
Their Evidence of Authorship and Origin

ALEXANDER KEITH

A SCOTS professor of the blunt old school was asked in company what he thought of German philosophy. Bored as much by the subject as by the conversation, he retorted with the epigram, "Water that's drumlie is nae aye deep." The professorial deliverance is an appropriate vent to the impatience of students of the traditional ballad at the ingenious theories of ballad origins which during the past generation have come to be the fashion. The simplicity and naturalness of the popular ballad, justly and universally extolled, are not recaptured in the treatises of those who concern themselves with its beginnings and its history. For the moment it is considered highly improper, in most realms of investigation, to prefer ancient opinions to modern; yet it is a fact, admitted by every collector of ballads from oral popular tradition, that Walter Scott's *Introductory Remarks on Popular Poetry*, written in March 1830, are nearer the truth of the matter than all the many volumes on the subject which have appeared since. The reasons are four in number and perfectly sufficient. Scott had more than the average endowment of common sense; he was steeped in the essential spirit of the old balladists; his knowledge of ballads was gathered from observing them personally in their natural environment; and in substance our available knowledge of traditional minstrelsy has scarcely increased since he and Shortreed made their "raids" into the fastnesses of Liddesdale. The purpose of this essay is belligerent. It is an endeavour to confute the notions of origin and authorship with which ballad criticism teems. Miss Louise Pound, Professor of English in the University of Nebraska, has already—in her *Poetic Origins and the*

Ballad (1921)—joined battle on their own ground with the supporters of the communal theory of balladry's beginnings. The present writer will supplement her arguments with others derived from a fairly close study of Scottish ballads, both as they exist in popular circulation at the present time and as they have been recorded by the collectors of the past. The internationality of the ballads is so extensive, their characteristics so similar in every clime where they flourish, that in examining the ballads of Scotland the researcher might be investigating those of any country; and arguments drawn from the traditional minstrelsy of Scotland can with equal pertinence be found in the balladry of England, of Germany, or of Scandinavia.

The student of ballads whose material is confined to the 305 items in Professor Child's *English and Scottish Popular Ballads* is at a certain disadvantage. Child's work is magnificent and invaluable, but it does not clearly differentiate between ballads taken directly from oral tradition and ballads which may or may not have been traditionally current, but of which the only extant examples are preserved in broadside and chapbook prints or in early manuscripts. On the evidence of print or manuscript, unsupported by traditional versions or by explicit testimony that such print or manuscript was compiled from oral delivery, we are not entitled to class a ballad as traditional. It may have been, but we do not know. So little of our knowledge of ballads is absolute that everything of the savour of doubt has to be excluded from our material. On the other hand, there are ballads, of which our first versions are printed, like "The Elfin Knight" (broadside of about 1670), which have been recovered from tradition time and again. Whether the traditional texts are derived from the print, or the print was based on contemporary tradition, cannot be ascertained. We know that in the eighteenth and early nineteenth centuries it was a common practice for enterprising Scottish printers to get traditional ballads "written up" by hacks, cheaply printed, and sold by hawkers from door to door or at fairs throughout the country. In such cases nice distinctions may be dispensed with, and the general rule applied that ballads in oral circulation are traditional ballads.

In ballad criticism the fundamental questions of beginnings and authorship are hotly disputed. If we fix the approximate period of the ballad's appearance we go a long way towards solving the problem of authorship. The first recorded versions of ballads in Scotland, taken from tradition, do not go back beyond 1700. Previous to that date British ballad versions existed, in England for the most part, in manuscripts and cheap prints, but we have assurances that traditional singing was encountered in the fourteenth century. John Barbour, writing in 1376, mentions a folk-song, on an historical episode, which may or may not have been a ballad; in the *Complaynte of Scotland*, 1549, we read of a number of "pleys and storeis," of which twenty seem to be of British folk-character, which were "told" by the shepherds and their womenkind, and of thirty-seven other pieces ("sueit melodius sangis of the antiquite") which were *sung* by the same company. Most of the twenty "storeis" can be linked up with traditional ballads, and among the "sangis" there are historical ballads of which versions have been recovered since—"The Battle of Otterburn," "The Hunting of the Cheviot," and "The Battle of Harlaw." Of a score of popular ditties mentioned in *Peblis to the Play*, *Colkelbie's Sow*, and Douglas's *Eneados*, not one is of the narrative, or ballad, type. In Child's collection, only eleven texts can be dated with certainty before 1600, and although none of them looks like a ballad taken from oral circulation, we need not quarrel with the assumption that they were "popular." Some of them doubtless were traditional. The Percy Manuscript, the first solid collection of English ballad material, dates between 1620 and 1650, and appears to have been compiled from oral sources.

The unassailable facts at our disposal regarding the emergence of the ballad are, therefore, that prior to the middle of the fifteenth century we have no ballad text of an indubitably traditional quality, and that until 1500 the evidences of ballads in oral usage as folk-songs are faint indeed. The date of the oldest Danish ballad text is about 1450, and the late W. P. Ker, the leading literary authority of our day on the Dark Ages, put the period of the ballad's emergence at a point not earlier than 1200, when written history was temporarily suspended. That the ballad did not appear in a night, or arise suddenly like Aphrodite from the sea, is obvious. It was a development of some earlier type, and that development, in view of the intellectual conditions, may have been slower than is usual in other literary forms. It is not unreasonable to suggest that three centuries before 1550 were consumed before the transition from the unidentified parent form, or forms, to the ballad as we now know it was accomplished. For three centuries after 1550 the ballad form was fairly stable, but within the last generation or two, it is interesting to note, another change began to work, shorter and more concise versions of the older, lengthier ballads making their appearance.

A certain number of ballads can be dated with rather more precision than the rest. When a ballad centres upon an historical event we at least know that it could not have preceded that event. There is, of course, always the possibility that older ballads may have been altered to fit fresh incidents, but it is no more than a possibility, and is shown, by a study of ballads influenced by occurrences subsequent to those which provided their main themes, to deserve much less emphasis than has been placed upon it. There is significance in the following facts. "The Battle of Harlaw" was not recorded from tradition till four hundred years after the battle itself; over a century elapsed between the engagement of Otterburn and the appearance of the first English and probably traditional text of the ballad of "Otterburn," while the first Scottish record is two hundred and fifty years later; the earlier Robin Hood ballads occur in manuscripts at least two hundred years subsequent to the outlaw's death—if he ever existed; whereas "Sir Andrew Barton" follows the last fight of the Scottish seaman (1500) at a short interval of only fifty years, and the burning of the House of Towie, in 1571, gave rise to "Captain Car" within a very few years. Thereafter, historical ballads come hard on the heels of the events they commemorate. In Child's collection, excluding the Robin Hood group and some late chapbook and broadside doggerel, there are sixty-nine ballads dealing with actual personages or historical occurrences. Of these, thirteen refer to pre-1500 events and persons, the subjects of six lie between 1500 and 1550, and only one or two of the remaining fifty are later than the period 1550–1700. This circumstance also indicates that before 1550 the art of making and singing ballads was only coming into fashion, and that the "golden age" of the ballad commenced after that date, and lasted through the seventeenth century. Professor Kittredge pleads that many medieval ballads must have been lost, by accident or for want of collectors; but it is curious that the ardent antiquarians of the seventeenth and eighteenth centuries could not recover more than a handful of specimens 200–300 years old, when in the beginning of the twentieth century, with traditional minstrelsy fallen into decay, Scottish collectors could find many versions of ballads concerned with events of three hundred years ago.

The analogies between British and Continental ballads have provoked a great deal of speculation since Robert Jamieson first pointed out similarities between certain Scottish and Scandinavian versions. Professor Gummere noted three distinct theories of explanation: mutual borrowing; "a common European or Aryan fund of popular tradition"; and "spontaneous and independent production of similar narratives." Cautiously refusing to commit himself definitely to any one theory, Gummere accepted Mullenhoff's proposition that "every song, every tale, legend, myth, must be studied primarily on its own ground in its own local associations." Separate examination of each individual ballad is essential, but to go no farther in the study of balladry as a whole is to shirk the main question. The common stock of atavistic tradition may have mixed some small ingredients in the minstrelsy of various peoples, but we cannot explain by its means such close coincidences of detail as occur in "Binorie," "The Duke of Perth's Three Daughters," and "Hind Horn," and their European parallels. "Independent production of similar narratives" is also probable in view of the nature of ballad plots, which are frequently and obviously drawn from occurrences common in the ordinary experience of semicivilized communities; but it does not account for the large number of similarities both in subject and expression.

Mutual borrowing, however, does fit the vast majority of parallelisms. Such give-and-take is, as I shall show presently, an integral part of the processes of tradition. Between British and Scandinavian ballads the closest likenesses are found. From very early times there was much political intercourse between Scotland and Denmark. From the sixteenth century onwards a second line of communication, in trade, was established; England also opened diplomatic and commercial relations with the north. From the middle of the seventeenth century the business intercourse between the northeast of Scotland and Norway became so intimate that in Bergen a regular colony of Aberdeenshire people was founded, from members of which Edward Grieg, the Norwegian composer, was descended. And it is clearly significant, in the light of this fact, that of all British ballads those of Aberdeenshire are most reminiscent of Scandinavian versions. The resemblances between Peter Buchan's Aberdeenshire gleanings and Danish ballads were so frequent and striking that a translator of the latter, three-quarters of a century ago, was moved to accuse Buchan of stealing from the Danish versions. Of modern parallels a single example will suffice. Of Child's twenty-seven versions of "Binorie" (the Twa Sisters), two are from Aberdeenshire. These two and one other in his collection make the elder sister "dun" and the younger a blonde, as in most of the Norse versions. Eleven Aberdeenshire versions recovered since Child's death have the same characteristic. Again, in none of Child's records does the drowning sister refuse to give up her lover to her rival and murderess; some of the Norse forms contain this refusal; and it occurs— for the first time in the British ballad—in four of the eleven recent Aberdeenshire texts. From Scottish history alone, without reference to the annals of England, we know that after the institution of the Scots Universities many of their graduates and alumni travelled the Continent; from the sixteenth century onwards Scottish soldiers of fortune, lairds' sons, students, and traders were moving in large numbers throughout the Continent; and that they were the agents who introduced into Scottish ballads the influence of the Continental forms, and vice versa, no one who is acquainted with the habits of tradition will doubt. These influences, it will be noted, were at work during the period which I have concluded to be the zenith of the art of balladry.

The second and most vexatious problem of ballad origins, that of authorship, has come to be drenched in a fog of speculation. This riddle, at least, has not been "wisely expounded." Three solutions have been suggested—composition by the folk or festal throngs, composition by homogeneous groups of individuals, and composition by single individuals, worked over time and again by various minds subsequently. The first is Grimm's theory. It is vague, and has in any case affinities with the fairy tales in which he specialized. As it became the parent of the second an effort has been made to defend it, not on the ground that it is probable but on the plea that it cannot mean what it is held to mean. Gummere, Kittredge, and many other commentators, without accepting Grimm's theory to the limit, have nevertheless, perhaps unconsciously, constituted it the landmark towards which they have directed their steps. There is, indeed, little to choose between the Grimm conception of a festal throng and the Gummere-Kittredge idea of a homogeneous group—dance party, family party, or what not— spontaneously or in collaboration composing ballads. Gummere is the chief protagonist of the communal theory, although his system differs considerably in detail from the "throng" conception of Grimm. And Gummere's fundamental postulate, which he attempted with vast learning and inexhaustible skill to prove an axiom, is that poetry at its beginnings is communally composed in the excitement of dancing.

In his *Popular Ballad,* a most ingenious and stimulating study, he sought to identify ballads as the last survivals of that primeval poetry. Primitive men, it is argued, cannot create individually until they have created communally or chorally, and in support are cited the song-and-dance of the Botocudos of South America, and improvisations of the Faroe Islanders and of cigarette makers in South Russia, and children's gamesongs of civilized countries, all these being taken as examples of uncultured versification. Miss Pound, as I have said, met the communalists on their own terrain with the facts that such savage races of the present day as the Akkas of West Africa, the Andaman Islanders, the Australian Bushmen, the Maori, the Semang of Malaya, the Seri of Mexico, the Esquimaux, and the North American Indians, dance without singing, sing without dancing, or possess individual bards who provide the tribal poetry. What has been called improvisation by children at play never extends to more than a word at a time, and then either one of the children suggests the word, or it is adopted from a previously-learned phrase. Permitting the utmost latitude of probability to the cited instances in favour of communal authorship, the evidence amassed by Miss Pound from various sources must be accepted as so contradictory that neither side proves its case.

In the shepherds' pastimes, recounted in *The Complaynte of Scotland,* the "pleys and storeis" are first recited, then the "sueit melodius sangis" are sung, and then "eftir this sueit celest armonye, tha began to dance in ane ring." "Robene hude," "thom of lyn," and "johnne ermistrangis dance" are three titles of dance tunes which may be connected with modern ballads—"thom of lyn" being taken as the tune of the modern "Tamlane," which is catalogued as "the tayl of the young temlene" among the "pleys and storeis."

In view of the alleged alliance between ballads and dancing it is singular that among the shepherds the narrative of "Tamlane" should not be sung, and that the air for the dance should have a different name. It requires a great deal of special pleading to prove that either narrative and tune or ballad and dance were bracketed together. It is quite within the possibilities of popular tradition that Tamlane or Thom of Lyn should have come to be regarded as a living personage, like Arthur and Robin Hood, most of whose exploits and personality are mythical, or like Sir James the Rose, who never existed, yet fought in the traditional "Battle of Harlaw"; and that dance tunes were named in his honour as a result of his ballad fame. It may be that considerations of this kind have impressed the communalists with the weakness of certain parts of their own theory, for their deductions are curious. None of the principal members of their sept claims definitely that ballads are dancing songs; Professor Kittredge goes as far as to say that our extant ballads were not communally improvised. Their case is that the ballads are derivations or developments from dancing songs, which were composed by companies. What would literary critics have to say of an historian of the drama who reasoned that, because both in Greece and in England the first attempts at dramatic construction were bound up with religious observances, the plays of Shakespeare, Congreve, and Shaw were written for the same purpose and are essentially religious in character? Yet that is the method of deduction adopted by the adherents of the communal theory of ballad origins. Gummere and, more emphatically, Professor Kittredge admit that the individual theory is consistent with common sense, and straightway proceed to rally in support of the opposite assumption, Faroe Islanders, school children, and Russian cigarette makers. They defend themselves by contending that if the individual solution is right, "all boundaries of the subject are obscured, the material is questionable, and a haze at once fills the air" (Gummere), or by declaring that the individualist explanation "is far too simple" (Kittredge). It cannot be both simple and obscure.

Everything has a beginning somewhere, and it is ridiculous to suggest that, at a hypothetical gathering where song was invented, the individuals present were each incapable of composing verse until by a spontaneous and instantaneous impulse they all burst into poetry together. The ballads themselves—setting aside the broadside and chapbook specimens, which were not composed by syndicates—present to us in every instance the credentials of individual origin. That they are almost without exception anonymous does not affect the point; a vast mass of early poetry is either anonymous or of uncertain authorship, and Scotland's finest songs before Burns are in like case. No one would venture to assert that "Andro and his cutty gun," or "The Wowing of Jok and Jynny," or "Sumer is i-cummen in," was written by a gathering, convivial or philosophical, simply because the author is unknown. Most people in Scotland, including Burns enthusiasts, associate "Annie Laurie" and "Mary of Argyle" with Burns; and, indeed, the folk do not worry themselves over nice questions of genesis. The "Old Lady's Collection" of traditional songs and ballads, for instance, contains poems by known authors, including "Tullochgorum" Skinner. Doubtless she learned these poems orally, without the aid of print. Henryson's "Bludy Serk" and "Robine and Makyne" and Scott's ballad emendations prove that the true spirit of authorship in the popular traditional manner is not inconsistent with high poetic art. There are ballads of which we have no versions worthy to be called poetry, and there are ballads of which there are versions that deserved to be classed among the higher reaches of poetry. One of the reasons for the depreciation of Peter Buchan's collection is that it contains so much of the first type. I am sure that the former class emanated from petty versifiers, inglorious but not mute Miltons of village and field, while the nobler ballads were the work of poets either of local or of national reputation, or deserving of such fame. Despite the unconsciously rough usage which continuous contact with the popular mind entails, ballads have come down to the opening of the present century, purely by traditional agency, which have preserved gems of narrative, description, and poetry. "The Douglas Tragedy," "The Lass of Roch Royal," "Johnnie o' Braidisleys," "Edom o' Gordon," and a score of others have retained in the latest recorded versions the cream of the first texts discovered.

That the finer ballads were not composed by any "son of the soil" is, I think, adequately demonstrated by a comparison between an early traditional version of any great ballad and a ploughman's or "bothy" ballad of recent times. "The Barnyards o' Delgaty," one of the most widely known and an average example in the northeast of Scotland of the ploughman's ballads, runs thus:

> In New Deer parish I was born,
>   A child of youth to Methlick came;
> And gin ye doot me to believe,
>   The session-clerk will tell the same.
>   Lintrin adie toorin adie,
>   Lintrin adie toorin ae.

> Good education I did get,
>   And I did learn to read and write;
> My parents they were proud o' me,
>   My mother in me took delight.

> To bide upon my father's farm,
>   That was never my intent;

I loved the lasses double weel,
    And aye the weary drap o' drink.

As I cam in by Netherdale,
    At Turra market for to fee,
I fell in wi' a thrifty Scot
    Fae the Barnyards o' Delgaty.

He promised me the ae best pair
    I ever set my e'en upon;
When I gaed hame to the Barnyards
    There was naething there but skin and bone.

The auld black horse sat on his rump,
    The auld white meer lay on her wime,
And a' that I could hup and crack,
    They widna rise at yokin' time.

Meg Macpherson mak's my brose,
    Her and me we cann gree;
First a mote and syne a knot,
    And aye the tither jilp o' bree.

But yet when I gang to the kirk,
    Mony's the bonnie lass I see,
Prim sittin' by her daddy's side,
    And winkin' owre the pews to me.

I can drink and nae be drunk,
    I can fight and nae be slain,
I can coort anither's lass,
    And aye be welcome to my ain.

My can'le noo it is brunt oot,
    The snotter's fairly on the wane;
Sae fare ye well, ye Barnyards,
    Ye'll never catch me here again.

Obviously this ditty never came from the sources out of which the great ballads arose, yet it was conceived in a mind as rustic and imperfectly educated as those which composed—if we believe the communal theorists—the triumphs of metrical tradition. It is full of traditional characteristics: the meaningless refrain, the phrases "child of youth" and "weary drap o' drink," the penultimate stanza (which Burns lifted bodily from a folk song current in his day), and the pseudo-moralizing of the final verse. "The Barnyard o' Delgaty" and its many frightful peers illustrate several of the insignia of popular tradition, and point the searcher away from the confines of the folk for the origins of the great ballads. The Pharisee and the publican were not more radically different than this sort of thing from "Clerk Saunders," "The Lass of Roch Royal," and "Barbara Allan."

The two styles are occasionally found united in a single ballad, the tenth-rate stuff having been stitched on to the true fabric by some blundering clown. In the first quarter of the nineteenth century, Kinloch got from James Beattie a pretty ballad, already known, called "The Gardener":

> The gardner stands in his bower-door,
>   With a primrose in his hand.
> And by there came a leal maiden,
>   As jimp's a willow wand.
>
> "O lady, can you fancy me,
>   For to be my bride,
> You'll get a' the flowers in my garden
>   To be to you a weed," &c.

About the same time and again three-quarters of a century later, the same ballad was found in oral tradition, with his incubus thrust upon it:

> There lived a lass now near han' by,
>   Who many sweethearts had,
> An' the gardener laddie viewed them a',
>   Jist as they cam an' gaed.
>
> The gardener laddie viewed them a',
>   An' he said he hadna skeel,
> "But an I wad gae as aft's the rest,
>   They wad say I were a feel.
>
> "I'm sure she's nae a proper lass,
>   Neither handsome, tight, nor tall";
> But another young man that stood by
>   Said, "Slight her not at all,

"For we are a' come o' womankin',
    If we wad call to min',
An' it's unto women for their sake
    We surely sud be kin'."

"Well, if I thought her worth my pains,
    Unto her I wad go,
An' I could wad a thousand pounds
    She wadna say me no."

Lady Margret stan's in her bower door,
    As straight's a willow wan',
An' by it cam the gardener lad,
    Wi' a red rose in his han', &c.

The amalgam in "The Gardener" represents the disparity between even second-rate ballads—for "The Gardener" is no more than that—and popularly made "poetry." These inserted stanzas, like "The Barnyards," reveal in their attitude to women a philosophy of the sexes which used to be universal and is still common in rural areas; but it is quite at odds with the chivalrous treatment of women in the great ballads—another proof that the latter were conceived outside the ruder society of the folk.

Three of the constituent features of ballads in general have been taken as proofs of communal origin—"incremental repetition," commonplaces, and refrains. "Incremental repetition" is defined by Gummere as "the lingering" over details of the narrative, "the succession of stanzas or of verses, mainly in triads, which are identical save for one or two pivotal words." Incremental repetition "supplies a visible link between oldest choral repetition and actual text"; it "points unerringly back to choral conditions, to a dance where the crowd moves to its own singing, and where the song, mainly repetition, got its matter from successive stages or shifts of what may be called a situation rather than a story." More than one student has pointed out that in the ballads this "incremental repetition" is not found in the earliest specimens preserved, that it occurs most frequently in broadside versions, and that it is a frequent characteristic of other kinds of lyric poetry. In traditional ballads incremental repetition is inextricably mixed with the commonplace and the refrain, and a study of its vagaries in oral usage reveals an aspect quite different from that which appears in an examination of printed texts without experience of actual singing or recitation. In the very long narrative ballads we look for incremental repetition, for the simple reason that the singer requires an occasional respite for breath. Ballads are not in this country sung communally. Some one sings a ballad and the others join in with the refrain or with any stanza they happen to be familiar with. Ballad versions run in families. The procedure, as described by a member of a family that has produced folk singers for many generations, was in this fashion. "They met at somebody's house one evening, the women taking their knitting. All sat round in a circle, while some one of the company sang a ballad, the whole assembly joining in *or* repeating the last line of each verse in order to give the singer time to get breath for his next verse. Then some others contributed, and all the while a large pot boiled on the fire, cooking kail or turnips which were ladled out on to a beremeal scone before the guests departed. Then another evening they met in another house, and repeated the performance, with perhaps other ballads but the same hospitality."

The refrain performs two technical functions. It may either fill out the words to fit in with the air:

> There was a king's daughter lived in the north—
> Hey the rose an' the linsie O—
> An' she has courted her father's clerk—
> An' away be the greenwood sidie O.
> (The Cruel Mother);

and in "The Elfin Knight," "The Twa Sisters," "The Fair Flower of Northumberland," "Hind Horn," and many others. Or it may be for the double purpose of rounding off the verse and at the same time affording the singer a breathing interlude:

> A bonnie May went out one day
>   Some fresh fish for to buy,
> An' there she spied a wee toon's clerk,
>   An' he followed her speedily—
> Ricky doo dum dae, doo dum dae,
> Ricky dicky doo dum dae.

The latter type is more common in the later than in the older ballads. The commonplace has also a dual quality. In popular minstrelsy certain actions, objects, and emotions are described in set terms. This is in accordance with the habitual expression of all whose vocabulary is limited, besides being parallel with the customs of speech in all matters where procedure has become stereotyped. Just as chairman after chairman of public meetings refuses to "stand between" the audience and the star speaker; just as a shareholder in a public company who has been asked to move the re-election of a director "begs to propose" or has "much pleasure in proposing"; so the balladist invariably calls water "wan water" and a page "a bonnie little boy" and a note "a braid letter," pronounces the curse "an ill death may you dee," and so on. When this formal mode of expression is extended from single words and short phrases to whole stanzas, we reach a second duty of the commonplace. Certain instructions—a call for a horse, an order to carry a message—and certain situations—the receipt of a letter, a swift journey—are narrated in terms hallowed by long application. When the ballad singer reaches such passages, the audience know what is coming and join in. This heightens the social effect of ballad singing.

In about fifty per cent of the cases of incremental repetition the commonplace is included. In all cases, however, incremental repetition is susceptible of being interpreted as a factor of the narrative, without any reference whatever to the movements of hypothetical dances. The repetition, substantially verbatim, of the words of a stanza—not necessarily in triads, for often the stanza is repeated but once, at times the increment is fourfold—permits the audience to join in, just as the appearance of the commonplace does. It has a further effect which has not, I think, hitherto been noticed. Much has been made of the artlessness, the simplicity, of the ballad, and these qualities are certainly predominant in the vocabulary and the details of the "plot." But when a ballad is sung it communicates sensations not in their kind essentially different from those aroused by a novel or a play. The interest of the audience is firmly, if subtly, won, and in the development of the story in the lengthy ballads incremental repetition tends towards a result resembling that attained by art poetry. The marking-time of the repetition whets the appetite for the crisis that is to follow; it is a pause in the action before the narrative hastens towards the usually tragic culmination. The Porter Scene in *Macbeth* is an interlude different in quality but not different in fundamental character from incremental repetition in the ballads. How involved may become the employment of commonplace and incremental repetition is exemplified in "Love Johnnie." Johnnie desires to send a message to his sweetheart, the King's daughter:

1. "It's where'll I get a little wee boy   (*Commonplace,*
     That will win gowd an' fee,   *2 lines*)
   That will run on to the King's castle,
     An' come quickly back to me?"

2. "It's here am I, a little wee boy,   (*Incremental*
     That will win gowd an' fee,   *repetition*)
   That will run on to the King's castle,
     An' come quickly back to thee."

3. "It's where ye find the brigs broken,   (*Commonplace,*
     Ye'll bend your bow an' swim,   *4 lines*)
   An' where ye find the grass grow green,
     Ye'll slack your shoon an' rin.

4. "An' when ye come to the King's castle,
     Ye'll ride it roon about,
   An' there ye'll spy a lady fair
     At the window lookin' out.

5. "Ye'll bid her fess wi' her the silken shift *   (* *Commonplace*)
     That her ain hand sewed the sleeve,
   An' ye'll bid her come on to the good green woods *
     An' speir nane o' the high man's leave.

6. "Ye'll bid her fess wi' her the silken shift   (*Incremental*
     That her ain hand sewed the gare,   *repetition, 3 lines*)
   An' bed her come on to the good green woods,
     An' Love Johnnie will meet her there."

7. It's where he found the brigs broken,   (*Incremental*
     He bent his bow an' swam,   *repetition of st. 3*)
   An' where he found the grass grow green,
     He slacked his shoon an' ran.

8. An' when he came to the King's castle,   (*Incremental*
     He rode it roon about,   *repetition of st. 4*)
   An' there he spied a lady fair
     At the window lookin' out.

9. "Good-day, good-day," the little boy said,—   (*Lingering*)
   "Good-day, good-day," said she,
   "Good-day, good-day," the lady she said,
   "An' what's your will wi' me?"

10. "Ye're bidden fess wi' you the silken shift   (*Incremental
    That your ain hand sewed the sleeve,   repetition of st. 5*)
    An' ye'll come on to the good green woods,
    Speir nane o' the high man's leave.

11. "Ye're bidden fess wi' you the silken shift   (*Incremental
    That your ain hand sewed the gare,   repetition of st. 6*)
    An ye'll come on to the good green woods,
    Love Johnnie will meet you there."

The quotation is from a seventy-year-old version, but another text, from the same district but recorded one hundred years earlier, has a stanza breaking the repetitional sequence between 1 and 2, omits stanzas 3–6 (obviously a lapse of memory), and omits stanza 9 (which is not essential to the story); otherwise it is practically identical.

Tautology and clichés are both insistent tempters of the human being who desires to express himself, but in their every manifestation they are each bound to have had a beginning somewhere. Repetition, the overwhelming weight of evidence goes to show, was a development of ballad expression subsequent to the invention of ballads, and it scarcely needs to be stated that the aptness of a particular phrase in an early ballad led to its adoption in similar circumstances in other ballads, and that thus the commonplace grew and spread. The refrains are either onomatopoeic—e.g. "a riddle a in aldinadie, A riddle a in aldinee"—in assonance with a sequence of notes or with the sound of a musical instrument, or they are meaningless phrases—like "fine flowers in the valley," "lay the bent to the bonnie broom"—which had been lifted more or less corruptly from other nonnarrative ditties. But from none of the three appurtenances of balladry—repetition, commonplace, and refrain—can evidence be drawn more compatible with communal than with individual composition.

Only one theory of authorship can pass all tests of probability and available knowledge. The ballads were originally composed by individuals, the best ballads by poets of culture and artistic power. Recited, sung, or in some way communicated by their authors to a wider circle, they were memorized by various members of these audiences, and by them orally transmitted to others, and thus gradually disseminated throughout the community. Farmers, sailors, shepherds, drovers, harvest hands following their vocation up and down the country, beggars, itinerant merchants, all sorts of travellers, and in more recent years navvies, have carried the ballads hither and thither from shire to shire, and even across the seas; while the chapbook and broadside printers with their cheap publications lent to the process of broadcasting an assistance that could well have been spared. The ballads thus circulated acquired local colour and associations: "Edom o' Gordon" has an English, a Lanarkshire, and an Aberdeenshire setting. They suffered all sorts of vicissitudes. Faulty recollection on the part of a new singer or reciter resulted in alterations; indifferent hearing or intelligence had a similar effect; persons who had, or imagined they had, a flair for verse could not be expected to refrain from changing rhymes, substituting phrases, interpolating fresh stanzas, in the ballads of which they acquired versions; collectors like Percy, Scott, and Jamieson furbished up their collections; the occurrence of an event broadly similar to one recounted in a ballad would naturally lead to the adaptation of that ballad to the recent incident; and few of those, in short, through whose minds the ballads passed, did not unconsciously or intentionally impress their own mark upon them. In the traditional version of "Harlaw" (which cannot be traced beyond 1800 and has every appearance of eighteenth-century origin), the mailed Lowlanders become "redcoats"; the Forbeses, who were not in the battle, shared the leadership of the Lowland forces with those two mythical worthies, Sir James the Rose and Sir John the Graeme; and the scale of the battle, including a few hours' interval while Forbes's servant runs home for his master's harness, is quite Homeric, and might have originated in the Hellenic enthusiasm of such a one as Robert Forbes, whose translation, "Ajax's Speech to the Grecian Knabbs," appeared in 1742. The historical ballads dealing with the Scottish feuds of the sixteenth and seventeenth centuries are all the work of partisans, usually of the discomfited faction. In short, while individuals were responsible for the first drafts of the ballads, which are lost, so many additions and alterations have been made in the course of traditional descent that the ballads as we have them today may accurately be termed of folk authorship, but the composition was incremental, cumulative, and haphazard, not communal and instantaneous. The last argument against the communal theory is found in the ballad airs, which in every way resemble the ballads in their development and vagaries, but which would hardly be claimed by the most rabid communalist as the product of festal throngs or homogeneous companies. That subject, however, is beyond the purpose of this essay.

ii

****

THE METER AND MUSIC
OF THE BALLAD

———————

6

✳✳✳✳✳✳✳✳✳✳✳✳✳✳✳✳✳✳✳✳

The Part of the Folk Singer in the Making of Folk Balladry

PHILLIPS BARRY

FOLKSONG is one of the great paradoxes of human experience. It is the possession of a people or *folk*, yet it was not made by the people. Nor is it to be regarded as the expression, in some mystical way, of the emotional life of a people. On the contrary, it is rather the cumulative result of expression of individual artistry through the work of the more or less indefinite number of folk singers who have brought it to its present status. It is perfectly proper to say of all folksong, and in particular of the folk-music drama which by inherited usage we still inaptly call the ballad, that it exists in a kind of fluid state, so that we say of any folk song: "there are texts, but no *text*; tunes, but no *tune*." Just because it is so different, so unlike, let us say, the songs of Stephen Collins Foster, every one of which however widely known and sung has its own authentic text and air not to be changed by any singer, a proper way has been sought to account for its existence. Thus the genesis of folksong has been carried back speculatively to a super-primitive state of society in which the making of the arts, including poetry and music, came about through the collective action of the folk.

Attempts have been made to visualize the process of communal or collective composition of song. The first such attempt, under the influence of the romantic movement, gave rise to the "play theory." We were asked to believe in a singing, dancing throng, making verses while engaged in play following toil—a hunt for wild game, a battle, or what not—re-enacting in verses experiences of the occasion living in memory. The adherents of this theory were at the same time both very cautious

and very incautious. Originality may be said to be the one thing they de-
sired least to be given credit for, so eager were they to show that their
dogma of communal composition belonged to that class which to a theo-
logian is expressed by the formula, *quod semper, quod ubique, quod ab
omnibus.* Thus they imputed to eminent authorities of the past, such
as Aristotle, Montaigne and the brothers Grimm, vague reflected
echoes of their own speculation which would have made these worthies
tear their hair, could they have come back from the Elysian Fields to
discover how untruthfully their minds had been read. Yet at the same
time they were cautious: while they conceded the singing of ballads, or
at least never went so far as to deny it, they did not stultify themselves
by attempting to visualise the collective composition by a throng of
even the simplest melody. Of course the logical weakness of their
theory is patent to any open mind. If it be made to work at all as a
hypothesis, as it has been made to work after a certain fashion, this
result is attained only by concession of the pre-existence of a melody to
act as a self-starter in every case of possible collective composition. Once
such pre-existence of melody is admitted, the whole theory falls into a
logical collapse. If *das Volk dichtet* be a true formula; if the folk, or
the singing, dancing throng ever made any songs by the collective action of a group mind, it should have made the music at the same time
as the words. If it did not make the music, and the best exponents of
the dogma declare that it did not, then the folk composed only poetry
and not folk-song. Perhaps it is this logical fallacy, hardly less than the
devastating barrage of facts launched by recent studies of individual
song-histories which should be set down as the principal reason why we
do not now hear so much about the singing, dancing throng and are
likely to hear less.

Yet escapist theories die hard. If the singing, dancing throng is
passing into the limbo of forgotten things, we have something like its
ghost still with us. Not a playing throng any more, but, in the opinion
of the Russian Tchemodanov, a working throng made the first folk-
songs. We are again asked to hark back to that prenatal stage, so to
speak, of society when the group mind so perfectly dominated the individual mind that there was no place in the economy of things for the
creative artist as an individual—to imagine the throng engaged in
collective labor. The inarticulate grunts and ejaculations of each worker,
set to the rhythm of the motions of the task, should in time emerge as
articulate words carried by an articulate melody. We submit that, no

less than the play theory, the work theory of communal composition begs the question. There are still work songs, plenty of them. But if there be any evidence of setting motions of labor in a fixed pattern held fast by rhythm and melody, as the theory demands, all such evidence is clearly on the side of domination of the group by a superior mind. Nothing in the way of a work song is less communal than a sailors' shanty: the shantyman dominates the group as a measure of necessary efficiency. Such domination of the group by the individual is shown to even better advantage in Lomax's "Steel-Laying Holler." One could not ask for better evidence in any work song of intelligently directed and regimented labor under a superior mind: the song consists wholly of the orders of a gang boss to his docile and obedient crew. Again the song is a means of maintaining efficiency of labor: steel rails, each weighing a ton or more, are not for haphazard juggling and can be handled with efficiency and safety only under such intelligent direction.

More than thirty years ago, we made the suggestion that it might be proper to go to the folk singers to find such evidence as might lead to the solution of some of the many—not the one—ballad problems. We were not surprised to meet with academic defeatism. It had been held that ballads were no longer *recited*—nothing was said about the singing of them, so firmly fixed was the notion that ballads were poems and not songs—hence there were no *reciters* to go to. True, it might be that occasionally a person would be found who could recite a ballad from memory, but there could be no escape from the supposition that he had learned it from print. Undaunted, however, we began our search: we found the ballads, as we found the folk singers, and we have been learning of the folk singers ever since.

The first thing we learned is that they sensed no distinction and tried to make none between the ballad of situation developed in dialogue form and the ballad of pure narration. The next thing we learned was that the folk-singer, however much he be keeper of a tradition, is never for a single moment dominated by it. He learns his songs and in his interpretation of them does exactly what he pleases with them. Often as temperamental as a prima donna, he is the most passionate of individualists. The way he sings a certain ballad is the *right way;* it may be sung differently by other singers whose deviations from his way may meet now with kindly tolerance, now with the bitterest intolerance. We have an authentic instance of two folk singers in Waterford, Ireland, who all but came to blows over the proper way to sing "The Old

Beggar-Man," an Irish version of Child's "Hind Horn." No song, new or old, may escape such re-creation by a folk singer; it is not even safe to say that folk singers *never* change text or air of Stephen Foster's songs. The evidence of a Vermont singer's manuscript collection, now in the Vermont Historical Society Library, shows that a Gilbertian "hardly ever" is closer to the truth. To put the results of our long sitting at the feet of the folk singer most briefly and concisely, the way of the folk singer is the way of the folk.

Let us take the case of a single ballad. Child's "Lord Randall" is very likely the most widely known of all the British ballads surviving in American tradition. Textually it shows the widest possible range of variation, though the plot is of the simplest. A young man dines with his true-love, who, for no apparent motive, gives him poison; he goes to his mother's home to die. One of the first versions of this ballad recorded by us, when we first sat at the feet of a folk singer, is the following, obtained in 1903 from a young woman who learned it of her grandmother in Fredericton, N.B.:

Dear Willie

"Oh, where have you been, dear Willie, my son?
 Oh, where have you been, my darling young one?"
"I've been to see my sweetheart, mother, make my bed soon,
 As I'm sick to my heart, and I fain would lie down."

"What did your sweetheart give you, dear Willie, my son?
 What did your sweetheart give you, my darling young one?"
"Three little silver fishes, mother, make my bed soon,
 For I'm sick to my heart, and I fain would lie down."

"What will you leave your father, dear Willie, my son?
 What will you leave your father, my darling young one?"
"My coaches and horses, mother, make my bed soon,
 For I'm sick to my heart and I fain would lie down."

"What will you leave your mother, dear Willie, my son?
 What will you leave your mother, my darling young one?"
"My best milch cows, mother, make my bed soon,
 For I'm sick to my heart and I fain would lie down."

"What will you leave to your sister, dear Willie, my son?
  What will you leave to your sister, my darling young one?"
"Many rings and diamonds, mother, make my bed soon,
  For I'm sick to my heart and I fain would lie down."

"What will you leave your sweetheart, dear Willie, my son?
  What will you leave your sweetheart, my darling young one?"
"A rope for to hang her on yonder green tree,
  'Tis more than she deserves, for she's poisoned me!"

The nuncupative will is found in most versions of this ballad, but not in all, and not in some of the texts of oldest record. The question whether it was originally a part of the ballad need not concern us, but only the form in which it is cast. As it stands, it is an excellent example of what is called incremental repetition: the several legatees pass by, so to speak, in a more or less established order of succession, leading to the climax in the person of the false true-love, who receives as her bequest the proper meed of punishment, sometimes in this world, sometimes in the next. As far as the aesthetic and ethical demands of an audience are concerned, it is not at all clear why the bequest to the false true-love should not be enough: the suggestion that blood kin share in the deceased's estate, while a natural sequence of thought, is yet a sequence none the less.

Be that as it may, once the succession of heirs is started the psychological law of associated ideas is enough to carry the composition of additional verses through the succession of father, mother, sister. The width of the family-circle concept tends to vary directly with the association complex in the mind of the singer. Thus, the absence of the brother from the text of "Dear Willie" may be as much due to the absence of a brother for the child in the family in which it was sung, as mere forgetfulness on the part of the singer.

Usually the relative succession in "Lord Randall" stops with parents and siblings; rarely the grandmother is included. One text of unusual interest came to us two years ago from Northeast Harbor, Maine. The contributor, who learned it as a small child, recalls having asked whether any bequest was made to aunts or cousins, but at the time no reply was forthcoming. This instance enables us to understand the incentives for re-creation of a traditional ballad—the breaking away from tradition with the individual consciousness of the singer in revolt.

It shows the child suffering from a sense of outraged justice that a be-loved aunt or a favorite cousin should be cut off without even the proverbial shilling, and demanding a place in the picture for the omitted relative. Psychologically, the wish to include parental siblings and their descendants means that the associated units of the family circle were more numerous in the child's consciousness than in the singer's. There is nothing to stand in the way of a singer having the same thought as this child; we can only say that, as far as we know, no version of "Lord Randall" exists in which place has been so made for parental siblings or their descendants. Yet a Vermont text of the ballad shows how association of a different sort may lead to the composition of an adventitious stanza, which as far as we know is unique: the false wife's servant is willed punishment as well as her mistress. Accessory guilt is the factor in the association.

The universally familiar ballad of "The Hangman's Tree"—in one variation known as "The Golden Ball"—resembles "Lord Randall" in that the entire action is carried on through dialogue and in the use of incremental repetition involving association family units. Originally, the plot of the ballad forms a symbolic drama dealing with the loss of virginity—symbolised as a golden ball—by the heroine, who sym-bolically recovers the lost article from the only person who has it, her lover. In what may be called the adult type of the drama, the action must stop with the entrance of the lover; any action beyond this point would be anticlimax. Not so for the regressed infantile type recovered by us from tradition in Maine. The most interesting version of this type has, naturally, no suggestion of the meaning of the lost golden ball, which the heroine, a child, has not from a lover, but from her uncle, who charges her not to lose it, or she will hang on the old "brindle-brindle" tree. The array of relatives who pass in succession through the drama includes parental siblings and grandparents, four of the last. Since the children of the family who played the game of the golden ball had four living grandparents, place was made for them, and it is the "other grandmother" who finally saves the little heroine from hanging. Of the two sisters from whom we obtained the version in question, the elder knew what "hanging" meant when she played the game: the younger associated hanging with the family wash on the clothesline, and supposed accordingly that the child who lost the precious gift would be fastened by a clothespin to the brindle-brindle tree. A trifling detail, one may say, but it is none the less evidence of the individualism of a keeper of tradition.

While we are still concerned with matter of interpretation of ballad tradition by folk singers, we may profitably consider the case of what may be called the regressive form of the ballad of "The Two Sisters." Let us consider the following version, recorded a year ago in Vermont:

The Youngest Daughter

There was a man who lived out west,
Lived out west, lived out west;

There was a man who lived out west,
He loved his youngest daughter best.

He bought for his youngest a gay gold ring;
The oldest she hadn's anything.

He bought for his youngest a beaver hat;
The oldest she was mad at that.

One day these girls went down to swim;
The oldest pushed her sister in.

First she sank and then she swam,
Until she reached the miller's dam.

The miller put out his line and hook,
And caught her by the petticoat.

The miller took off her gay gold ring,
And threw her into the stream again.

The king and his son were riding by,
They heard the youngest daughter cry.

And so the riders pulled her out,
To see what she was crying about.

Next day the old miller was hung for her sake,
And the eldest daughter burned at the stake.

As compared with some of the older versions of Scottish and Scotch-Irish tradition, printed by Child, this text of "The Two Sisters" appears very clearly on the downhill road. The ballad itself, with which we hope

to deal exhaustively in an extensive monograph now in preparation, is
based on a very ancient theme, having to do with the possible tragic
issues of family life in which *three* sisters take part. The original
form of the plot, featuring not two sisters but three, is in Polish and
sporadically also in Scottish and Scotch-Irish tradition. The form of the
plot as we have it in the foregoing version differs from the normal
tradition in that the cause of murderous jealousy is not grounded in
love for a suitor, but in a pathological attachment between father and
daughter. Now there are in American tradition, three types of the
normal plot: (1) in which the miller is the lover of the murdered sister; (2) in which the miller takes the younger sister from the pond
while she is still alive, strips her of clothes and jewels and throws her
back to drown, for which he as well as the elder sister is put to death;
and (3) a variant of (2) in which only the miller is punished. In both 2
and 3 we find the regressive form of the plot, with the gradual and
finally total disappearance of the lover, together with the pathological
relation of father and daughter, evolving as a by-product of traditional singing. The reason for this development is that a certain number of persons who have sung the ballad have been sufferers from
frustrations, soured on the world, and as a result of their pathological
make-up, have come to forget those stanzas which relate to the part of
the lover; the very stanzas which should be the least likely to be forgotten. We even have the curious case of a copyist who not only omitted
the lover stanza but even inserted asterisks to show the gap. The text
was printed by Child as "Y": he never verified the original, in the
Percy mss., or he would have discovered the omission.

While we still have the foregoing text of "The Two Sisters" fresh
in memory, it may be noted that it consists wholly of narration, not a
word of dialogue, introduced or unintroduced. In this respect it is
not in any way different from the following recent woods ballad:

Samuel Allen

Ye tender-hearted people, I pray you lend an ear,
And when you have my story heard, you can but drop a tear
Concerning Samuel Allen, a man both strong and brave,
And on a stream called Rocky Brook, he met with a watery grave.

He was both tall and handsome, his age was twenty one,
And if I do remember right, he was an only son;

His father bade him a fond farewell, as the Gibson train rolled by,
And then walked slowly homeward—the tears bedimmed his eye.

I'll tell you now of Rocky Brook, that sad and dismal place;
No matter where you work on it, death stares you in the face;
The rocks stand up like mountains high, for miles along the shore;
'Twould fill your heart with misery, to hear the waters roar.

'Twas on one Monday morning, the sun was shining clear,
When Samuel Allen last attempt, with neither dread nor fear;
He went up to the rolling dam, to see what he could do,
In trying to get the boom prepared, to sluice the lumber through.

He looked first up and down the stream, a-looking for a jam,
When the water made an awful rush and tore away the dam;
The boom that he was standing on, was quickly torn away,
And soon within the raging tide, his lifeless body lay.

'Twas ten o'clock in the forenoon, he received his fatal blow;
Some people think he lost his life while in the undertow;
He was cut and bruised about the head, his body it was bare—
O, what a sight it must have been for comrades who were there!

They took him to his father's house—'twould grieve your heart full sore,
To see the people mourn for grief around the cottage door;
There was one fair form among them, I will not speak her name,
Who had hoped to be his wedded wife, when home again he came.

But hope gave way to dark despair, when she beheld the form
Of him who promised all through life to shield her from the storm;
And hand in hand no more to roam the hills of Gerick Vale;
Both night and morn this maid forlorn her saddened fate bewails.

He leaves an aged father, quite well along in years,
Likewise a fair young sweetheart to wait for him in tears—
He took her by the hand that day, when he left his father's door,
But little did he think that he would never see her more.

His body in the churchyard, to rest is laid away,
A-waiting for the Savior's call, on that great judgment day,
When friend and foe must rise and go at the Archangel's call,
And there abide, the Lord beside, the Father of us all.

We have applied the term "folk-music drama" to such ballads as "Lord Randall." Does the term apply equally well to "Samuel Allen"? We submit that it does, though the dramatic technique is quite different, and we are content to rest on the precedent set by the world's greatest masters of drama, the tragic poets of ancient Athens. They had and used both kinds of technique, dialogue and narration. The reaction of Oedipus and his mother to the discovery of the relationship in which fate had placed them is too inspiring of pity and fear to be acted on the stage: the audience is permitted but to hear of it, as we hear the fate of Samuel Allen, from a narrator. In the case of such calamity ballads as "Samuel Allen" and the more familiar "Jam on Gerrow's Rock," there are also technical difficulties which stand very much in the way of presenting the situation except through narration by a third person.

The danger of going astray by making artificial distinctions is illustrated by the case of "The Two Sisters." If by some odd chance no version had survived except the single one in which the action is depicted wholly by narration, if we had none of those earlier oldcountry texts in which the apparel of the much over-dressed heroine is described in a series of sometimes tedious incremental stanzas, the makers of artificial distinctions and ballad aristocracies would deny the ballad the right to be classified as "pure folk." It is the story, not the manner in which the story is told, which in the last analysis accounts for the fact that a certain song is a folk song.

Usually the author of a folk song and the composer of the music are unknown; herein lies one of the lesser reasons for the escapist attitude which sought refuge from perplexity in theories of communal origins. About twenty-five years ago, Professor Lomax printed a ballad in his *Cowboy Songs,* of a young white woman, kidnapped by Indians, rescued from torture and death by the chief of the tribe who fell in love with her and offered to go to the stake in her place. We may assume this ballad, authorless as it was then, fell in the category of those songs which seemed to have grown up as mysteriously as the grass on the plains.

The true history of this ballad is now known. In the summer of 1818, a young graduate of Dartmouth, afterwards known as the Reverend Professor Thomas Coggswell Upham, who for over forty years held the chair of Moral Philosophy at Bowdoin College, was spending his vacation in the hill country of New Hampshire. On

July 19 he had seen a meteor of brilliant red color and unusual size and brightness, which attracted great interest among all who saw it. There was something portentous, even to an educated man, in a falling star that seemed as large and "bright as the full moon at rising," to quote the words of Professor Hall of Middlebury College observatory. On September 19, the following poem by the young college graduate, inspired in part at least by the awesome meteor, appeared in the *Columbian Centinel* (Boston):

Olban

The moon had gone down o'er the hills of the west,
And her last beam had faded from *Moosehillock's* crest,
'Twas a midnight of horror—the red meteor flash'd,
And hoarse down the mountain, the cataract dash'd.

At intervales came in the hollow wind's sigh,
The hoot of the owl and the catamount's cry,
And the howl of the wolf from his lone granite cell,
And the crash of the dead forest tree as it fell.

The watch-fire was lighted, and fann'd by the breeze,
Its red embers shone on the evergreen trees;
And fiercer the looks of the plum'd savage seem'd,
As the light on his features of bronze dimly gleam'd.

At the foot of the hemlock the wild game was flung,
And above from its branches the rude armour hung—
From battle and plunder, the warrior repos'd,
And the toils of the chase till the morrow had clos'd.

Ere the blushes of morning again should return,
In torture *Amanda* was destin'd to burn—
Amanda, the pride of her village and home,
Who far up the Merrimac's waters had come.

In war led a captive, unfriended, forlorn,
Her feet bath'd in blood, and her garments all torn;
She courted the vengeance and wrath of her foes,
And sigh'd for the day, when her suff'rings should close.

The faggots were kindled, the red torches glar'd,
Her hands they were bound, and her white bosom bar'd;
Around her stood waiting the merciless throng,
Impatient to join, the war dance and song.

Young *Olban,* the chief of the warriors was there,
With the eye of an eagle,—the foot of the deer,
And a soul that would scorn from a foeman to crave
A sigh for his suff'rings, a tear for his grave.

For a moment he hung on the charms of the fair,
Her dark hazel eye, now uplifted in prayer,
And her bright sunny locks, that in ringlets below
Half hid from the gazer her bosom of snow.

"Forbear," cried the chieftain, "your tortures forbear,
The captive shall live—by this Wampum I swear—
This night if a victim must burn at the tree,
Young *Olban,* your leader, that victim shall be."

To the arms of *Amanda,* as forward he rush'd,
The revelry ceas'd and the tumult was hush'd,
And mute stood the circle of warriors around,
While *Olban* the chains of the captive unbound.

On *Pemigewasset,* at dawning of day,
Their birchen canoe was seen gliding away;
And fleet as the wild duck that swam by their side,
In silence they rode down the dark-rolling tide.

At dusk of the evening, the white cot was seen,
And its smoke curling blue round the wild willow green;
One moment in parting they past on the shore,
And Olban, the warrior was heard of no more.

There is a great deal more of Thomas Moore and Thomas Campbell than of originality in this poem, but it is written in what passed in its day for good taste. Some folk singer chanced on a copy of the *Centinel,* read the poem, and exclaimed to himself in the words which we have met from time to time as the meed of praise by the naïve, "isn't that grand!" Too good for mere reading, it ought to be sung. There was an air in his mind, the air to an old-country ballad of the lady who hunted the farmer with her dog and her gun, because she was in love with him and wished to marry him. The folk singer tried this air—and Professor Upham's ballad is still sung to it, in various sets. We have found it in several versions in the Northeast, where it was a favorite song of the woodsmen. When, in the late 1860's, adventurous youths from Maine and the Maritime provinces laid aside axe and peavy and took up quirt and branding iron, they did not cease to sing of fair Amanda and the chivalrous savage. So now the Texas cowboy knows a neglected item of a college professor's juvenilia as an authorless folk song. The folk singer has made it a folk ballad: no one else. It has even undergone a certain amount of re-creation, some of it in far worse taste than the strained sentiment of the original. Upham left Olban a *noble* savage, renouncing love to keep his word with his tribe, though keeping it meant death by torture. No longer noble, of the savage it is said in one Texas version,

> All that he asked was shelter and food
> From the parents of Amanda for the chief of the woods.

How the mighty have fallen—to the depth of asking for a handout. Perhaps the folk singer responsible for this touch did not mean to be comic, but he showed one aspect of the way of the folk with its ballads, helped in their dotage to elicit more laughs than tears.

WE HAVE SAID that a song by Stephen Foster differs from a folk song in that it has its authentic text and air, whereas a folk song has *texts,* but no *text, tunes* but no *tune.* The interpreter of a Foster song has no right to deviate in the slightest degree from the author-composer's autograph. The interpreter of a folk song, however, has every such right, for the reason that, as he sings the song, he is something more than an interpreter: he is, together with every other folk singer who sings the song in question—past, present or future,—co-author with the author of the text, and co-composer with the composer of the air. He may, if he choose, render a certain ballad exactly as it was sung by the person from whom he learned it; the fact, however, that he does so render it gives us no warrant for the conclusion that he or any other folk singer is simply an animated dictaphone record. One of the happiest experiences of our field work in the Northeast was on the occasion when two folk singers, fellow townsmen and near neighbors, sang for us their respective versions of our favorite ballad of the woods, "Lost Jimmie Whalen." There were differences between the two texts but far more significant differences between the two sets of the air—one of the loveliest in American tradition anywhere. The singer whom we shall call Mr. A— sang a set in the Dorian mode; the traditional background of his version is demonstrably Canadian. Mr. B— sang a Mixolydian set, superficially seeming a distinct air. When, however, the two sets are collated note by note, their descent from a common original is perfectly clear, while the transformation of a Dorian melody to a Mixolydian is traceable through a variation, three times repeated in the course of the ballad, as sung by Mr. A—; this variation is of a kind that, to the extent to which it stabilises itself in memory, so breaks up the tonal associations of Dorian melodic structure that it cannot fail to affect the form of the air as a whole. Apparently Canadian singers who have transmitted "Lost Jimmie Whalen" have a preference for Dorian tonality which is not fully shared by singers in the States.

The first lesson to learn from the ways of these two friends who sang for us in the cool of a June evening a year ago is that it is always necessary to record the music to the entire ballad. To record the music of but a single stanza is better than following the old-school example of ignoring the music and trying to make sense out of ballads as literature. But it is no better for what we are trying to learn about ballads than taking only the text of a single stanza. Occasionally it is even possible to catch the re-creating folk-interpreter-composer in the very act. We recall the case of a dear old Irish lady who sang for us the only version ever recorded in the United States of the earlier tradition of "The Demon Lover"—quite distinct from the familiar "House Carpenter." A certain phrase of the air is pitched rather low; as she sang it the effect was not satisfactory to her. She repeated her singing; this time she lifted the phrase in question into an upper octave, making also such other changes in melodic sequence as were required to give a smooth progression. We had never before encountered this device, but its application enabled us to understand certain aspects of melodic variation which we had met with elsewhere and for which no explanation was forthcoming.

The foregoing evidences of changes in the structure of folk melodies as a result of definite preference on the part of folk singers are not by any means the only evidences we have. The late Gavin Greig made a statement which, at the time he made it, seemed very much open to question: he expressed his doubt that there were many independent airs in English traditional music. Now in the case of two ballads which we have made the objects of assiduous study, "The Two Sisters" and "The Golden Vanity," the excellent judgment of Greig seems very clearly vindicated. For the old-country tradition of "The Two Sisters," the bulk of the versions are sung to a Scandinavian air; the American tradition, with the familiar "bow down" refrain, is sung to a different Scandinavian air, to one set of which is sung the only known version of the Swedish ballad *De Tvo Systrarna* (The Two Sisters) hitherto recorded in this country. An examination of the sets of this air, recorded by Sharp in the southern Appalachians, shows the presence of great instability of mode: individual singers show the folk singer's individualism by singing at one time in major, at another in modal sequence— Dorian, Mixolydian or Aeolian. In the case of "The Golden Vanity," we are ready to make a cautious and tentative statement that nearly if not quite all traditional tunes of this ballad, of whatever form, have come from the original air "Sailing in the Lowlands," named in a seventeenth-century broadside; that this air has survived in derivative sets close to its original form in Vermont and in Missouri. The original air, we infer, in the major mode, had a puzzling kind of cross-tonality which literally forced folk singers to re-create it. Sometimes they changed the original air but slightly; at other times, they actually composed new tunes on the basis of single phrases of the old. The readiness with which a number of the modal tunes to this ballad may be shown to be such secondary improvisations, raises doubts in our mind as to the probable antiquity of much of the existing body of modal music. It may be a good guess that part of it is of relatively recent date.

Let us next consider the case of iteration of phrase in music. This is a device as perfectly established in the music of the folk-music drama as incremental repetition is in the texts. A sadly uninformed reviewer of *British Ballads from Maine*, who showed thereby his profound ignorance of all that Mr. Cecil Sharp has written on English folk-music, objected that too many of our tunes were "vitiated by the unenterprising repetition of simple figures"—whatever that may mean. Everyone who has more than a tyro's knowledge of folk music is familiar with what Béla Bartók has called the architectonic patterns, graphically represented by such formulas as ABBC and ABBA, just to mention two such patterns. These patterns are found not only in Hungarian and Rumanian folk-melodies, as Bartók has shown, but are equally common in Irish airs of the long come-all-ye type, favorites with folk singers of the North. There is a very distinct tendency observable among folk singers, to follow a line of least resistance in rendering these airs. That is, given an air of the ABBC type, in which the final phrase is not the same as the initial phrase, they change the air to the ABBA type by a kind of anticipation, as it were of the A-phrase with which the following stanza begins. Reduction of an air of this type to a single phrase is not unknown; herein is a lesson for the critic who venturesomely declares that the textual superiority of such and such a ballad or version is conditioned by the actual amount of incremental repetition. We do not deny that repetition is an artistic device which properly used is effective, whether in text or tune. In a text it may go on *ad nauseam*, as in Child's κ-text of "Lamkin" which degenerates into a series of stanzas inviting a succession of noble ladies to come down stairs and be bled to death, a succession which it has been said might go on until the "reciter" (sic!) could not think of any more women's names. It may be used for comic effect, as it certainly is used in a few versions of "The Two Sisters." What we do insist is that critics of the folk-music drama shall learn to discriminate between the sort of iteration of phrase in text or tune which has its proper place as enhancing aesthetic effect, and the sort which is a sign of decay and nothing else, the result, as any psychologist knows, of the rule that it is easier to repeat a familiar phrase than to memorise a new one.

If iteration of phrase in the form of incremental repetition, as we have it in the nuncupative testament of "Lord Randall" and in the relative sequence of "The Hangman's Tree," is in any sense whatever "the touchstone of the genuine," it is no longer possible to maintain the fiction of a closed canon of balladry by means of which this contention was originally established. We find incremental repetition developing over and over again, as a by-product of folk singing, in ballads which did not originally have it. Thus a Polish ballad (The Three Sisters), written in the 1820's by Alexander Chodzko and lately recorded by us in Vermont, has acquired the "ballad style" though the author's original did not have it. It is beside the point to argue that the "ballad style" does not develop in narrative ballads like "Samuel Allen" which use the device of the messenger of classic drama; in these there is no place for or need of it. Tunes also, even some of known authorship, show a clear and unmistakable tendency to acquire architectonic forms which they did not originally possess. In effect, all that any such phrase "the touchstone of the genuine" has any right to mean, is that, to be regarded as a folk song at all, a certain song must show evidences of having been sung by the type of singer who feels perfectly free to consider himself not merely interpreter but at the same time co-author and co-composer.

There is a great opportunity open to the psychologist who shall discover and define the operation of those psychological laws which govern the processes of re-creation of traditional ballads, particularly the music of these ballads. There are such laws; so much we wish to claim as our discovery. What is not known or only very imperfectly known is their operation. The preference for modal airs, we suspect, may be deeply rooted in the consciousness of the individual singer. Thus, it is possible that some singers are harmony conscious; that they sense tonal relationships in the form of chords, while others, being melody conscious, sense such relationships only in melodic sequences. The ancient Greeks, we know, were so completely melody conscious that they never made so much as a beginning toward the harmonic evolution of music as we understand it today. Our modal folk-tunes are of a pattern that has descended to us from the Greeks through medieval ecclesiastical music. It has been shown that a part at least of traditional Danish ballad music is nothing more than an adaptation of Church tunes set in the ecclesiastical modes; until something of the same sort has been done for British folk-music, in order to separate the genuinely old from the more recent, it remains a rash notion to assume greater antiquity for modal folk-tunes than for folk tunes cast in more modern forms. What we wish to insist upon is that it is not enough to study the tunes; the singers also should be studied and the reasons for their individual preferences established as far as possible on psychological grounds.

For such researches as we have suggested, and others that will emerge as the work develops, the need is now urgent. Ten years ago we should not have been so insistent. Today, however, American folk-music faces the greatest peril to its continued existence. Only a few days ago newspaper reports carried the story that the folk musicians of the Ozarks were dropping their traditional fiddle tunes in favor of alleged mountain music made in Detroit, perhaps, and transmitted via radio! If such breaking down of the precious individuality of folk singers and folk musicians goes on long enough, American folk-music will soon be no more. For this reason we urge all possible activity, *now,* in making records and carrying on as intensively as possible the study of songs and singers. We might even save the singers and thus save the songs. Let it be literally cried from the house tops that the folk singer is a personality, an individual, and most of all a creative artist. In the name of good science and good sense, let us have done once and for all with calling folksong and folk balladry artless.

It was with no intention of setting up artificial distinctions that Montaigne contrasted popular poetry with the conceits and *tours de force* of the court poets, but those who have glibly quoted him have not taken the trouble to see that all he was talking about had to do with sincerity; that popular poetry was sincere in one way, the poetry of the learned and the philosopher in another way, whereas the insincerity of court poetry was its chief trait. That the fiction of artless folk-song should have endured so long is understandable in view of the fact that many of those who were writing learned treatises on it, including those who devised the theories of communal origins, never heard a folk singer sing in their lives. Even the earlier field workers ignored the music; so little was it understood what Oskar Wolff truly said nearly a century ago, "the folk does not speak in poetry, it *sings!*" And this brings us back once more to the paradox with which we started, that folk song belongs to the folk, but is made for the folk by the art of the individual—let us add, the passionate individualist folk-singer.

7

✳✳✳✳✳✳✳✳✳✳✳✳✳✳✳✳✳✳✳✳

The Interdependence of Ballad
Tunes and Texts

BERTRAND H. BRONSON

HISTORY, doubtless, has its logic, if a man could but find it out. After fifty years of arduous and enthusiastic effort in the collection of British folk-tunes, and, behind that, another hundred and fifty devoted with increasing scholarly intensity to the collection and detailed comparative study of ballad texts, nothing but the apparent unreason of history could justify the absurdity of recommending at this date that for their proper comprehension it is necessary to study texts and tunes together. For that is so logically and so obviously the initial point of departure! And before any other approach was thinkable an unnatural divorce had to be effected between two elements which had always existed, not side by side, but so inextricably interwoven that even Psyche's "confused seeds" were not more intermixed. The absurdity of urging an axiom for acceptance rests on a greater absurdity: namely, that the greatest scholar in the field, the acknowledged "prince" of ballad students, could all but complete his lifework on the subject without a single word of analysis or description of the traditional music—the vitalizing, breath-giving half of balladry.

Latterly, however, thanks to the sound work of individual collectors and folk-song societies, there has been plenty of interest in folk music, and some pious exhortation from older students of the ballad not to neglect the tunes. If I am justified in taking as my theme the elementary interdependence of ballad tunes and ballad texts, it is because throughout the country too many academic courses in the ballad still proceed on the basis of textual study alone, with perhaps for a final flourish an hour or so devoted to the concert rendition of a few selected numbers, or the playing of such commercial phonograph records, unaccompanied by critical remarks, as the instructor may have chanced to scrape together—with the acquiescence, one hopes, of a wife indulgent to his extravagance. But as for the exhaustive accumulation of records of the same song for comparative or analytical study of traditional variation, where are the English or Music departments that have budgeted for this?

Yet, I insist, if the student of the ballad is not prepared to give equal attention to the musical, as to the verbal, side of his subject, his knowledge of it will in the end be only half-knowledge. If he lacks the necessary acquaintance with musical rudiments or is indisposed or unable to enlist the active and continual collaboration of others properly equipped, he had better turn to other fields. For he dismisses the ballad music at his peril. In spite of the scanty and undependable records which have survived from earlier centuries, there is always a possibility that some illumination may be thrown on a particular problem by what is known or can be deduced from ballad music. And, for our own century, for the study of the ballad as something else than a fossil deposit, there is available a fairly large mass of evidence awaiting critical examination. In the present brief survey, I shall devote most of the space at my disposal to supporting these contentions by characteristic examples.

Take first the elementary matter of the ballad stanza, the unit which matches each complete repetition of the tune, of which it must be the exact counterpart. What is the nature of this unit? What is its irreducible minimum, what are its constituent parts, how is it to be divided? How is a scholarly editor to dispose it upon his page? Ordinarily, as every one knows, it consists of fourteen stresses, with a pause after the seventh, set off by a rhyme between the seventh and fourteenth. The pause may be, and frequently is, filled in by another stress, in which case a corresponding stress will also be added at the end. Metrically, the iambic is the usual pattern, but other types of feet are so freely substituted in easygoing popular verse that it is best not to overemphasize the metrical unit. Hymnodists call these two varieties of stanza "common metre" and "long metre," respectively, or CM and LM. In actual length, however, they do not differ, because the length of the added foot, or stress, in LM—that is, the eighth and sixteenth stresses—precisely equals the length of the pause or sustained note in

CM. Both forms, that is to say, are sixteen pulses long. The pause which occurs at the halfway point of the stanza corresponds with the most obvious structural feature of a tune of this sort, the mid-pause or middle cadence, which in the majority of our tunes comes on the dominant—musically the most satisfying point of rest after the tonic.

As ballads are generally printed, the stanza is divided into four lines, alternately of four and three stresses or, in LM, of four and four. And for this division also there is as a rule musical justification; for subordinate pauses or cadences ordinarily occur in a tune at just those points, so that we feel a natural division into four musical phrases. This pattern is so ubiquitous in English and Scottish folk song that where it does not occur—unless the departure is according to some well-defined pattern, as in the case of five-, six-, or eight-phrase tunes—we may almost assume that something has gone wrong with the traditional machinery, whether from forgetfulness of text or tune, or from some extraneous influence.

There is no sign that there has been any appreciable variation in this structural norm for ballad tunes since the beginning of the record. During its whole known history, that is to say, the ballad tune has shown no inclination to transcend or exceed in any manner the structural bounds that we know today. But also, during its whole history, this folk-tune pattern has shown no preference for ballads, or *narrative* songs, over any other kind of traditional song text, whether work song, carol, or personal lyric. There is no evidence or inherent probability that in the beginning it belonged to the ballad alone, unless we maintain that in the beginning there was only narrative ballad—which is to me unthinkable. Without stopping to muster arguments, it seems obvious that the narrative ballad in the form in which we know it—and be it remembered that we deny the name when the form is lacking—cannot have existed before the musical vehicle which sustains it had been invented. By definition the ballad is a song. The first ballad, therefore, was sung to a tune. Regardless of whether that particular tune came into existence simultaneously with the first ballad, the form of the tune—this ubiquitous musical pattern found with nearly every kind of popular song—was already in existence. For the proponent of the theory of communal ballad origins it is even more necessary to believe this to be true than it is for the believer in individual composition. For a group can join in communal singing only when the members of it are in approximate agreement about the tune.

I do not propose to enter upon the question of communal origins. At this distance from Harvard University I dare, indeed, to call the theory metaphysical moonshine, in so far as it has any bearing upon the popular ballad of recorded history—the ballad as represented, for example, by any known variant of any of Child's three hundred and five, including "The Maid freed from the Gallows." Let me then revert to the four-phrase musical form which we take as the norm for our ballad of tradition.

When we find a ballad text which notably fails to conform to this pattern of a minimum of four equivalent phrases, what is to be concluded? Child, following Motherwell, prints his A text of "The False Knight upon the Road" (3) in this fashion:

1. "O whare are ye gaun?"
     Quo the fause knicht upon the road:
   "I'm gaun to the scule,"
     Quo the wee boy, and still he stude.

2. "What is that upon your back?" quo, etc.
   "Atweel it is my bukes," quo, etc.

3. "What's that ye've got in your arm?"
   "Atweel it is my peit."

And so on. Now it is obvious that the first and third lines are in general abnormally short. To lengthen them, nothing seems detachable from the alternating refrain lines, because we can hardly borrow less than the two-stress phrases, "Quo the fause knicht" and "Quo the wee boy," and borrowing so much would leave us in worse case than before, with only two stresses for the refrain-lines. Moreover, the refrain lines look as if they were to be regarded as proper four-stress lines as they stand. Can we, then, put any trust in this text as one actually sung? On the contrary, when we turn to Motherwell's Appendix of tunes, we find a tune for this ballad with variant words for the first stanza as follows:

"O whare are ye gaun?" quo' the false knight,
     And false false was his rede.
"I'm gaun to the scule," says the pretty little boy,
     And still still he stude.

The evidence of this variant suggests that the first was given inaccurately, either to save space or to avoid unnecessary repetition. Unless there was a sharp cleavage in the tradition, we should suppose that "quo the false knicht" was after all part of the first line, and was repeated to fill out the second. Thus:

> "O whare are ye gaun?" quo the fause knicht
> [Quo the fause knicht] upon the road:
> "I'm gaun to the scule," quo the wee boy,

and so on. Motherwell's giving "quo, etc." on the same line of text, after the first stanza, might hint corroboration. Looking for further light, we come upon a North Carolina variant collected by Sharp in 1916. (The first, of course, was Scottish, 1827.) The first two phrases of the music carry the following text:

> "Where are you going?" says the knight in the road.
> "I'm going to my school," said the child as he stood.

A Virginia variant confirms this pattern, as do two others, from Tennessee and Indiana. A connection in the melodic tradition can be traced through all these with one another and with Motherwell's tune. One would consider the case closed, therefore, were it not for an odd little circular tune preserved by Macmath from Scottish tradition about the end of last century. This tune has the look of being much worn down in tradition, but as it stands it carries the exact counterpart of Motherwell's first text, and so ought finally to settle the question of line adjustment. Well, it does! It proves that the stanzas should be printed as long couplets, and that it is a violence to split them in two. For the tune is one of those which forego any real first and third cadence, and bring you to the mid-point without a break. Any fixing of first and third cadence would have to be arbitrarily determined by the words, for it would have no musical significance. Musically, an arbitrary cadence point would be possible on any one of four successive beats— which is but to say again that there is no real cadence. If we divided exactly in half, which would be the musical norm, we should get the textual absurdity of

> "O whare are ye gaun?" says
> The fause knicht upon the road.
> "I'm gaun to the scule," says
> The wee boy; and still he stude.

But the musical phrase, I repeat, begs not to be divided at all: then why should the words? There is, I might add in lieu of further discussion, a melodic connection between this tune and a Nova Scotian one; and since that is connected with the Appalachian variants, we can link the whole series onto the traditional melodic chain—though not in a straight line of descent.

A textual problem of a somewhat different sort arises in connection with the ballad of "Clerk Colvill" (42). Child's A text of this ballad comes from the famous Mrs. Brown of Falkland, who supplied Jamieson and Scott with some of their choicest and rarest texts. A few years ago, Ritson's transcript of a lost manuscript collection of Mrs. Brown's ballads was turned up in the auction rooms, was bought by Dr. Rosenbach, and presented to Harvard. The transcript preserves the tunes to which this lady sang her ballads, set down, unfortunately, by a confessedly inexpert hand, but, in the lack of anything better, a valuable record, as indeed anything of the sort back of 1800 must necessarily be. "Clerk Colvill," it will be remembered, is the ballad of a mortal man who meddled with a beautiful water-sprite, incurring her enmity with fatal results. A headache set in, which only grew worse when she gave him a piece of her sark to bind about his head for a cure. He had barely time to reach home before death overtook him. Keats's "La Belle Dame" is perhaps an educated cousin of this ballad. Mrs. Brown's text is in LM, quatrains of four-stress lines, rhyming on the second and fourth. There is no refrain, internal or external, and there is no indication in the manuscript that a refrain was sung. The words are not written under the notes: the tune is given first, by itself, and the text follows after, separately. Now, the tune is composed of two phrases of equal length followed by a repeat mark, and then a longer phrase, also marked for repetition. It is hard to see how a quatrain could have been sung to such a tune. A line of text corresponds well enough to either of the first two phrases. Then what of the repeat? It is quite against custom to sing the first two lines of a stanza through twice. The repeat, then, must mean that the second half of the stanza was sung to the same two phrases. But that leaves the second part of the tune unaccommodated with words. Two lines of text could with an effort be squeezed into this second part, but there are convincing reasons against it. One is that there is no phrasal correspondence between the first and second part of the tune. Another is that the second part must be divided just where two notes are tied together (by the only tie which the writer took pains to insert in this half). A third is that the second half is four bars long, as against six bars in the first half—a very odd fact, if equal lines of text are to be carried by it. And a fourth is that the second half is felt to be naturally only one long phrase. It appears to me, therefore, that no part of the text as we have it was sung to this second half. The only deduction possible, then, is that it must have carried a refrain which Mrs. Brown's copyist, her nephew, never bothered to set down. Presumably, if the words or syllables had made sense, he would have done so: we may infer that they were nonsense syllables. And for such a case there are parallels in Greig's collection of Aberdeenshire tunes.[1] But the fact that Mrs. Brown's nephew left out the refrain without the least hint of omission raises a question about other ballads which have come down from her, only one of which in this manuscript has a refrain. Two, in particular, are in the form of tetrameter couplets. Now, so far as I am aware, although it is a common practice to omit an alternating internal refrain after the first stanza, in printing, so that the rest of the ballad *reads* in short couplets, no ballad has ever been taken down from actual folk singing, by careful and accurate collectors like Sharp and Greig, in this short-couplet form. If the refrain comes inside the quatrain, on lines 2 and 4, there is of course no sign of the fact in the tune alone. The fact that the tunes of these ballads of Mrs. Brown appear to be of the usual four-phrase sort (in one case *abab*, or two phrases repeated) consequently throws no light on the question. But in view of the general rule, and the all-but-demonstrable omission in the case just discussed, it appears strongly probable that Mrs. Brown sang "Willy's Lady" (6) and "Gil Brenton" (5) with an interlaced refrain. Moreover, the same probability appears to me to hold in all similar cases of early texts in short couplet form, taken down without their proper tunes. Such a conclusion would affect, to name no lesser things, the A* text (*ca.* 1450) of "Riddles Wisely Expounded" (1), supposing it to have been sung, and "Earl Brand" in its first and most important text. But the same would *not* hold for the long couplets—really a half-stanza to the line—of "St. Stephen and Herod" (22), "Judas" (23), and "Bonnie Annie" (24).

The question of patterns in refrain has obvious importance for the melodic tradition of a ballad. Had Child been concerned to establish the singing tradition of his ballads, it is clear that he must have given more attention to their refrains than he did. In many cases, such concern would have resulted in a rearrangement of his variants. For, obviously, where there has been a shift in the type of refrain, as from

interlaced refrain at the second and fourth lines to refrain as an
added fifth line, or to a more complicated interlacing, there must also
have occurred a corresponding alteration in the melodic vehicle. A
change of this kind could not be a gradual transition, such as produces
the multiplicity of related variants. It must have been single and sudden, a conscious shift from one tune to another. This sort of aberration
is not ordinarily included in the conventional description of the traditional process. Nevertheless, the evidence is sufficient to show that,
whatever the motives, the phenomenon is not uncommon; and it must
be reckoned with as an important factor of change in oral transmission.

For illustration we may use "The Twa Sisters" (10), a ballad unusually rich in changes of refrain. One would guess from the record
that the earlier type of refrain here was the simple interlaced pattern
at the second and fourth lines. The earliest English texts (of mid-
seventeenth century provenience) are of this kind, and the majority
of Child's Scottish and Irish texts belong to it. (In all, he takes account
of about forty texts.) All the variants of the "Binnorie" group fall
into this category. Incidentally, it might be noted that the currency
of the "Binnorie" refrain appears mainly in the wake of Scott's *Minstrelsy*, 1802. It does not appear in the Herd manuscripts, nor in the
Scots Musical Museum, and Pinkerton is the only authority—he is not
often entitled to the name—to make use of it before Scott. And Scott,
as his manuscripts prove, engrafted it upon his primary copy of the
ballad from another.

Of this same type of refrain we have various styles: "With a hie
downe downe a downe-a" (in the seventeenth century); "Fal the lal
the lal laral lody" (English of the nineteenth, and probably eighteenth,
century); "Norham, down by Norham," or "Nonie an' Benonie,"
coupled with "By the bonnie mill-dams o Norham," or "Benonie";
"Hey with a gay and a grinding O" and "About a' the bonny bows o
London"; "Cold blows the wind, and the wind blows low" with "And
the wind blows cheerily around us, high ho"; "Oh and ohone, and
ohone and aree" with "On the banks of the Banna, ohone and aree";
"Hech hey my Nannie O" with "And the swan swims bonnie I." The
last two styles are especially Celtic, and the swan refrain would be
particularly favored in Ireland, where they go in for swans. Child's
suggestion that the explanation of the obscure name, "Binnorie," may
possibly lie in the phrase, "On the banks of the Banna, ohone and aree,"
is supported neither by the rhythm nor by the Irish tunes, which appear

fairly distinct from the Binnorie group. As a final example of this type
of refrain, a variant found in Michigan, in 1934, might be cited: "Viola
and Vinola," with "Down by the waters rolling"—wherein the proper
names turn out to be those of the rival sisters. It is to be hoped that the
gloss of commercialism on these names is too high to be perpetuated in
traditional memory.

This ballad still persists in vigorous life in our own country, especially in the Appalachian region. There its association with dancing is
attested by the words of a refrain of a different type, prevalent wherever the "play-party" tradition has been current, and probably elsewhere. Here the pattern is of a stanza of double length, the interlaced
refrain coming on the second, fourth, seventh, and eighth lines. There
is a threefold repetition of the first line of text, on lines one, three, and
five; so that the narrative advances only two lines with each stanza.
Here is a characteristic example, from Kentucky:

> There lived an old lord by the Northern Sea,
>> Bowee down!
> There lived an old lord by the Northern Sea,
>> Bow and balance to me!
> There lived an old lord by the Northern Sea,
> And he had daughters one, two, three,
>> I'll be true to my love,
>> If my love'll be true to me! [2]—

a canny proviso.

Musically, this stanza implies a double-strain, or eight-phrase air,
with the middle cadence coming after the second element of refrain.
It is especially apt for dancing, for the greater length gives space for
the figures to develop, and the slow rate of narrative progression permits concentration rather on the dance than on the story. Many of the
seventeenth-century English country-dance tunes in Playford and elsewhere are of this form. But it is older than the seventeenth century
and has associations with a number of early ballads and songs, such as
"The Wedding of the Frog and the Mouse," "The Friar in the Well,"
"The Three Ravens." That its perennial serviceability is not yet spent
is proved by the currency of "Mademoiselle from Armentières"
("Hinky Dinky, Parlez Vous"). And that the demoiselle is in the
direct line from an Elizabethan daughter of Eve can be proved by a
morality play of about 1568. In William Wager's *The Longer Thou
Livest the More Fool Thou*, Moros, whose head is stuffed only with

idle mischief, enters singing snatches from the popular songs he has picked up from his pothouse companions. He gets through the first stanza of one of these, as follows:

> There was a mayde cam out of Kent,
>> Daintie loue, daintie loue,
> There was a mayde cam out of Kent,
>> Daungerous be:
> There was a mayde cam out of Kent,
> Fayre, propre, small and gent,
> As euer vpon the grounde went,
>> For so should it be.

That is the earliest appearance of the full-blown "Twa Sisters" stanza known to me; but there may well be earlier cases, for many early carol texts, assuming natural repetitions, would fall into the same form. It is doubtless evidence of a depraved taste to confess that one would give the rest of Wager's play in exchange for the rest of Moros's ballad.

As for "bow and balance": how old are the names of these postures in the dance can perhaps be settled by the historians of that subject. In its present connection, the question is complicated by several ambiguous possibilities. The earliest trace of the Appalachian refrain which I have noted with this ballad goes back to Kent, as it happens, about the year 1770. Among the Percy papers there is a copy of that locality and date, with refrain on 2, 4, 7, and 8 as follows:

> . . . Hey down down derry down
> . . . And the bough it was bent to me
> . . . I'll prove true to my love
> If my love will prove true to me.

There can be no doubt of the connection between these refrains. But the earlier one has no indication of the dance-step. From a Yorkshire variant of the later nineteenth century comes a new suggestion:

> . . . Low down, derry down dee
> . . . Valid we ought to be
> . . . And I'll be true to my love
> If my love will be true to me.

Here are neither bent knees nor bent boughs. But in another variant of about the same time and place as the last comes this:

> . . . Bow down, bow down
> . . . As the bough doth bend to me

> . . . And I'll be true to my true love
> If my love will be true to me.

This last gives us a consistent reading, but it is not easy to prove that it is the original consistency. Certainly "hey down down derry down" has ancient precedent behind it, notably in the Robin Hood cycle; whilst "low down" in such a context has little or none. Nor does "low down" seem likely to have led to "bow down." Yet "down" by itself contains the suggestion of "low"; and if "hey" were ever pronounced "hi" by singers, someone sooner or later would be sure to change "hi down" to "low down." Again, there is on record among such singers the pronunciation "bo" for "bow": "he bo'd his breast and swum." The sequence is therefore possible, if barely so. On the other hand, "the bough was bent to me" might of itself induce the "bow down" of the other line; and in its turn "bow down" might suggest in oral tradition the other image, as it obviously has in one recorded variant, "Bow your bends to me." From this to "bow and balance" is but a skipping step in a dancing community. But the "Valid we ought to be" can hardly have been corrupted *into* "balance and bo(w) to me": it must have been the other way round, where the dance terms were unfamiliar. So that a greater antiquity may be indicated for "bow and balance" than any of which we have record. Nevertheless, *boughs* that bend, and *bows*—whether elbows or bows of yew—have ancient and legitimate connections with balladry, and may well contain the radical images. Moreover, the American variants continue the confusion between *bows* and *boughs*. *Balance,* however, comes not in such a questionable shape; and when "the *boys* are bound for me," as in certain late variants, they wear their folk etymology upon their sleeves.

At any rate, the variants with these refrains—there are between three and four dozen of them on record—all belong to one melodic family, which can never have been related to the "Binnorie" group. The "bow down" pattern has shown an occasional tendency, as exhibited in about a dozen additional recorded variants, to abridge itself to a six-phrase pattern, generally by omitting one repetition of the first line, together with the second element of the refrain. As thus, in a Berkshire version:

> A varmer he lived in the West Countree,
> With a hey down, bow down:
> A varmer he lived in the West Countree,

> And he had daughters, one, two, and three,
>   And I'll be true to my love,
>   If my love 'll be true to me.

That this is not actually a new pattern, but a corruption of the former one, is proved by the fact that every case of it is an incomplete and usually disordered member of the same melodic family.

Finally, a separate Scottish tradition as old as the eighteenth century makes use of the same eight-phrase interlaced stanza pattern, but with place names for the refrain, and (apparently) a distinct melodic tradition. Thus Mrs. Brown's text:

> There was twa sisters in a bowr,
>   Edinburgh, Edinburgh,
> There was twa sisters in a bowr,
>   Stirling for ay
> There was twa sisters in a bowr,
> There came a knight to be their wooer.
>   Bonny St. Johnston
>   stands upon Tay.

The same refrain is found with several other ballads.

It will perhaps be a relief if I turn to another aspect of my subject, another way in which texts and tunes are interrelated. It not infrequently appears that, just as a refrain will get attached to more than one ballad, so variants of one and the same tune will be discovered in association with the texts of different ballads. What are the possible explanations of such a phenomenon, and what legitimate inferences may be drawn from it?

There are undoubtedly certain tunes, or tune families, which are so strongly and ineradicably rooted in traditional singing that, like the commonest sorts of weed, they tend to crop up everywhere and take possession of any available space, crowding out the less hardy plants. Such, for example, are the common tunes for "Lady Isabel and the Elf Knight" (4) and "Lord Thomas and Fair Eleanor" (73), which are found all over the ballad landscape. From these I can draw no significant deduction, other than the obvious one that certain tunes are so catchy and easy to remember that, once heard, they cannot be shaken off. Like burrs, they cling to every passer-by and are carried far and wide.

But there are other tunes which require a congenial soil for transplantation, and sometimes reveal an interesting lineal connection. There may be fortuitous resemblances between tunes which cause them to gravitate and coalesce. Equally, there may be verbal or narrative connections between ballad texts which facilitate a borrowing by one ballad of the other's tune. Or, again, there may be tunes which, from a relationship half-consciously sensed by the singer, act as the disintegrating and reintegrating agents that gradually win away elements of a ballad, and re-establish these in new contexts, modifying the conduct of the narrative, or otherwise effecting a crossing that produces a new and different species. Many of these textual interconnections have been remarked in Child's head-notes. But it can hardly be doubted that the tunes have been responsible for the linkages perhaps as often as have parallels of situation.

Sometimes related tunes suggest or lend confirmation to a suspected connection between ballads. A case in point is Child's no. 27, "The Whummil Bore." Child introduces it with the dubious remark: "This ballad, if it ever were one, seems not to have been met with, or at least to have been thought worth notice, by anybody but Motherwell." As the piece is very short, it may be quoted here:

1. Seven lang years I hae served the king,
    Fa fa fa fa lilly
   And I never got a sight of his daughter but ane.
    With my glimpy, glimpy, glimpy eedle,
    Lillum too tee a ta too a tee a ta a tally

2. I saw her thro a whummil bore,
   And I neer got a sight of her no more.

3. Twa was putting on her gown,
   And ten was putting pins therein.

4. Twa was putting on her shoon,
   And twa was buckling them again.

5. Five was combing down her hair,
   And I never got a sight of her nae mair.

6. Her neck and breast was like the snow,
   Then from the bore I was forced to go.

This appears to be an example of pawky fun at the expense of high romance, like "Sir Eglamore," "The Twa Corbies," (26) or "Kempy Kay" (33). For this sort of thing there is, of course, high precedent in Chaucer's "Sir Thopas," to name but one out of multitudes. "The Whummil Bore" appears to me a by-blow of a serious romantic ballad. The evidence of its tune indicates where its affiliations lie. Here is Motherwell's tune:

The Whummil Bore

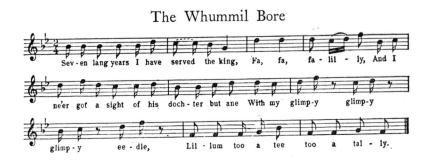

If the order of the first and second phrases is reversed, the result is a fairly close parallel to Miss Minnie Macmath's tune for "Hind Horn" (17), amounting almost to identity in the third phrase. The Motherwell tune, flown with insolence, repeats its third phrase with variation, and ends with a fifth phrase which would supply an equally appropriate termination for the Macmath tune, which in fact seems to have forgotten its proper conclusion:

Hind Horn

Child, incidentally, did not miss the fact that some versions of "Hind Horn" contained a curious reference to Horn's seeing his love through some small aperture, e.g., an augur bore or a gay gold ring, and conjectured that the detail was borrowed from "The Whummil Bore," where it manifestly comes in more appropriately. He did not, however, suggest that a much greater obligation lay in the opposite direction, which to me appears altogether probable. "Hind Horn" is an ancient and honorable ballad, and its tune, in one variety or another, is well established and consistently associated with it.

The ballad of "Lizie Wan" (51) is one which has not often been found. It first appears in Herd's manuscripts and has been recovered once or twice in our century in this country, and once in England. As Herd gives it, it tells an unpleasant story: Lizie sadly confesses to her father that she is with child. By comes her brother, and she charges him with equal guilt:

> There is a child between my twa sides,
>   Between you, dear billy, and I.

When he finds out that she has revealed her state, he draws his sword and cuts her to pieces. His mother asks him, later, why he acts so distraught. He replies, first, that he has killed his greyhound, and next, under pressure, that he has slain Lizie Wan.

> "O what wilt thou do when thy father comes hame,
>   O my son Geordy Wan?"
> "I'll set my foot in a bottomless boat,
>   And swim to the sea-ground."
>
> "And when will thou come hame again,
>   O my son Geordy Wan?"
> "The sun and the moon shall dance on the green
>   That night when I come hame."

The parallel in the latter part of this ballad with the much more famous "Edward" (13) is obvious. It is therefore interesting to find a similar parallel between the tune collected by Sharp in his Appalachian version of "Lizie Wan" and one of the tunes which he got in the same region for "Edward":

Edward

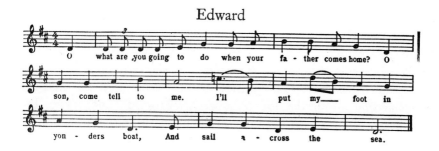

O what are you going to do when your fa - ther comes home? O son, come tell to me. I'll put my___ foot in yon - ders boat, And sail a - cross the sea.

The question of relationship between these two ballads opens up a fascinating field for speculation. Both, if not of Scandinavian birth, have important Scandinavian counterparts. Both appear in the Scottish

Lizie Wan

Fair Lu - cy sit - ting in her fa - ther's_ room, La -
ment - ing and a - mak - ing her mourn; And_ in_ steps her
bro - ther James: O_____ what's fair Lu - cy done?

record at approximately the same time. Neither has had currency in England or Ireland. Professor Archer Taylor, in a comparative analysis of all available variants, has shown that the Percy text of "Edward," from the point of view of tradition, is spurious and sophisticated.[3] The version next in date is later by more than fifty years in the record, and, although doubtless a good deal closer to tradition, still affected in the dénouement by Percy. The traditional versions of "Edward" do not implicate the mother in her son's guilt, and tell a tasteless story of brother-murder in a fit of anger devoid of tragic significance. The brothers fall out about a little bush that might have made a tree, which one of them has untimely cut down. Phillips Barry has suggested that the bush (holly or hazel in the Appalachian variants) is to be interpreted symbolically as a girl. This sort of symbol seems to me—I speak under correction—alien to the popular habit; and "Lizie Wan" shows how unnecessary it was to veil the meaning in such obscurity. Nevertheless, it is natural to suppose that originally the ballad of "Edward" had a more compelling narrative core than appears in extant tradition. And certainly the murder of a sister as a *crime passionel*, or of a brother out of jealous rivalry, would provide a plot sufficiently Aeschylean. It is a fact that some Swedish texts of "Edward" make the sister the victim, whether this means much or little. "Lizie Wan" is one of four ballads in Child on a similar theme, and its roots are undeniably deep in northern tradition. It might, incidentally, have been expected that a connection would be found between "Edward" and "The Twa Brothers" (49), where the same brother-rivalry and fratricide occur. And in some texts of the latter ballad such a connection is in fact disclosed. (Child 49 D, E, F, and G.) But the melodic connections in the latter case do not support the association. Instead, they mainly lie rather with "Little Sir Hugh" (155), and apparently rise from a similar opening of schoolchildren playing ball. But, without being dogmatic, I would only remark further of "Edward" and "Lizie Wan," that if, granting contamination of one ballad by the other, we attempt to establish a priority, the claims of "Lizie Wan" to being more deeply rooted in early Scandinavian lore, and inherently less likely to have derived from "Edward" than the reverse, are claims not to be lightly dismissed.

Another interesting case of possible crossing occurs between "Young Hunting" (68) and "Lady Isabel and the Elf Knight" (4). The melodic tradition of "Young Hunting" is rather perplexed and hard to make out, whilst that of "Lady Isabel" is unusually clear. But a small group of variants of "Young Hunting" makes use of a distinct variety of the "Lady Isabel" tunes, and the texts of this group commence in a very particular way:—with the sound of a distant horn, and the conflicting emotions stirred up by that music in the breast of Young Hunting's sweetheart. Elsewhere, the ballad generally opens abruptly with her invitation to come in and stay the night. Now, in the current variants of "Lady Isabel" there is no mention of a horn. But formerly, as in Child's A text and in various Continental analogues, the horn had a most important and necessary function to perform in that ballad. It was elfin music, and it had such power of magic persuasion that before the heroine ever saw the creature who blew it, she was ready to run away with him. No other ballad, I believe, makes such introductory use of a horn except "The Elfin Knight" (2) which Child supposes also affected by "Lady Isabel." The occurrence of the horn in "Young Hunting," then, may be an intrusion from "Lady Isabel" and may have drawn the characteristic tune with it; or the tune may have brought the horn over to the other ballad, from versions of "Lady Isabel" formerly in circulation. It is worth notice, moreover, that both ballads, besides sharing the theme of a sweetheart's killing her lover (albeit for very different reasons), make prominent use of a talking bird. In "Young Hunting," this bird has been understood to be a relic of former belief in metempsychosis, the bird being the soul of the slain lover.[4] It plays a vital and significant role in the narrative. But in "Lady Isabel," the parrot that chatters idly when the heroine comes safely home before the dawning, and has to be bribed to silence with the promise of a cage of ivory and gold, performs no office essential to the plot and is doubtless an importation. There may be here a borrowing in the opposite direction, underlined perhaps by the similar promise of reward from Young Hunting's mistress, if the bird will not reveal her guilt. However it be, there appears sufficient evidence of a hitherto unnoticed crossing of these ballads in tradition, signalized by the melodic convergence.

Much, again, can be learned about the ways of tradition, both textual and musical, from what has happened within the last three hundred years to the ballad of "Sir Lionel" (18). Back of 1650 lies the earliest known text of this ballad, in the Percy Folio manuscript, a very defective text, without a tune, and not certainly known to have been sung. In spite of serious deficiencies—there are two large lacunae where pages have been torn out of the manuscript—this is still our fullest text in narrative content, and a serious treatment of a theme of high romance. Except for a nineteenth-century Scottish text recorded by Christie, all the other versions of this ballad which have been collected, whether from English or American tradition, tend in varying degree toward the farcical. The Percy version is in quatrains, with an interlaced refrain at lines 2 and 4—the refrain, incidentally, echoing a song that has survived in a manuscript of Henry VIII's time.

In the present century, but doubtless going back in family tradition a hundred years or more, there appears in this ballad a marked change of pattern as well as of mood. Instead of the staid refrain of the older form, we find a series of nonsense syllables, fitted to the elaborate eight-phrase scheme already met in "The Twa Sisters." This new (but ancient) pattern is exemplified in a Wiltshire variant, published, without a tune, in 1923:

> Bold Sir Rylas a-hunting went—
> I an dan dilly dan
> Bold Sir Rylas a-hunting went—
> Killy koko an.
> Bold Sir Rylas a-hunting went—
> To kill some game was his intent—
> I an dan dilly dan
> killy koko an.[5]

This, with occasional abridgment, is the nearly universal stanza form of the ballad in current tradition. Now, obviously, there has either been a complete break here with the older tradition, or else the traditional antecedents of the modern ballad are not adequately represented in the examples printed by Child. What has happened to the narrative will support the latter alternative.

Child pointed out that "Sir Lionel" had much in common with the old metrical romance of "Sir Eglamour of Artois." This relationship is clearest in the Percy Folio text. There we have a lady sore beset, whose knight has been slain by a wild boar; a fight between Sir Lionel and the boar (implied, but lost with the leaf or leaves gone from the manuscript); a rencounter between the giant, who owned the boar, and Sir Lionel, in which Sir Lionel is worsted but chivalrously granted a forty-day respite to prepare for a new combat; Lionel's return to fight with the giant and rescue the lady; and, finally, in the last portion (again missing, but baldly summarized in Christie's version), the defeat of the giant. All these elements had appeared in the old romance, which, however, Child carefully abstains from calling the original of the ballad.

Now, in the nineteenth-century English versions, the giant's place has been supplied by a "wild woman" whom the hero treats as unmercifully as he had earlier treated the giant. The central incident, however, has become the boar fight. The lady in distress is barely mentioned, and is easily confounded with the wild woman who owns the boar. In the more recently collected versions, she appears only long enough to tell the knight that a blast of his horn will bring on the boar; or (as usually in the American variants) she makes no appearance whatever. The wild woman in some variants does double duty for gentle and savage; but she, like her predecessors, also tends to drop out of the story. What finally remains is the single episode of the boar fight, told now as riotous farce.

At some time in the seventeenth century, apparently early, another ballad on the subject of Sir Eglamore became popularly current, and was perpetuated on broadsides. The first known copy seems to be that in Samuel Rowlands's "The Melancholie Knight," 1615, and Rowlands may have written the ballad. By the last quarter of the seventeenth century it was widely known and was circulating independently of print. It had a catchy tune which went about in variant forms, as popular tunes unshackled by copyright laws will do. One form of the tune—with new words, but identified by its proper name—was printed in Nat. Thompson's *180 Loyal Songs* (1685), page 276, as follows:

Sir Eglamore

Another was copied into a manuscript of approximately the same time, and now lies in the Edinburgh University Library, hitherto unprinted (MS DC. 1. 69):

Sir Eglamore

In nearly identical form, this variant later appeared in Durfey's *Pills,* with the following text:

> Sir *Eglamore,* that valiant Knight,
> *Fa la, lanky down dilly;*
> He took up his Sword, and he went to fight,
> *Fa la, lanky down dilly:*
> And as he rode o'er Hill and Dale,
> All Armed with a Coat of Male,
> *Fa la la, la la la, lanky down dilly.*

> There leap'd a Dragon out of her Den,
> That had slain God knows how many Men;
> But when she saw Sir *Eglamore,*
> Oh that you had but heard her roar!

> Then the Trees began to shake,
> Horse did Tremble, Man did quake;
> The Birds betook them all to peeping,
> Oh! 'twould have made one fall a weeping.

But all in vain it was to fear,
For now they fall to't, fight Dog, fight Bear;
And to't they go, and soundly fight,
A live-long day, from Morn till Night.

This Dragon had on a palguy Hide,
That cou'd the sharpest steel abide;
No Sword cou'd enter her with cuts,
Which vex'd the Knight unto the Guts.

But as in Choler he did burn,
He watch'd the Dragon a great good turn;
For as a Yawning she did fall,
He thrust his Sword up Hilt and all.

Then like a Coward she did fly,
Unto her Den, which was hard by;
And there she lay all Night and roar'd,
The Knight was sorry for his Sword:
But riding away, he cries, I forsake it,
He that will fetch it, let him take it.[6]

Here we have the stanza pattern of the current ballad of "Brangywell"
or "Bangum and the Boar," as "Sir Lionel" is called today; and the
tunes sung in our century will prove to be variants of the same melodic
idea as "Sir Eglamore," with such shortening and rhythmical modification as might be looked for in its translation from country-dance usage
to its present solo form. A characteristic example from Kentucky is
the following:

Bangum (Sir Lionel)

It is plain, then, that both in spirit, in narrative, and in melodic tradition, the recent forms of "Sir Lionel" are primarily descendants of the "Eglamore" ballad, and only secondarily of the ancient romance ballad. Any who wish for that reason to exclude it from the authentic traditional canon may do so, not I.

The foregoing will serve as examples of a common melodic tradition between different ballads, and of characteristic results of such a crossing. What further of the contrary case, where a single ballad is sung to different tunes? One aspect of the problem has, of course, already arisen in this matter of deflecting crosscurrents. But we should like to know more about what might be called the sharp corners in tradition, where tune or text, or both, appear suddenly to have taken a new direction. What is the nature of the prism which must be hypothesized at these nodal points? It is a mechanism that cannot be examined at first hand: we can only deduce it from its effects. But no subject of human inquiry is more open to all the winds of chance than that of folk song; and it is altogether probable that not one but many prisms have produced these deflections. So that any generalizations are likely at best to account only for a limited group of phenomena.

What, for example, can be deduced from the fact that a ballad is sung in Scotland to one melodic tradition, and in America to another? There are cases of this kind, where no relationship can be discerned between the melodies current or on record in the old world and the new, but where the text is recognizably close. The ballad, we must presume, was brought across the ocean by singers, for the Bell Robertsons who remember only the words are black swans in balladry. And if the tune were dropped overboard on the way, the reasonable inference would be that the ballad came West on paper and not in the head. Then the water barrier, we conclude, is of no real significance: the melodic tradition turned the corner either before or after the ballad crossed the Atlantic. We are thus faced with the original problem: Why is the same ballad, continuously handed on from singer to singer, never heard without its air and committed to paper during such transmission only as an aid to verbal memory—why and how is this ballad found with different tunes?

The conventional explanation would probably be that these songs had been so long in circulation, uncontrolled by an authoritative original version, that the variants had drifted farther and farther apart. The older the song, the wider the differences; so that where we find no traits of resemblance between two or more tunes of a ballad, we may infer many generations of traditional transmission behind its present state.

To such a conclusion I should myself grant only a tentative and very limited assent, for I do not find that the available evidence at all justifies so sweeping a generalization. There is plenty of evidence, I believe, to support a contrary position: that where a melodic and textual tradition is solidly established, vigorously and continuously alive, its identity will be perpetuated, with a notable consistency in its main outlines, for long periods of time. Such has been the way, for example, with the melodic traditions of "Barbara Allen," and "Lord Lovel," and "Lord Thomas and Fair Eleanor." I do not speak of the texts in these cases, which have been more or less subject to the control of print. Conversely, I believe it sometimes to be an indication of a late start that a ballad displays no dominant melodic tradition. Thus, it strikes me as a suspicious circumstance that "Sir Patrick Spens" (58) shows no such melodic continuity anywhere. It is quite clear that Johnson, when he first printed a tune for this ballad in the *Scots Musical Museum*, knew no traditional setting, for he put it to an unsingable pipe or fiddle tune which has never since been found with it in tradition, although it has been several times reprinted from Johnson. It may, in fact, be a point of real importance that the musical record of this ballad seems to show—I do not positively say does show, for the variants are not abundant enough for proof—a gradual convergence in the last century and a half. Contrary to what we have been taught to expect, the period of widest diversity here is the earliest, since which time the traditional tunes of the "Spens" ballad have appeared to exhibit a tendency, as yet indistinct and uncertain, to drift toward a relatively similar melodic form. Indeed, I throw it out as an open question whether, in the decline of folk song which we must inevitably expect as more and more of the population becomes corrupted by musical literacy, as it already has been by verbal literacy—for literacy and culture are very different—whether, I say, all folk music will not evince the same tendency to drift toward a single, universal, indistinguishable, ultimate tune. The one process which seems to be universally operative in the realm of tradition, however it be by fortunate circumstance obscured or delayed, is, alas, no "epic process," but the process of abrasion, which tends always from complex to simple, and more simple, until the iniquity of oblivion, or soon or slow, shall have completed her office.

I believe, nonetheless, that the natural conservatism of the folk singer—admittedly very impressive in particular cases—has been greatly exaggerated as a universal phenomenon. It is of course just the cases of extraordinary tenacity which would strike a collector most forcibly, whereas the opposite tendency would be relatively little subject to remark. The evidence, in its total recent bulk, seems to me to point to a greater independence, or potential infidelity to strict tradition, than has heretofore been allowed. The rate of change, involving unconscious, semiconscious, and even wilful alteration, may have been considerably more rapid than most students suppose. The coefficient of change—speaking now particularly of consistent and not disruptive change—is the level of intelligence of the folk-singing community, and the liveliness of its artistic sensibility. The higher that level, the more unwilling—indeed, unable—a singer will be to serve merely as a passive transmitter of the songs that he has loved. Those students who have maintained that there was, hundreds of years ago, a creative period of oral tradition, but that since the sixteenth century or thereabouts tradition in balladry has been on the road downhill, have really been saying the same thing. But their view of the matter has been conditioned and limited by the fact that they were looking almost exclusively at the texts. Faced on the one hand with a number of superior early ballad texts, and on the other by the spectacle of increasing dilapidation in the multiplying evidence of the variants collected from recent tradition, their conclusion was in fact almost the only rational one possible. The spread of literacy has drawn off into other channels a large proportion of the creative energy which once went into the ballads. The later generations of ballad singers have for the most part lacked the gifts to do more than perpetuate in a relatively unenlightened fashion the verses they had received, so that, speaking generally, the negative influences of forgetfulness, confused recollection, and imperfect comprehension have been the major influences at work on the ballad texts. But the musical tradition has not been subject to anything like the same rate of decay. Beyond the reach, until very lately, of any sort of written or recorded control, it has persisted, to a surprising degree, in its primitive vitality. That this assertion is hardly open to contradiction is demonstrable in the vast number of beautiful tunes which have been gathered in our own century from illiterate, or nearly illiterate, singers on both sides of the water. It is possible for an uneducated, even a comparatively unintelligent, singer to reach a level of comparatively high musical culture, within the circumscribed limits of traditional song:—a power of melodic discrimination, a subtle sense of rhythmical effect, an artistic sensitivity of no mean musical order; to display, in fact, what may fairly be called creative ability, subject again to the unwritten canons of an ancient tradition. I do not mean that many, or perhaps any, of these singers could deliberately create at will a new and original folk tune. But, in spite of themselves, their musical sensibility and instinctive knowledge of the values they seek inevitably result in constant modification and variation which is effectually creative, or, more strictly, re-creative. They essentially remember; and the falling short of exact recollection has, as yet—it may not continue long to be so—been more than compensated by a power of miniature invention sufficient for their habitual needs, and of which they appear but dimly aware. Moreover, what they have in their minds is not a note-for-note accuracy as of a written tune; but rather an ideal melody, or melodic idea, which is responsive to the momentary dictates of feeling or verbal necessity. What else can we conclude from the evidences of constant variation, recorded by meticulous collectors like Sharp, in successive stanzas, or successive renditions, of the same song? Sharp's blind singer, Henry Larcombe, of Haselbury-Plucknett, Somerset, is an extreme case of this re-creative ability. Whenever Sharp asked him to repeat a phrase or a stanza of a song, he got a new variation in return, many of them beautiful, ingenious, and resourceful—and this without the singer's realizing, apparently, that he was not giving what was requested. Joseph Laver of Bridgwater was another singer of the same kind. Now, if any other folk singer had learned a song from the lips of a singer like these, what else could he possibly have carried away in his memory but the *idea* of a tune, the general pattern or form of it which resides in a more or less constant melodic contour and rhythm? When we are told that a singer hands on his song exactly as he learned it, what other exactness than this is possible to conceive? Since the song was never sung twice in exactly the same way, and since it is humanly impossible for the memory to make an indelible and phonographic record of a single rendition, stanza by stanza, it is obvious that exactitude in this realm bears a very different meaning from what it does when a Schnabel gives us the results of his study of Beethoven's manuscript of a sonata.

Larcombe and Laver are cases at one extreme; but they are not for that reason any the less genuine and authentic folk singers. At the other extreme, and equally genuine and authentic, are the singers with a low coefficient of artistic sensibility, who can neither improvise nor invent, who only dimly remember, and who by dint of desperate effort manage to hang onto a single phrase, or perhaps half a tune, which they repeat at need until so much of the text as they have kept for themselves has been sung through. These, in varying degree, are the singers who most easily get sidetracked onto another tune of which they have a clearer notion; so that, by the hooks and eyes of unconscious suggestion, be it of rhythm, of melodic cadence, or verbal commonplace, a ballad is slowly or rapidly transformed to something other than it was. But these, again, are doubtless most often the deleterious influences: they are in general the disrupters, not the reintegrating and positive forces in traditional transmission. Probably they, in the main, are responsible for the most abrupt and inexplicable departures from established patterns. Their influence must not be minimized, for mediocrity is commoner than talent. Nevertheless, the evidence both of tunes and texts in balladry can lead only to the conclusion that, leavening the undistinguished mass, there have been, even up to our own time, more Larcombes and Lavers than we have any record of; and that, formerly, their verbal counterparts, so to put it, constituted a phenomenon common enough to have molded into familiar forms that body of narrative song, at once naïve and yet capable of the most poignant beauty, which has been enshrined in Child's *English and Scottish Popular Ballads*.

8

✳✳✳✳✳✳✳✳✳✳✳✳✳✳✳✳✳✳✳✳

Prolegomena to a Study
of the Principal Melodic Families
# of Folk Song

SAMUEL P. BAYARD

THE present essay is intended to serve as a prelude to studies that may be described as efforts directed principally at melodic identification; i.e., the distinguishing of variant forms of different individual folk tunes in tradition. The objects of study will be those tunes which appear to be the ones most commonly associated with folk poems sung in the British Isles and (by speakers of English) in North America. Our natural starting point, of course, is with tunes sung to songs in English; but it is impossible to confine attention to the traditions of any one British language. The tune-families to be considered are apparently broadcast over the British Isles, and are often sung to songs in Gaelic, Welsh and Manx, while some of their versions will be found still farther afield in Europe.

Our discussion cannot be historical, strictly speaking, because the data are fragmentary for the present and recent past, and are entirely lacking for the remoter past. That is, there do not seem to be any versions of these melodies which are traceable definitely to the Middle Ages, or which were recorded in times so distant. However, the discussion will try to set forth a number of considerations which were borne in upon the writer from a rather long study of the musical material; and will endeavor to clarify the meanings of certain terms used throughout. Thus, this essay will be concerned with what might be called "background" considerations applying to the material studied, the conditions under which it is studied, and the methods of approach. The national melodic traditions involved will be characterized roughly and their important overall features set forth to the best of the writer's ability. Records of the observations of various collectors will explain the impetus of this study, and the bases for some of the assumptions under which it was begun. The writer's own experiences and observations as a collector—which correspond rather closely with those of others—will naturally be drawn upon also.

Collectors and editors of folk music in the British Isles, from the earliest to the latest, have testified to their perception of tunes widely current in whatever localities they explored, and known in more than one variant form. So, for instance, with certain eighteenth-century Scottish collectors such as the Gows[1] and Patrick McDonald;[2] and nineteenth- and twentieth-century students such as William Chappell,[3] Alexander Campbell,[4] Simon Fraser,[5] G. Farquhar Graham,[6] John Glen,[7] George Petrie,[8] W. P. Joyce,[9] Gavin Greig,[10] Father Henebry,[11] and Cecil J. Sharp,[12] to name only some of the more prominent ones. So also, apparently, the Irish collectors Pigott and Forde[13]—and, in fact, all the eminent collectors with the sole exception of Edward Bunting,[14] whose views are the more unaccountable inasmuch as his experiences must have closely paralleled those of the others. The list of students who have recognized the presence of cognate versions of melodies occurring in British tradition could be enlarged; but these names will perhaps suffice.

The testimony of these writers agrees remarkably in substance. Sometimes a tune has been easily perceptible in many forms, widely scattered, and seemingly well known. Sometimes, on the other hand, differences in versions have so obscured the relationship that it went unobserved for a time, but suddenly became apparent when the student had learned more tunes and had gotten their outlines better fixed in his mind.[15] The fact that substantial agreement existed between students and collectors about the power of survival of some tunes in tradition, and the circumstance that my own observations so often agreed with theirs, were my initial warrants for assuming that in this British-American material we have strong individual persistence of tunes. In studying a collection of English folk songs with their music, which I had gathered in southwestern Pennsylvania and northern West Virginia, I attempted to pay some adequate attention to the music as well as the words, and to such special aspects as had rarely been accorded attention before: namely, the diffusion, textual associations, and different forms of individual tunes in their aggregate of variant settings. Only Phillips Barry and Greig-Keith had gone much into these aspects.[16] My own musical discoveries were such as to make me realize that the study of our folk tunes was neither short nor simple; nor was it bound up, necessarily, in an inseparable manner, with the study of our folk texts. Indeed, it became increasingly apparent that, in some way, the melodies would have to be considered first independently of their text associations; and that their intrinsic nature and interrelations, so therefore their identities, would have to be better determined, before it would become possible fruitfully to study the folk songs as text-tune complexes with both their elements, verbal and musical, taken together in a balanced consideration. As a result of my deciding thus, my attention became concentrated especially on the melodies, which manifestations proved exceedingly complicated when subjected to a closer scrutiny.

Stated as curtly as possible, the broad result of some years' study of British-American folk song melodies has been my eventual belief that the number of distinctly different folk melodies in circulation among our modern folk singers is somewhat smaller than I had at first believed; that the groups of variants, versions, and otherwise closely related airs are correspondingly more inclusive; and that these derivative forms, with relatively few exceptions, are current wherever folk songs in English are sung. I believe that it is possible to indicate cognate relationships between groups of tunes not before suspected of such affinities; and if this belief seems warranted by what follows, the conclusions to be drawn from such a fact should be highly interesting to all who study the phenomena of folk memory and the processes of creation in oral folk arts.

My concentration on music has revealed, I think, that it is perfectly possible, by studying the song tunes apart from their texts, to throw light ultimately on the entire composite tradition of folk song. For these tunes to all appearances have a very real life independent of text associations. They are capable of travelling about, of being varied, of undergoing influences and attractions from other music, and of being elaborated or simplified by various performers no matter what their textual associations may be. And despite what has been said about the "inseparability" of air and words in a folk singer's mind, it is perfectly evident that tunes have been carried in the minds of musical folk without reference to any words, and that many folk singers can and do separate words and air with ease.[17] Perhaps, then, the study of tunes in at least partial divorcement from their texts will be found to have some justification. In their mass, as well as individually, they seem to have had a development along lines which have, strictly speaking, no complete correlation with the occurrence and diffusion of individual folk-song text versions, insofar as can be observed.

In attempting, then, to identify specific melodies in as many of their variant forms as possible, I have proceeded along lines already laid out by previous investigators. But in trying to go as far as possible along one path, I trust that I have not failed to appreciate the value of other approaches to knowledge of our folk music tradition. This particular method of attack seemed capable of casting sufficient light on that subject to justify the effort expended upon it. It appears to be a worthy partner of tune-indexing efforts; a logical precursor and accompanier of melodic-variation studies, analyses of musical style, inquiries into the migrations and history of songs, and studies in the relations of melodies and words. It may also possibly illuminate that elusive quality called "national style" in folk music, and those thus far mysterious categories known as "types" of melody in our traditional song.

The results of my inquiries must be presented with full realization of the uncertainties of the subject and the liabilities of error. Hence, statements which may sound arbitrary are not really intended to be so; to make them straightforwardly is the only way of insuring that what is erroneous about my conclusions will in time be corrected by someone with deeper insight than mine. An attempt such as this at analyzing a folk music tradition has to be based on a working theory. Mine is that, by and large, our folk songs are (and perhaps always have been) sung to a limited number of tunes whose variant forms—apparently originating in oral transmission and re-creation—may be found all over the area where these folk songs are sung, and in some parts of the world where they are not.

Having done with this *apologia*, let us pass on to some considerations of the character of our folk song melodies as a whole. These considerations embrace such matters as (*1*) the nature of our information about the individual melodic items, and the evidence we have to work with in making conclusions about their affinities; (*2*) the nature of the melodic alterations that always confront a student of folk music, and are, of course, abundant in our own melodies; and (*3*) the general aspect of the tune-repertories known in the British Isles and in this country.

To begin with, it is apparent that an examination of folk tunes must be primarily descriptive. We cannot speak with exactness about stages in the development of any tune, for our records are still too incomplete and too recent; and back of every folk-melodic item lies a history of transmission and cultivation that remains quite unknown. Besides, we are all aware of the fact that the time when any folk-tune variant is recorded has no reference to the real age of that variant. So far as I have been able to discover at present, none of the important (i.e. widespread, much-used) tunes of our folk singers' repertories can be traced back beyond the early sixteenth century; most of them seem untraceable beyond the eighteenth. Again, we must always realize that our record of collectanea is rather uneven. Some regions have had careful collecting done in them, whereas others have been comparatively neglected. I shall not pause here to discuss the accuracy with which folk music records have been made in the past.[18]

About the history of individual melodic items we generally know nothing that is really helpful. When, in present-day collecting, we can trace a tune-variant at all, it is usually for only a generation or two back, and in some family line or restricted locality. The development of that variant, its time and place and cause of branching-off from some widely known air of which it may be a form, its routes of transmission and diffusion, its alterations from singer to singer and generation to generation—these are data with which the singers cannot supply us. We can often see what look like links between widely divergent forms of the same tune; what may *seem* to be stages of development between those forms, and illustrations of the steps by which one version gradually became transformed into another. The links are certainly there; but when we see them, we have to remember that they are actually not *stages* in the formal development of the tunes, so far as we really know. They cannot be regarded as such, because we have no idea of the time element involved in their creation, nor have we any starting point from which to calculate the order in which they might have appeared. Each tune-item is presumably an end product of variation, with its own partially independent line of evolution behind it. We have no record, consequently no idea, of either the course or the rate of development for these items; hence, we cannot tell by what exact steps they evolved into the forms we know. One version or group of variants may be older than another; but we have yet no way of telling which is which. One form of a tune may have evolved and become widespread before another appeared; but at the present day we cannot safely distinguish between them in this respect. There is every opportunity for older tunes to be remodeled in accordance with the requirements of a later musical influence, and for newer tunes to be re-created along lines (or after fashions) of melodizing that go rather far back. So far as we are concerned, then, these folk melodies are *parallel*, not successive, as they occur and are noted down from tradition. And the fact that batches of them have been collected at various times, in different regions, and without specialized inquiry, hence, doubtless, without proportional representation, does not help to clear up our ignorance about the stages of their growth and change.

We are thus for the most part thrown back on the tune-records alone, and our evidence about their kinship must be almost purely internal. The witnesses to their relationship must therefore consist of those resemblances in structural and melodic features which have survived a period of continuous re-creation by countless anonymous singers of an unknown number of generations. There can be no doubt about the fact of oral re-creation; neither can there be a doubt that resemblances of the sort just indicated do exist. But there is really no logical place to start in our analysis of the versions of any air; we simply make a beginning with some perceptible variant-group and thence proceed to others, being careful not to assume that one version is derived in direct line of descent from another.

The sorts of resemblances we look for, to guide us in disentangling separate tunes one from another, are those of tonal range; of rhythm; of melodic progression, or melodic line; of order (or recurrence) of corresponding musical phrases; and of order (or recurrence) of stressed notes or tones. These various kinds of resemblances are not of equal importance or dependability. Pre-eminent among them are the correspondences in melodic line and in the place and succession of the stressed tones throughout the compass and course of individual melodies. Range, rhythm, and phrase-order are all variable, and less dependable than similar melodic lines and the presence of corresponding stressed tones. If these latter two are relatively constant per phrase, we can be comparatively well assured that we are dealing with a group of cognate or closely related melodic items. But though these features may be enumerated and roughly evaluated, they cannot be looked for one by one, or taken into account separately in the endeavor to identify tune-versions. They must all be considered together. And before such phenomena can be used most beneficially, the investigator must, by immersing himself in the tunes, have impressed on his mind the identifying features of various members of perhaps many different tune-families. Thus, the business of recognizing tune-versions is bound to be gradual and cumulative. The obvious members of a version-group will be perceived at once and easily. Later, when the salient and relatively persistent features of the basic tune are firmly fixed in mind, the identity of the less apparent forms will dawn on the student's comprehension. Folk-tune investigations are full of these sudden discoveries of hitherto unsuspected affinities. Ordinarily, the more often a student re-reads a good-sized collection of folk airs in our tradition, the more members of cognate version-groups he will discover. I have no doubt, therefore, that many versions of familiar, widespread melodies have passed under my eye undetected—especially when I have been able to examine a collection of tunes only once.[19]

The identifier of tunes is really up against a somewhat harder task than the identifier of folk song text-variants. The former does not have recurrent corresponding stanzas, or runs of stanzas, a correspondence or identity of situation and thought, and a perceptible story to guide him, as the textual critic has. Instead, he is confronted by a multitude of fluid and variable melodies, usually much shorter than the song texts to which they are set, and presumably not bound to follow any special lines in the course of their inevitable variation. Among these brief and ever-changing little artistic creations, he tries to confirm what seem to him to be relations of a genetic sort. In order to accomplish this, he has to take into account whatever he can find out about the ways in which the tunes vary: this in order to ascertain, if possible, whether the resemblances which meet his eye are the products of chance or the actual manifestations of some fundamental individual design that endures throughout repeated alterations.

One of the inevitable results of oral cultivation in any folk tradition, whether of texts or music, is the development of a number of congenial idiomatic expressions which are at once functional and artistic in their purpose and use. These are the verbal and melodic formulae—long known in folk poetry by such names as "the ballad tags" or "the ballad commonplaces," and clearly perceived also in the folk tunes, though not designated by any special names. I call them "congenial" because they suit the people who evolved them, and harmonize with other similar manifestations in the folk songs. They are "idiomatic" because their incessant use and continual recurrence confirm them as the regular, accepted idiom—musical or textual—of the folk-song art. They are "artistic" because to their users they are evocative and expressive, and constitute the proper and formally (or conventionally) fitting special means of utterance in verse or melody. They are "functional" in that they are employed in verse to outline situations, designate actions, indicate feelings, provide transitions, and fill structural or formal gaps. In music the formulae serve similar purposes. They are used to start a melody; to end it; to progress from one point to another, according to conventional practices associated with the various scales (which practices also dictate largely the ways in which ascent to, or descent from, a given point in the melody is to be managed); and to provide, as it were, a carrying-on matter between two especially expressive or artistically valuable points in a melody. In short, if, as Professor Entwistle says, "ballad language is formula," [20] then we may also say "ballad music is formula"—and with the same reservations that we should expect to be applied to the verse. For neither folk songs nor tunes are simply chance collections of formulae; and like the ballads, the several separate folk melodies are distinguished by strongly imprinted features. They are, in fact, quite individual musical creations, with varying content and message, just as folk ballads are individual poems telling different stories. But in the case of poems and airs alike, the messages are conveyed to a great extent by the help of formulae. And formulae can best be recognized as those features which tend to recur, as occasion arises for their use, in any piece of traditional verse or music, despite incalculable variations.

The fact is worth emphasizing that most of our folk tunes cannot be regarded primarily as bundles of formulae combined momentarily or on occasion in a semi-extemporaneous way. The presence of numerous cognate tune-versions in our tradition closes the door on that possibility. But neither must we allow ourselves to assume that formulae have a sort of fixed order of recurrence in single tunes, so that, for instance, if an air commenced with formula A, then formulae B, C, and D would inevitably follow in that order, and the tune would be promptly identifiable by its opening notes. This assumption is not borne out by the features of tune-versions. Such an assumption would also necessarily include the idea that the melodic formulae are clearly definable and isolable—which, in fact, they are not. In folk tunes, as in other works of art, the parts are subordinate to the whole, and the formulae are in all cases inseparable components of the entire melody. They are welded together; they merge with one another to build up the coherent and organized musical composition (however brief and simple); and though they may be seen to recur, it is a mistake to suppose that they can have boundaries set to them. Even when they evidently interchange in different tune-versions, they are so naturally woven in that the exact limits of the interchange cannot be definitely set. No one can take a musical formula in folk song and set it apart as one can a formulaic line of folk verse such as "An angry man was he," or "An ill deid mat he die," and say "Here, for all time and for all purposes, is the formula." If anyone disbelieves this, let him take any ordinary folk melody and try to draw a circle around every formulaic element he sees—*setting thereby its limits,* in the tune or out of it. The logical end result of an effort of this sort will be that the formula definer will have at last a series of isolated single notes which mean and reveal nothing. Folk melodies are living musical form and movement—not mechanical compilations of musical odds and ends.

The reason why so much must be made of formulae is that formulaic resemblances among folk tunes have played an important part in previous attempts to identify or classify—or index—the tunes. In being turned to these uses, I think, such resemblances have been given an importance beyond their due. Sooner or later we must face the fact that our folk-musical tradition is pervaded not only by unmistakably formulaic details in the tunes, but also by versions of quite individualized melodies. The outlines of these melodies are strongly ingrained and persistent. Formulaic variation does not easily, or ordinarily, derange them. On the other hand, the interchange and alteration of formulae can easily derange the outlook of a student who gives them paramount importance in his examination of the folk music, and who fails to look beyond them, so to speak, and take into his view the folk-music items in their entirety. In doing so, he at once deprives himself of any fixed point from which he may contemplate our folk music in its broader aspects.[21]

I realize that the remarks in the foregoing paragraph can be made only under the assumption that the more persistent tunes discernible in our tradition are the logical starting place for an examination of the nature and content of our folk-tune stock, and for a study of the processes of its oral re-creation. As it happens, however, under present circumstances, this assumption—whether immediately justifiable or not —is the inevitable, and in fact the only possible one. It gives us our sole attainable point of reference in dealing with the really significant elements in this music as a part of the larger tradition that includes the folk poems and their melodies together. At the present time, our folk music, because of its complicated and unravelled tangles, has to be used with the greatest caution in attempting to extend knowledge about the traditional history of our folk songs. All work with any folk song version and its tune is at present inhibited by our lack of a broad view which takes in, on the one hand, the occurrences and other uses of the tune, and on the other the associations of other versions of the text with different tunes. Of course it is possible—such is the fundamental ambiguity of folk-music records—that even after we have learned much about the manifestations of the tunes in version-groups over a wide area, we might find the music of only limited usefulness in solving folk song problems. However, we continue to hope otherwise.

A mention of the involvement of melodic formulae in efforts to classify folk tunes brings to mind at once the word "type," one of the most ambiguous, loosely used, and generally troublesome terms in the English language, as applied to traditional melodies. During the years when the priceless volumes of the *English Folk Song Society Journal* were appearing, the musical notes furnished by the editors were necessarily inspired by data which were growing too fast for leisurely study. There was no time for elaborate folk-music investigations, nor would they have been very beneficial in that stage of the work of recovering the material. As a natural result, in their efforts to draw attention to tune-records which seemed worthy of comparison, the editors overused and misused the word "type." It was a term easily employed—though not so easily defined.[22] Later students have not been overcareful, either, to define this vague word so that only one meaning could be taken from its use. Hence, no one can be sure now whether the word "type," when used, refers to the function of a version; to rhythmic pattern; design (order, arrangement) of phrases or themes; melodic range or contour; cadential or other formulaic resemblances; modality; "national" stylistic features; or to any combination of any of these traits in a tune, or in tune-groups.

Thus, the confusion is complete; for it is not certain that any two folk-music investigators employing the word "type" have ever had in mind approximately the same meaning. The use of this term in relation to folk tunes has been quite on a par with its use in reference to folk texts: e.g., in the expression "ballads of the Child type"—a phrase of which the meaning is unknown.[23] Because of these circumstances, I have tried to avoid altogether the use of "type" in my remarks and—in keeping with my fundamental aim of distinguishing versions of individual melodies—have preferred to use the word "tune," or even better, the term "tune family," as being more expressive, less ambiguous, and altogether more accurate. A definition of the term "tune family," however, will have to wait until we have considered further aspects of our musical tradition in these remarks.

The word "style" is another dangerous one for investigators of British-American folk music to use in connection with groups of similar airs, since it can be so employed that it can hardly be distinguished in meaning from any of the possible meanings of "type." The late eminent scholar Béla Bartók some time ago made this pronouncement about styles in Hungarian folk music: "At the time when a certain style is in full bloom, a great number of tunes identical in build crop up; each one shows one or several stereotyped features of a certain kind. . . . An abundance of very similar tunes supplies the decisive proof that we are confronting a fully mature style. . . ." As a footnote to this, Bartók adds: "When we have to deal with a very great mass of tunes similar in character, it is sometimes difficult to determine whether one is a variant of another or should be considered independent. One is led to one of two extremes: either to consider all these tunes as forming one group of variants, or to treat them as independent tunes that differ from one another only in a few of their curves." And later in the same work: "During the heyday of a style of peasant music a great number of tunes closely resembling one another (and indeed almost impossible to differentiate) arise. . . . That every one of these, differing from the remainder only in a few melodic details, should ever have been . . . inseparable from one . . . text, is . . . impossible." [24]

These words of Bartók express with unsurpassed accuracy one of the immediate major difficulties besetting a folk-music student. The problem Bartók sees and states is also our problem. It is true that in discussing music, one's language is always bound to be rather vague: musical examples alone are adequate to reveal and illustrate the phenomena under discussion. However, it is surely not out of place to point out that this language about "styles" of music could also be understood to refer to "types" of melodies; and in English our confusion is great enough without the addition of any such new troubling element. Nevertheless, the alternatives Bartók presents call for a fundamental decision one way or the other by every student of every folk music, according to the facts observed in the particular musical tradition under study. The features which Bartók enumerates as characterizing a mature and fully developed style we also observed in British-American folk tunes. And they at once pose for us the question: Do we have here a large number of tunes composed independently along very similar lines, or a large number of versions, variants, and forms otherwise derivative of some original fundamental melodies?

It is obvious, of course, that if the phenomena of our own folk music be interpreted as the independent outgrowth of the influence of various musical styles, each producing its crop of closely similar, yet genetically unrelated melodies in multiple parallel production, we must bid farewell to the effort to identify and trace any individual tunes by means of their variant forms. Instead, we must concentrate on an effort to find out how the styles (?types) arose. However, when we apply this attitude, suggested by the language of Bartók, to our own folk-tune records, we encounter what appear to me to be serious difficulties— which I wish to review at once.

First, if we subscribe to this view, we must then assume that the testimony of practically every eminent folk-tune collector in the British Isles is all wrong in one respect: that they treated their material as consisting in large part of versions of individual melodies, of which they were accustomed to hear various sets in tradition. This blanket indictment applies not only to those who had grown up among folk-music traditions and inherited them naturally (e.g., Patrick McDonald, Simon Fraser, W. P. Joyce), but likewise to those other collectors, from George Petrie down to Miss Anne Gilchrist, whose observations are no less valuable because they approached the musical tradition from the outside, as conscious investigators. From the utterances of those named (and others) we may infer that they have never dreamed of such a thing as a succession of musical styles impressing themselves upon the peasantry and producing each in its turn a crop of inseparably similar melodies. Rather, they saw in their traditions a number of separate tunes—sharing alike the traits of a common musical idiom which they were apt to call the national style of their folk music, and showing structural similarities which made their students endeavor to classify them roughly into various "types."

Second, we are decidedly conscious of the presence in our traditional music of "stereotyped features"—they are perhaps most prominent in opening and cadential passages. However, these features are common not only among the members of certain closely resembling tune-groups, but in practically all the folk melodies. I take such features to be *formulae*—as they certainly interchange, and generally appear to have no decisive effect on the prominent melodic outlines of members of the closely resembling tune-groups.

Third, those clusters of airs in our tradition whose resemblances suggest relationship have in common (as I have already pointed out) a close correspondence of melodic outline or contour; of melodic intervals; and of recurrent accented tones. These correspondences persist across differences of rhythmic pattern and of mode. Thus, if these tunes exemplify the growth and spread of a "style" of music, then each of the folk-musical styles we know must have arisen and developed in complete independence of modal and rhythmic characteristics; and we must infer that such characteristics cannot be taken into account as features of any style of music found in British cultivation. This would be difficult to explain.

Fourth, it is exceedingly hard to see how the features enumerated in the preceding paragraph as possessed in common by closely similar tune-groups can be parts of any style, unless that style is underlain by—and has its foundation in—one archetypal, individual *tune*, of which all the members of the groups would then be variants or derivatives. If a style having these melodic characteristics were *not* derived ultimately from a single tune, then, in order to account for such persistent features, we should have to believe in simultaneous identical inspiration among the folk on a wide scale (in fact, internationally), but applying only to *tone-interval steps* in the construction of melodies, and having no reference to the part that rhythmic and modal patterns might play locally in the formation of any melodic style. Here we should have a dark mystery indeed.

Fifth, whereas similarities in tone-interval (i.e., melodic) outline enable us to see groups of airs that resemble each other strongly, *differences* of the same sort likewise make perceptible other and different groups of airs. Each of these various groups shows strong interresemblance among its component melodies. All these groups share certain stereotyped and idiomatic features in common, but are otherwise quite diverse. If, then, these separate groups of tunes stand for "styles," we have not only two or three of them to deal with: at the very lowest count, and making all the allowances of which I am capable at the moment for traditional divergence, I reckon that no fewer than thirty-five of these "styles" must at various times have had their heyday in British folk music.

If that be the case, the observed distribution of the tune-items themselves is puzzling. One would naturally expect, I believe, that a style of music would normally have a single starting place, or region of beginning development, and thence would spread abroad. Accordingly, one would also expect to see certain styles especially prominent in certain regions, and to find more scattered examples of their products penetrating into the music of other regions. Also, one might expect to find one or more styles predominant and universal, while others, giving evidence of greater antiquity, would appear to be dying out— would be surviving, for example, in peripheral areas or especially remote or backward parts of the country, preserved in the minds of relatively few people, and fast being forgotten. Phenomena of this sort were certainly detected by Bartók in the regions where Hungarian folk music was cultivated.

But this is emphatically not the state of affairs we note in connection with our well-known clusters of similar tunes in British-American folk-music cultivation. Here, on the contrary, we find members of the well-known different clusters of interresembling tunes mingled together everywhere. Furthermore, in most regions, we find these clusters well represented, by the currency of rather diversified forms of their members. If they stand for styles which arose in any successive way among the British peoples, we must conclude that the styles spread without ousting one another, or without popularity at one another's expense; that they were all accommodated side by side in the folk-tune repertories of the singing people. In short, if these groups of melodies are "styles," we have no evidence whatever of the order in which they spread, or the routes they took in their diffusion. There is nothing associated with these groups of airs *as* closely resembling groups, which would in any way connect them each with the spread of a separate popular style of folk music.

Another observation regarding style-characteristics may be made in connection with the foregoing paragraph. In British-American folk music, our tunes are nearly all divided into parts of exactly or approximately equal length, and these parts generally differ, or contrast in some way one with another. Most commonly in our tunes, these parts are only two in number, and could be labelled A and B (variant renderings and internal subdivisions of both in any tune-item are of course to be expected). Without trying to exhaust the possibilities, we may say that the most common tune-patterns among our folk songs, with reference to the ways in which these parts alternate, are the following: AABA, AABB, ABAB, ABBA. Perhaps to be regarded as traditional derivatives of these, among the closely resembling tune-groups, are the phrase-orders AAAB, and the apparent reversals, BBAA and BBBA, *inter alia*. Now the point is that, among the aforesaid clusters of closely resembling melodies—which have in common their strong accented-tone and melodic-interval similarities per phrase or per section—we can observe the variant orders of parts just outlined. Their alternations do nothing to lessen the interresemblances between the tunes; they merely change now and then the succession of the phrases. So, for instance, among these groups there will be some examples in which part A corresponds to the first and second tune-lines (or phrases), and others in which part A will be the first and fourth of these lines. Thus, one member of such a group will have the order AABA; another, ABBA. This means that if we are inclined to take the pattern of phrase-recurrence in a tune-item as showing a trait of any specific musical *style*, we cannot apply that particular stylistic criterion to version-groups among our traditional melodies either. The mutual interresemblances of tune-groups override the order in which tune-phrases may occur. Thus, another feature, in addition to rhythm and modality, would have to be discounted in our efforts to connect styles of music with each of these tune-groups; and, in fact, our definitions would have to be very narrowly circumscribed if we wished to identify these melodic clusters each with a particular musical style.

The sixth, and final, objection to the identification of closely resembling tune-groups with special styles is this: There remains to be answered the question of how to regard tunes occurring *outside* British tradition (especially in the folk music of the Scandinavian peoples) which are still seemingly or manifestly members of these British groups. These scattered airs themselves are apparently merged into closely related local groups of tunes. How shall we account for their presence or their features? Are they cases of accidental convergence, in whole or in part? Are they remnants of older styles once widespread, but now scantily represented (perhaps largely displaced)

in Scandinavia, yet still flourishing in the British Isles? Or are they
"wandering melodies"—much more genuinely so than Tappert's [25]—
which have migrated from their homeland? If so, which way have
they migrated, and where is the homeland of the styles they represent?
Did an air migrate from Scandinavia to Britain, there to become the
nucleus of a new folk style? If we decide thus, we put ourselves in
the position of assenting to the fourth point raised above: that such
styles are derivatives of a single melody. Or, perhaps, has the style
spread from Britain to Scandinavia, but never become universally
popular there? In that case, what should we call these Scandinavian
melodies—examples of a style, or members of groups or versions,
cognate, in their northern homes, with widespread British airs? In
short, the "style" approach to these groups of basically similar airs in
our tradition raises more unanswerable questions than does the approach
which assumes that these airs are descendants of single melodies which
have doubtless had their rise in certain musical styles, but which do not
necessarily own the preservation of their marked and salient special
traits to the integrity or the preservation of such styles. I shall therefore continue to talk about tunes, tune-versions, and tune-families, in
these remarks, and shall treat the material discussed as consisting of
groups of melodies which are derived ultimately from single originals.
There is apparently no time on record when the British folk-music
traditions have not consisted essentially of individual tunes living in
many variant forms.

My own opinion regarding national and regional musical styles is
that there certainly are such things in the British tradition; and that
sometimes these styles are quite noticeable. Such common national and
local idiomatic features as deserve the name of "musical style" affect,
but do not obscure the identity of, the numerous members of the tune-
version groups that are common to the folk music of different British
nationalities. Though these styles remain largely unanalyzed, it is
plain that the individual melodies, wherever they are found, naturally
bear the imprint of the prevalent local musical idiom. However, no local musical idiom can be said certainly to have affected the currency of
the individual melodies. The tunes do not regulate the regional styles
in the British Islands; instead, they are adapted to the styles, for the
greater part. Nor are the tune-versions, to all appearances, instantane-
ously translated from one stylistic idiom into another as soon as they are
transported from one nation or region into another. On the contrary, in

their free movement from person to person and locality to locality, they seem occasionally to have carried what may sometimes be regarded as the stylistic characteristics of one region into another area—thus confusing still more the already vague enough picture of developed regional musical idiomatic features. In short, national tune-repertory is not found to coincide with what can be recognized as national melodic style in British tradition; hence we infer that the styles in themselves neither conserve the identity nor restrict the diffusion of a folk tune in this area.

I guess that we shall ultimately ascertain the regional musical styles of British folk song cultivation to be based upon inherited mannerisms of melodizing—stocks of little *motifs* or successions of tones of the same character as the tetrachord a-g sharp-f-e, which is so much heard in oriental music—mannerisms that have been developed or adopted and become habitual among the British singers. Doubtless these have been exchanged among groups of people; but some would probably tend to become especially favored by one group and relatively little used by another. Favorite scales and formulae used habitually among Irish singers, for example, would be those singers' ordinary way of making music; and what would be more natural than that these formulae and these modal characters should slip into versions of airs learned from some other people and received into traditional currency among the Irish? As examples of such formulae, let me cite a few progressions commonly found in Irish folk music, and apparently much esteemed. With a tonic of G, in order to progress to the D a fifth above, Irish tunes quite often use the succession G-A-C-D; and so also in reverse to descend. When rising from A or B (with the same tonic assumed) to G, numerous Irish melodic versions go thus: B-D-E-F sharp-G; whereas in order to descend in the same compass, it is quite common practice to slide down by means of G-F (sharp, natural or neutral)-D-C, and so to B or A. These little conventional mannerisms, while not entirely confined to Irish tunes in British music, are still exceedingly popular among Irish singers. It is such details as these which seem to me to furnish the best guide to detection of folk-singing styles in this tradition; not the currency of organized tunes which may be internationally known, and may sound English in England, Irish in Ireland, and Hebridean Scottish when they have penetrated into the northern Highlands and Isles.[26]

There is also a seeming preference for, and especially common use of, one or another diatonic scale among these British nationalities. The English singers, for instance, would appear to be particularly fond of what we call the Dorian mode (D to D), since they have used it so incessantly and artistically. On the other hand, we observe what seems to be a similar decided fondness among Irish singers for the so-called Mixolydian mode (G to G, with neutral F); while Hebrid Gaels and American Appalachian mountaineers are often well satisfied with scales of five or six tones, presenting gaps at one place or another.[27] Our internationally known tune-versions, accordingly, are found in forms modified by all these different musical preferences: they may be detected in Dorian, Aeolian, Ionian (or Major), Mixolydian guise; pentatonic, hexatonic and heptatonic scales alternate in their variant manifestations; and all without destroying the fundamental successions that make the basic air discernible.

I realize that the foregoing remarks about style comprise a mere glance at matters of much complexity, and are in part expressions of personal opinion. However, it seems that they are borne out by what may readily be seen among versions of widely known folk tunes in British repertories. I take it to be inevitable that folk artists will alter tunes learned and transmitted by ear in the direction of the idiosyncrasies of music-making most habitual and familiar to their ears and congenial to their acquired artistic tastes. And there seems to be good testimony to this in the diversified forms assumed among different peoples of the British Isles by the tunes current internationally.

But in order to be varied in tradition, a tune, needless to say, does not have to be borrowed by one people from another. Slight variations —minute changes, or exchanges, of formulae—go on, of course, all the time. It might be that if we really could isolate the formulaic passages, we should find that each of them, likewise, was one of a little cluster of variants. We actually do not know what proportion of this variation is unconscious or involuntary, and how much is conscious or intentional. In some folk singers we seem to see mere repeaters, unaware of their few slight variations, and to some degree mechanical; in others we apparently are face to face with artists playing with their material, and expending upon it all the resources of their inherited traditional knowledge and aptitude. However, it seems as though certain rather important recurring types of melodic variation can be perceived; of which all may entail still further variation in the melodic formulae found in tune-versions. Thus, these types of variation may seemingly also be in themselves causes of variation, at times, and of some very important after effects. I take the types in question to be at least eight in number, as follows:

First: An unusually long melodic jump up or down. This generally necessitates some re-arrangement of the melodic line immediately following, and is likely to be compensated by another jump, or a progression, in the opposite direction. But sometimes, also, the skip can be perfectly accommodated without significant additional alterations of the melodic line.

Second: A strong alteration in the tempo or pace of a tune. This is ordinarily caused by the adaptation of the tune to a quite different text, or to a different function. There is apparently no inevitable correlation, however, between the function of a tune-version and its relative degree of ornateness or simplicity. A fast dance-version may be ornate; a quick song-or-game-version may be simple. Slow versions may be furnished with many decorative graces or passing-tones, but these do not necessarily obscure the basic formulae. Rhythmic changes may accompany alterations in pace (e.g. between $\frac{3}{4}$, $\frac{3}{2}$, $\frac{6}{4}$, $\frac{4}{4}$, $\frac{6}{8}$, etc.), being also associated to some extent with function, and probably also bringing along melodic-line variation. To all appearances, these alterations in pace may be brought about either deliberately or involuntarily.

Third: A marked alteration in rhythm, and a contraction or prolongation of tune-line or phrase (see the preceding point, which overlaps this). Tune-lines may be altered to suit the varying number of syllables or main accents in lines of verse; and may thus present the appearance of having been either "drawn out" or "telescoped."

Fourth: The translation of a tune-version from one mode into another. That this has happened often among our traditional airs there is no doubt whatever. And, as Cecil Sharp pointed out long ago, the change is in the nature of a "free translation"; [28] i.e., the formulae most suitable to (or habitually associated with) the mode into which the version is being altered will tend to appear in the recast version, which thus will not be entirely or purely an interval-for-interval transposition. The use of neutral or quarter-tones in our folk scales would seem to facilitate this modal exchange. Although the demonstrated presence of these neutral tones in our folk music [29] may somewhat confuse the picture for the student of modality, it does nothing to obscure the main outlines of the various individual tunes.

Fifth: The influence of other melodies contemporarily current in tradition. Very probably, all melodies in oral tradition side by side exert some influence on each other; but such influence (?contamination) is hard to talk about, since it so often cannot be definitely traced or proved. However, there are cases—which one might call examples of melodic "attraction"—where it seems perfectly clear that a strain of one well-known, strongly individual tune has had a pronounced effect on a strain of another. To this, also, we may perhaps attribute some of the instances in which the first half of a melodic item will belong unmistakably to versions of one large tune-family, while the second half pertains just as clearly to another. Such cases are confusingly frequent in our folk dance music, somewhat less often encountered among song-tune versions. There are also even more perplexing cases of seeming fusion in some tune-sets, where one may be puzzled about whether to account for the facts by means of "attraction" or to consider that the versions one sees are examples of older melodies out of which (by traditional divergence) have emerged two or more distinct tunes. Cases of this kind I shall presently discuss further.

Sixth: Repetitiveness—I call it this for lack of a better term. The presence of this feature can be convincingly attested only by the detailed comparison of a number of variants of a tune. Its special interest seems to me to lie in its apparent close analogy to the repetition of phrase, line, couplet, or stanza which is such a notable feature in traditional song texts. By means of what I call "repetitiveness," a formula characteristic of one place or point in a folk melody may be repeated in another place (sometimes the corresponding point in another phrase, sometimes immediately before or after the regular or expected occurrence of the formula), with the consequent displacing and discarding of the formula otherwise normally occurring in that second place. This repetition-with-replacement may alter only a few notes of an air; or it may affect whole phrases or lines. Perhaps it has been the cause of a good many of the alternating-formula examples we see among various versions. On the other hand, it is not to be confounded with such features of tune-structure as the repetition of a phrase with differing cadential formulae, or the occurrence of two differing phrases, one following the other, but both furnished with the same ending notes. The occurrence of variants in which a short passage common to other variants is omitted, with the "gap" filled in by repeated material, is sporadic on the whole; and it is this fact which leads me to surmise that this type of variation is caused by "repetitiveness." If such features were not merely occasional, we should have no way of guessing whether the repeated bits were original features in the variants, or later developments. As they occur, however, they have the air of being not ordinary, organic phrase-repetitions, but the intrusive repetition of material worked into the phrase from somewhere else in the tune.[30]

Seventh: The transposition of tune-phrases or strains, already discussed above.

Eighth: Corrupt rendition, the result of faulty learning and bad performance of a tune. Corruption we can actually see only when it thoroughly upsets the balance and coherence of a tune. But it may also give occasion for redeeming re-creation. In a process like that, however, any tune may conceivably be varied so much that its original feature may be lost, and another tune evolved. I suggest that some of our folk tunes may possibly have arisen from just such processes—which by their very postulated nature would, of course, be impossible to trace.

Perhaps under the heading of "corruption" might go the phenomenon which Barry called "wearing down." [31] The expression refers to a progressive loss of content by a melody in tradition, so that eventually some versions will appear shortened and lacking in variety—sometimes both monotonized and unbalanced; at other times, simply abbreviated, with no loss of organization. The theory of this occurrence is easy to set down on paper; but the actual process itself is often hard to demonstrate, because we cannot by any means always tell when a melody has been "worn down" and when it has been "built up." Presumably, in oral transmission, a tune can be either augmented or curtailed; but the sort of evidence we have for both procedures is far from satisfactory, and editors have varied greatly in their attitudes toward melodies which have been recorded some times in a longer, sometimes in a shorter form. Dean Christie, for example, was so certain that every tune should properly consist of two "strains," and was originally so composed, that he set himself to provide second strains for all the tunes he conceived lacking them in his own and his father's collection.[32] Keith, on the other hand, was convinced that the "one-strain" versions of his ballad tunes were the correct older or original forms, and that second strains had been supplied by unknown revisers after the tunes had circulated awhile in tradition.[33]

The actual condition of our orally cultivated tunes three or four hundred years ago, naturally, is unknown—even assuming that most of the ones we now encounter were in existence at that time, a speculation that may as well be dismissed, because there is no evidence either for or against it. The original form of any widespread folk tune of our acquaintance is also unknown. Tunes of varying lengths are current in present-day singers' repertories, as also tunes which at one time we hear in a longer form, at another time in a shorter. We therefore are in no position to maintain offhand that any one (not to mention the bulk) of our folk airs was or was not originally composed of two complementary strains of equal length.

These "strains," as normally written down in our folk music, would ordinarily amount to about eight bars each, covering the two lines of a rhyming or assonating couplet (four bars to a line). Some exceptions are furnished by tunes in 9/8 time; by tunes whose phrase-ends are curtailed, or which are otherwise rhythmically disturbed; by tunes that accommodate lengthy refrains; and by a group of melodies adapted to songs which make their lines only three bars long, with their "strains" (halves) becoming consequently six bars in length.[34] Aside from these, however, the two-strain or one-strain tune, with eight bars to a strain, is normal, and holds for association with folk-song texts whether the texts are set down in stanza-form as two-line couplets, as four-line couplets (with or without refrains), or as four lines with two couplets side by side.[35] This means that under ordinary circumstances it is not always possible to tell by the verse form of our folk poem texts whether their accompanying melodies did (or should) consist of two of these "strains" or of only one.

Sometimes we meet with a four-line, two-couplet stanza sung to only one strain of music, which is repeated in order to cover both couplets. These cases are often made perceptible by the practice of ending each stanza pointedly with the same or a similar line, or with the same phrase [36]—a textual feature that sometimes lets us know when lines of a song-version have been lost in transmission, but which tells us nothing, necessarily, about the proper form of its tune. Sometimes, on the contrary, to a song customarily written down in stanzas of four lines and one couplet, we find a two-strain air joined; and the presence of an uneven number of these couplet-stanzas is then apt to cause the singer simply to ignore and drop one strain of his tune somewhere in the course of the song. The same may be said for songs in four-line, two-couplet stanzas: here, half a stanza may be missing somewhere, hence half the tune is also dropped for the nonce. The so-called "common ballad stanza" (four lines, one couplet) is very apt to be

sung to a melody which covers it exactly, and is repeated with variations for every such stanza in a folk poem so written down. In other
words, the common ballad stanza generally goes to a one-strain melody,
of which it may be impossible to tell whether the recorded form was
previously longer (two-strain) or not. Where, then, are our bases for
assuming such a phenomenon as the "wearing down" of a folk melody?
Or for saying, as I did above, that some tune-versions, worn down, will
be monotonized and unbalanced, and others simply abbreviated?

To answer these questions, we must explain some conditions not
always easy to describe. I shall commence with the simplest and most
explicit sort of record. Vaughan Williams testifies that when singers
grow old, they often "sing only the second half of a tune." They commence a song set to a two-strain air; but after singing awhile, they
abandon the first strain and continue the song to the second only.[37] I
also have seen this occurrence, and so, doubtless, have other collectors.
Often repeated, this sort of performance would tend to fix a worn-
down, one-strain version of the tune on popular memory locally, and
start such a version out on a line of traditional cultivation.

Again: a tune design lending itself easily to such modification is
one in which the two main phrases, A and B (see above), are organized
as follows: ACBd, A'cBd—that is, with variant cadential closes, or variant
half-phrases at the end of each separate phrase, and an additional
variation of the A-phrase. The two strains, being rather close in resemblance, can become simplified into one, and that one repeated for
all couplets of the verse; so that such tunes just as often appear as
ACBd alone, or A'cBd alone—or also as ACBC and ADBd. The next observed occurrence that we shall consider will explain why we sometimes feel justified in saying that the longer form of a folk air does
not present a lengthened or elaborated rendering of the shorter.

Suppose that we have two different folk songs, x and y, both being
often—perhaps usually—sung to versions of the same air; and suppose,
in addition, that the air has the phrase-design ABB'A (for tunes of such
phrase-design often have a variation of the B-phrase on its repetition,
amounting to a sort of climax). Versions of x and y will be found
scattered about over the English folk-singing world. Depending on how
thorough the collecting has been in any region, we may expect to find
some texts of x and y recorded often in some regions, but scantily
represented in others. As to musical records, we may expect to see only
a fraction of the recorded texts accompanied by recorded tunes; but

most of these tune-sets will be recognizable as versions of ABB′A. Among the texts for which our tune (with its ABB′A form) has been recorded, some will show association with the full air; and this association is likely to be observed wherever the poems have been found. But right along with those forms of x and y will be found other variants which are not set to our tune ABB′A in its entirety; on the contrary, they will be joined to melodies which, when compared with ABB′A, will reveal themselves as consisting of such combinations as the following: AAAA, BBB′A; AB; B′A, etc. The tune-phrases will be unmistakably the same as those making up the air ABB′A as it occurs with other versions of x and y; but in some cases a phrase will be lost; in other cases, the arrangement will be altered so that the balancing occurrence of the phrases, and their peculiar alternation-pattern will be sacrificed; and in still others, what will be recognized as only the first or second half of the tune will occur—so that a whole stanza of x and y will now be set not to ABB′A, but to AB *plus* AB or B′A *plus* B′A. It may happen, too, that versions of x and y will get taken down differently by different recorders, so that some appear in stanzas of two couplets apiece, others in stanzas of only one couplet. In the latter case, the tune-versions AB or B′A will constitute the whole recorded melody.

In circumstances such as these, and taking into account what has been observed of the strain-dropping tendencies of some folk singers, we may often be correct in inferring that sets of a tune which have lost some of their regular design-features and perhaps their melodic balance and variety, are *worn-down* sets of the air which may elsewhere be noted in a fuller and more highly organized condition. But we may not feel safe in assuming this wearing-down in every case we meet of the seeming occurrence of full-tunes beside half-tunes. All possible factors connected with the continuing association of versions of one tune with versions of a certain text, *plus* the use of that tune in various sets along with other texts, have to be weighed before we may unhesitatingly say that any tune-version is present in a worn-down form. There is no external evidence to tell us whether the very first, original, set of a melody had one or another of the several recurring melodic phrase-patterns now broadcast among our traditional tune-versions, or was originally longer or shorter than we find its sets to be at present.[38]

It may have seemed a piece of gross oversimplification to assert, as I have above, that most of our melodies are made up of two separate phrases that could be labelled A and B; and to discuss our tunes as if they invariably consisted of A- and B-phrases in various alternation-patterns. What of those tunes (it may be asked) which manifestly consist of *four* differing phrases, and thus present themselves in schemes of ABCD? They are certainly noticeable in Anglo-American folk music wherever it is recovered, and they cannot be ignored.[39] Nor do I propose to ignore them; but before dealing with them it was necessary to make the preceding explanations about A-*plus*-B designs, because of the peculiar relations between airs with those designs and the airs with schemes of ABCD. Keeping in view what has been said about the tunes generally, we can make the following observations about these tunes with ABCD phrase-pattern:

I remarked above that internal subdivisions of any phrase in the make-up of a folk melody were to be expected. Now the fact stands out that in the repertories of our folk-singers, a number of the melodies apparently having the independent pattern ABCD are actually found to correspond with one or the other half of longer tunes in the melodic stock—and these longer tunes show phrase-patterns of ABBA, AABA, etc. In other words, the AB of one of these ABCD-tunes is really discernible as equalling the A of a longer air, and the CD is similarly found to correspond with the B of the longer air. This means that, either originally, or through re-creation and varying development, certain tune-phrases have traits that divide them clearly into two subsections which are found everywhere in the variant forms of these phrases. These subsections, also, may on occasion serve as entire phrases themselves. The situation, then, with regard to ABCD-pattern tunes, is often as follows:

Taking the ABBA pattern merely as an example, one of the longer-form airs will show:

$$\text{I.} \quad \text{A} \qquad \text{B} \qquad \text{B} \qquad \text{A}$$

which is found, upon closer examination, to be approximately equivalent to

$$\text{2.} \quad \text{ab} \qquad \text{cd} \qquad \text{cd} \qquad \text{ab}$$

This, in turn, we find to correspond with

$$\text{3.} \quad \text{AB} \qquad \text{CD}$$

of some shorter airs, or with

$$\text{4.} \qquad\qquad\qquad \text{AB} \qquad \text{CD}$$

of others—where the AB - CD of these latter melodies actually corresponds to the cd - ab, or BA, second-half pattern, of the versions of the longer melodies. I freely admit that the foregoing explanation is both generalized and simplified; but it had to be in order to indicate intelligibly a phenomenon that recurs continually in our recorded folk music. To sum up: tune-items with phrase-patterns of the ABCD may themselves often be shortened (?worn-down) forms of longer tunes in which is customarily found some alternation-pattern of phrases that could be distinguished by the designating letter A and B (*cf.* the examples set forth in footnote 38).

As a result, we are unable to say definitely that ABCD-patterns are always those of full, independent, properly complete tunes; nor can we declare these patterns to be entirely separate from other A-*plus*-B arrangements found generally in our folk music. It is true that certain melodies consisting of four different phrases may be regarded as retaining their proper, full-length forms.[40] But such tunes do not by any means all do so. And thus, the mere phrase-pattern of any traditional tune-item cannot in itself teach us anything about the original form, or the proper form, or even the usual form, of the tune of which that item may be a variant. Hence, we have to conclude either that folk melodies in our tradition do not belong to "types" on the basis of their phrase-order patterns only, or else that—even if we arbitrarily classified them thus—such "phrase-pattern" typology cannot serve to identify versions of individual melodies in British-American folk song. As shown above, differences of phrase-order pattern may, and do, exist aplenty among the versions of any individual folk melody, with the result that either the single phrase or the half-tune is the real unit with which we have to work when attempting to identify melodies by means of the highly important features of melodic-interval (melodic-line) and stressed-tone correspondences. Observing the recurrence of those complexes of phrases that stick together as distinct entities in themselves, we arrive at the conclusion repeatedly stated above: that our musical tradition is essentially one of organized, integrated, individual tunes, whose fundamental identities remain perceptible throughout many vicissitudes of oral transmission, re-creation, and reorganization.

Perhaps I have said enough to indicate that while the phenomenon which I call "wearing down" cannot always be satisfactorily detected or determined, the actual presence of tune-versions of varying length and phrase-arrangement in our melodic tradition is a very real fact.[41] Whether a tune was originally in one or another form, or to what extent lengthening or shortening has taken place in transmission, are interesting questions which may or may not become important. But the existence of shorter or longer tune-versions, and the transposition of phrases or entire halves of tunes in tradition, are facts of the first importance to a student either of the music or of the association between the music and the songs.

It occasionally happens that a group of variant texts of a single folk song will appear at first glance to be sung to a number of different melodies. But upon further comparison of all the tunes to those variants, and of other resembling tunes joined to other texts in the tradition, we are sometimes enabled to see that the musical settings to the texts of our song are really diverse forms of a single air—in which variation, transposition of phrases, and shortening-or-lengthening of the entire tune have produced differences that can entirely mislead a hasty or superficial observer. In such cases, it sometimes takes a quite extensive tune-examination of the sort just indicated before we see that the melodies on which we happen to be concentrating are actually all cognates. A discovery similar to that just outlined is one which an investigator of British-American folk song tunes may expect to make repeatedly. Such an experience furnishes one of the most cogent arguments for the study of the music by and for itself, before any large-scale plunge is taken into the exceedingly complicated problems of the history of folk song variants as text-tune units. What the organized knowledge of our folk music, when attained, may do to help us with problems of ballad text history is hard to predict. But at least, it should considerably refine our approaches to those problems.

In the preceding paragraphs I have been endeavoring to describe some of the salient variation-phenomena that a student encounters when he pays close attention to our folk music. I must now turn to still other features of oral variation; among them, some which practically force us to theorize about what has happened to our tunes in their passage down the generations. The student often finds himself at close grips with music to which almost anything may conceivably have happened in oral transmission; yet he is deprived of any record of just what actually *has* happened, outside of such information as he may glean from the music itself. And this internal evidence is apt to be profoundly ambiguous just where an investigator wishes it were most explicit.

While the student is trying to envisage clearly all the possibilities lying behind the record, the realization naturally haunts him that all reconstructions of processes which he may make are conjectural. In the presence of alternate possibilities, there are often no unmistakable indications that will enable him to fix on the correct alternative. This situation yet again forces him to rely on thoroughgoing resemblances between collected tune-items. They in turn, by their continual reappearance, convince him anew of the real existence of separate melodies, widespread in tradition and split up into large families numbering many variant forms. Just as the principal folk tales may be detected through the multitudes of floating traditional stories by the recurrent combinations of their respectively component *motifs*, so certain distinctive folk melodies in this tradition reappear amid the welter of oft-used melodic formulae. This is not remarkable in itself; by analogy with other folk arts, it is to be expected. But what really is remarkable is the overtowering importance of these distinctive tunes in the tradition—their prevailing use wherever the tradition lives.

I stated above that apparent cases of melodic attraction between airs, and instances where an actual mingling of two otherwise usually distinct melodies would seem to have taken place, can often confuse an investigator. It is in precisely these cases, naturally, that one is most troubled by inability to decide between possible alternatives—through lack of clear evidence. These cases merit some effort at brief analysis.

Occasional and passing resemblances between two undoubtedly different airs are to be expected in folk music, of course, and do not cause much trouble. But in cases where a really inextricable fusion of two ordinarily distinct tunes may be seen, we simply cannot discover with any certainty the actual course of events behind the seeming fusion: the possibilities are too many, the indications too few—or entirely wanting. For example, any such case may possibly be the result of what is really the exact opposite of "fusion." It may be a version of a melody out of which, by traditional re-creation, may have developed the two widespread distinct airs whose elements we discern in it. On the other hand, such a tune may represent simple confusion of memory on the part of a singer or singers somewhere along the line of transmission—by means of which two well-known different airs have been mingled unintentionally, and the product of this confusion passed on to other singers. Or, again, the combination of strains or elements from the different airs may have been made in full consciousness, and deliberately, by someone. Or, again, the tune in question may be the product of someone's effort to compose a new melody—in which, however, the would-be composer was dominated by the memory of a couple of important tunes already current in the tradition, and thus evolved something more imitative than original. In the presence of varying possibilities like these we find ourselves practically helpless.

It must be remarked, however, that what we discern in the versions of distinguishable tunes allows us to envisaged one general possibility: namely, that all these fused and indeterminate airs may actually be of later development than the comparatively clear-cut ones. Perhaps in such tunes we witness the beginnings of a newer tune-repertory, which by gradual growth and spread in time—if the tradition were undisturbed—might eventually displace the one out of which it grew. The only basis for a conjecture such as this is the "nonuniversality" of these mixed melodies. They certainly do not appear to enjoy a currency wherever the English folk songs are sung—as do many other airs whose recurrence we may reasonably expect anywhere in the English folk-song world. Melodies such as these mixed ones occur sporadically. They appear to be made up of the elements of airs known universally, yet they themselves are not so known. They might even be regarded as accidents of tradition, and as transient local phenomena—although any one of them at any time could conceivably become something much more important in the folk song culture.

One hitherto unmentioned aspect of traditional variation bears directly on these "mixed" tunes and upon the problems of melodic attraction in the folk music. It is a fact, clearly apparent to the student, that sometimes a change of mode may greatly increase the overall resemblance of a version of one separate tune to versions of another separate tune. This could easily lead to still more influence of the material of the one tune upon the other, and result in ever-increasing resemblance between some versions of one and of the other. Actually, it is probable that just as folk poems may change theme by theme and slide imperceptibly—and by subtle associations of ideas connected with the themes—into quite different song-families; so also some folk-tune versions, through crisscrossing of modal, formulaic, and general structural resemblances, can come to a point where it is impossible to say to which of two (or even three) large cognate groups they belong. They could be in any; are, in fact, strictly in none. It is also likely that versions of an originally independent tune may gradually become more and more like versions of another (in the way just outlined) so that eventually they are, to all appearances, and in all respects, versions of the tune to which they have little by little been assimilated.

In the British tradition we certainly find some melodies which are quite bewildering because of what look like the results of "multiple attraction" of some of their versions to more than one widespread tune-family. That group of interrelated and interresembling tunes generally sung in old-country English tradition to the ballad "Henry Martin" (Child No. 250) shows extraordinary variety among its members.[42] Now they will appear to be independent tunes; again, they will look like forms of the "Lord Randal" melody, one of the commonest of our folk-song airs; still again, they rather seem to resemble another such widespread tune-family, that one which I have arbitrarily christened the "Bailiff's Daughter" air. Some such remarks also apply to the tunes ordinarily sung to the ballad "Young and Growing"[43]—which display at once so much mutual resemblance and so many divergent developments that their actual relations one with another and with any single widespread family of folk tunes seem at present indeterminable.[44] It thus appears that sets of tunes in our tradition may be attracted toward more than one different melody current among folk singers at the same time. If such things actually happened—as seem reflected in the musical record—then the influence of certain melodies which attained universal popularity and continual use all over the British folk-singing world must have been considerable. Such airs would appear to have been prime examples of the folk musical taste and ideals; sources of inspiration and subjects of imitation; regulators of variation; and so, in a sense, shapers of creative melodizing among the singing people. Sooner or later the student of this musical tradition comes to the point of concluding that the power and importance of various universally known individual melodies are hard to exaggerate.

Another feature of oral variation, which is a fruitful source of confusion for uninitiated and experienced students alike, is the phenomenon which I have called "alternating cadential formulae."[45] I have already noticed these manifestations briefly. And I think that, for once, the term just given fits the phenomenon completely. A few words about this aspect of our folk music may be desirable here. It appears to arise through an exchange of formulaic cadential passages all of which may be substituted one for another in many of our tunes. It is, then, just another example of that exchange of musical formulae already discussed. Obviously, it is a melodizing trick that would present no difficulties to a practiced folk singer whose mind was filled with the common tunes of his traditional repertory and with the memories of how he had heard them varied. On the contrary, it is something that would be quite naturally and easily done. I have heard traditional singers substitute one cadential formula for another in the course of their singing one tune to stanza after stanza of a song; and evidently other collectors have heard the like, since such exchanges on the part of one singer of a tune-version also appear in published folk-tune records.[46]

The particular cadence-alterations under discussion at the moment have the effect of ending a phrase of a tune on *different notes* of the scale or mode in which the tune happens to be cast. This fact implies at once that they are not used at the closes of tune-versions—which is the case. Such alterations occur medially: sometimes at the end of the first phrase (mid-point of first strain); also often, at the mid-point of the tune (end of first strain). At these points, tune-versions that are unmistakably forms of one original melody will vary, turning now up, now down, according to the progression of the inserted cadence-formula.

Thus, there are three places where the melodic line of a tune-version may be confidently expected to vary: at the very beginning (sometimes the variation is considerable, here); at the very end; and at the mid-point cadence, or end of the first half of the set. A tune-version is not necessarily altered beyond recognition by changes at any or all of these points. Indeed, it may be conjectured that if a certain number of these alternating formulae come to be associated in the minds of various singers with the familiar strains of certain tune-versions, that fact itself might work as a conserver of the outlines of a tune. However, the formulae which interchange at these medial tune-cadences are not restricted—as to their occurrence—by rhythmic pattern, by pace or tempo, by strongly marked version-group characteristics, by the immediate function of a tune-version, or by the mode in which a tune-version happens to be sung at any particular time. In other words, we may look for certain variant medial-cadential turns to recur in any sets of any widespread melody, despite the alterations caused by variation of other kinds. Thus, this remarkable manifestation in our folk music actually helps the investigator to detect cognates of a tune as it floats hither and thither on the currents of tradition. On the other hand, it can also—taken with the "falling together" of versions of different folk tunes, due to their being by chance translated into the same mode—bewilder a student, no matter how careful he may be, and divert him from perceiving the main outlines of a given tune. It can disguise from a careless or hasty observer the true affiliations of some melodic item with some widely known family of variants.

However, there will always be some amount of indeterminate material in our tradition, no doubt. We are left in an ignorance of the past of our folk music which prevents us from being able to decide between the alternatives of dispersion *plus* variation; independent invention *plus* assimilative variation; and (deliberate or unconscious) tune-merging *plus* variation, in any attempt to account for the features displayed by some of our airs.

Judging from the testimony of the published musical records, our folk song tunes fall into three main classes, on the basis of the comparative number of their discernible cognate relatives. These classes are: (*1*) a few tunes which have formed very widely diffused and multiform families—consisting of inextricably interrelated sets that dominate the musical scene, and account for the majority of the tunes sung to the songs; (*2*) a fair number of distinct, independent tunes seemingly less well known, and recorded in fewer variant forms— hence, forming smaller tune-families; and (*3*) the "indeterminate" melodies just now being discussed.

Melodies of class (*2*) sometimes have their variants more or less concentrated; or they may show variants widely, but thinly, scattered over the entire area of the tradition. Those of class (*3*) are varied in their aspects. They are all in a recognizable style, or musical idiom, of the tradition. Sometimes they may partake of the characteristics or elements of various exceedingly well-known airs in the repertory, without yet being clearly members of any of the version-groups of those airs. At other times they are quite nondescript—arrangements of familiar melodic turns or passages—and seem to illustrate perfectly what Professor George Pullen Jackson calls "general melodizing." [47] Furthermore, to judge from published musical evidence, they are mostly not traceable in variant forms from region to region of the English folk-singing area—as are the tune-families of the widely known airs. On the contrary, they occur locally and sporadically—most of them are *hapax legomena*, in fact—so that it is not certain whether they have had any extensive currency, or whether any lengthy history of transmission lies behind them. (I have mentioned above some groups that seem to furnish exceptions to this general principle.) In brief, their occurrence suggests that they are, for the most part, "sports" of tradition—chance, hybrid products of variation—and not integrated, intrenched, widely accepted old melodies, strongly impressed on the popular memory. They seem not to travel about like the great tunes of the tradition; but to be current locally, perhaps temporarily. It may be that they represent the gradually accumulating elements of some exclusively local tune-repertories, or the products of some local worthies in obvious imitation of forms of the really important melodies in the general stock. Indeed, their character itself inevitably suggests that they are usually formed in imitation of (or under the influence of) those already dominant airs in our tradition, and hence cannot be of such age as the latter. If this be actually the case with these non-allocable airs, still another suggestion likewise becomes inevitable: that our folk-song-tune repertory, over its whole area, is not only composed, for the greater part, of diverse forms of a few individual tunes, but that it is essentially *individual tune based.* I mean by this that it gradually grows larger mostly by means of the occasional mergings and slow divergences in transmission of continually varied forms of the dominating, strongly impressed melodies.[48]

I have been trying, at great length, to set forth the most notable features exhibited by our folk music as a whole—especially, however, those aspects that illustrate the nature of the oral variation that our melodies have undergone. Considering those aspects, it seems as though we should fall into a considerable mistake if we tried to account for the rise of any one of the great "tune families" in our tradition merely by cumulative unconscious or involuntary oral variation of an isolated, single, simple melody. We have to recall two basic facts: first, that no traditional melody ever lives or is re-created in a vacuum—it is always liable to influence from other melodies co-existent with it; second, that there is no reason to suppose all variation unconscious—a good part of it may have been not only conscious, but even deliberate, on the part of the traditional artists whose property the music is.

For practically every one of our folk melodies of British extraction, the composer, and the time, place and circumstances of composition are alike unknown and unimportant. It is perfectly plain that the melodies, as we now know them, have been re-created time and again by persons of no mean organizing and artistic talent. It is also plain that—their original forms being unknown or undetectable—we cannot undertake to say how they first came into being. Possibly they were each composed as "new" tunes by some persons at some times in the past. Just as possibly, they arose by endless variation out of some older mass of airs—

and once a thoroughly congenial form or outline had been attained, it stayed in popular memory and spread by oral diffusion. Or perhaps some of them arose in the one way, some in the other; we cannot tell. We can be sure of at least two things: that our folk music, as far back as we can trace it, has always been alive and developing; and that certain tunes have managed to retain their identity in the face of oral re-creations that have fundamentally altered the esthetic character of many of their versions.

But from the occurrences and apparent tendencies visible in this music, it would seem not unreasonable to suppose that a big tune-family was built up by a succession—or a combination—of happenings somewhat like the following:

1. A tune, its form once comparatively settled either by original composition or by someone's distinctive revision, would appeal to a number of people, who would learn it and start to spread it abroad orally. During this diffusion it would at once commence to be heard in variant forms; and throughout its subsequent life in tradition, it would never cease to be varied more or less by practically every one of its singers.

2. Because of its wide appeal—and perhaps its adaptability to many different song texts or uses—our hypothetical tune would become exceedingly popular, so that it could be reckoned one of the best-known melodies in the folk repertory.

3. The variant forms of this tune, travelling back and forth, would become known side by side—or in clusters—in many communities. Their similarity one to another would make it easy for singers to merge them involuntarily while performing; so that variant forms of one tune, found alongside each other in any community, would affect each other mutually, exerting influences one upon another of a most complex and subtle kind. The composite variant forms made by this confluence of more than one already existing variant of the tune might spread anew to other communities, where the process would be likely to be repeated.

4. This merging of parent and derivative variants would tend to fix the basic outlines and important intervals of a tune firmly in the minds of the singing people—so that the pattern and principal formulae of the tune would become a part of the way in which they habitually thought melodically.

5. The reinforcement of the tune's main melodic outline, combined

with constant slight variation, would in time cause a number of inextricably interrelated forms to appear—among which a form very
close to that of the original melody might or might not survive.

6. Bits of other concurrent melodies might get worked into some of
the forms of this group of variants, causing more or less divergence
from the common tune outlines, and facilitating the appearance of
versions of the tune. A change of rhythm, pace or mode (always possible when the outlines of a tune are firmly ingrained in a folk singer's
consciousness) would effect the appearance and further development of
still other distinctive versions.

7. The variation undergone by these related tunes—traceable both
to the influence of other airs and the interchange of elements from
their own sets—would make it practically impossible for many singers
to hear or think of their forms of the tunes in any single, unvarying
way. They would likewise tend to vary their forms by consciously introducing the formulae of other variants which they had heard.[49] And
this interchange of variant-material, in turn, would tend to increase the
number of usable and interchangeable beginning-and-ending formulae
which the folk singers would have at their disposal in performing any
of their traditionally learned tunes.

8. The formation of distinctive versions of the tune—by means of
alterations in rhythmic scheme, pace and mode—would not all be
natural or unconscious: some of it would be intentional. Some folk
musicians who thoroughly knew a form or forms of the air would be
able to adapt it to another function (marching, dancing, etc.) by deliberately recasting it—in the ways mentioned, or by the elaboration or
drastic simplification of its melodic line. The capabilities of certain
musical instruments might also exert an influence in this process.

9. Because of alterations of mode and interchange of formulaic
beginnings and strain-endings, melodies which originally had been
quite different from the tune whose development we are following in
theory, would be found resembling it much more closely. Some of these
melodies, or some forms of them, would become progressively assimilated to forms of our supposed "dominant" tune—until at length
they would be as indistinguishable from it, or as inextricable from the
mass of its variants, as if they had been forms of the "dominant" tune
from the beginning.

10. So deeply impressed would be the outline and basic structure of
the tune, throughout its many forms, that we might expect imitations of

it to appear. A person of no originality, desirous of composing a new tune (and this sort of person is by no means unknown in folk-singing circles), would be more likely to produce an adaptation of something already familiar to him. And his "new" composition could readily take one of two forms: either what amounted (or, in the course of variation, ultimately would amount) to simply another version or variant of our supposed dominant tune; or a hybrid, in which a part of one such dominant tune might be joined to, or mingled with, a part of another air equally widespread in the oral repertory. In this way, the array of versions would be increased by one; or else one of the non-allocable "nondescript" airs of the tradition would be produced.

11. As the derivative forms of the dominant melody continued to be perpetuated by tradition, some would become shortened; others, due to the adaptive faculties of talented folk musicians, might be extended or elaborated, or provided with additional full-length strains or refrain passages. All such alterations would tend (provided they lived and spread) either to establish yet another group of versions in oral currency, or to produce a form so divergent that it could be developed without difficulty into a quite different air.

12. In the course of time one would be able to find among folk singers some individuals who were alive to the likenesses and evident relations between close variants among the forms of this air which they knew; others who were oblivious of such features, and the less obvious versions of the air would be sung without suspicion that they were in any way related. All forms, however, would continue to be re-created by their singers. The derivatives of one traditional melody, cultivated along with others, would thus have multiplied and greatly enriched the communal musical tradition.

In accordance with the hypothesis just outlined in the above twelve points—a hypothesis itself depending on observable phenomena in our folk melodies—I can now offer my definition of a "tune family":

A *tune family* is a group of melodies showing basic interrelation by means of constant melodic correspondence, and presumably owing their mutual likeness to descent from a single air that has assumed multiple forms through processes of variation, imitation, and assimilation.

THE FOLK MUSIC of the British Isles is apt to impress one at first by its really astonishing variety, both of national repertory and of regional style.[50] Of repertories we can distinguish at least five among the land-dwelling population: those of the English, the Lowland Scots, the Welsh, the Irish, and the Highland and Hebridean Scots. To these must be added a sixth distinctive melodic repertory, not peculiar to any nationality: that of the tunes to the shanties, or marine work-songs. Among them all, the most stylistically distinct and melodically self-contained are the tune-treasuries of the shantymen and the Highland Scots.

"Style" in our folk music, or in any music, is terribly hard to characterize. Nevertheless, a few words more may perhaps be set down about the dominant perceivable styles in British traditional tunes. They do not—as has been pointed out at length—correspond necessarily with groups of versions or related airs, nor with any melodic repertories, strictly speaking. They belong to the sort of phenomena which may be often readily perceived, but almost never successfully described; and what one can say about them in words is bound to be exceedingly superficial.

Broadly speaking, and leaving out of account the shantymen's tunes, the folk music of the British Isles, as we have known it, appears in three distinguishable main styles. These we may term the *English,* the *Irish,* and the *Hebridean;* but these terms must be understood as being employed more for convenience than for any scientific reason. The English style, current in English counties and the northeast of Scotland (with local variations of melodic idiom), shows relationship in its mannerisms with Scandinavian traditional music. The two other styles may be roughly included under the term "Gaelic," and are rather closely akin in many fashions of melodizing. The Irish style prevails, naturally, in Ireland, and in the western Scottish Lowlands. The here so-called Hebridean style is that of the Scottish Highlands and the Western Isles. In this music also some observers have (not surprisingly) thought to see Scandinavian influence.[51]

Both English and Irish styles share some qualities to which I have already alluded: their tunes are generally couched in bisymmetric two- or four-line organizations, and have phrase-patterns of AABA, ABBA, ABCD, etc. I hope I have made it plain that the internal structure of these airs is much more varied, complex and subtly organized than any A-*plus*-B scheme of phrase-arrangements could indicate: these schemes are simply indications of fundamental models. The great popularity of the Dorian mode in English music has also been mentioned. In addition, we might say that the English style is characterized by a certain solidity of melodic build—an emphasis throughout the tune on the strong notes of the mode, like the tonic or dominant tones—and by a preference for the sort of melodic movement which "gets somewhere," which is not held up by hesitating progression or undue overlay of ornamental features. In general, the style is firm and forward-moving, with vigorous rhythm, bold, long-range sweeps, and simple melodism.[52]

Whereas the English folk poems are nearly all composed in stanzas of four main accents to a line, or in alternations of four accents with three, many Gaelic and Anglo-Irish poems are composed in lines which, from a musical point of view, might be said to contain three, five, or six principal stresses; consequently, we see tunes with five- and six-bar lines in music of the Irish style. Irish singers, as already noticed, seem to show as marked a liking for the Mixolydian mode as English singers do for the Dorian; and the English singer's leaning to relatively straightforward and simple melodic lines is counteracted in Irish tradition by a love of ornament, of multiplying notes, of varying rhythmic patterns by this sort of multiplication. Often, in Irish singing, the skeletal tune is so heavily overlaid with ornamental features that it becomes hard to recognize; yet, too, it is hard to call these features (cadenza-like runs, slides, rapid shakes, grace-notes of various sorts) an "overlay"—they seem to form an integral part of the melody, as well as of the style of performance.[53] This same ornamental tendency, plus the free-time rendition of many song-tunes, and the five- and six-bar line of many others, gives to Irish music in the purest style a quality which Padraic Colum also notes in Irish verse-structure: i.e., the most characteristic Irish song-tunes are "wavering and unemphatic" in their movement.[54] Contributing still further to this impression are two other marked features of Irish style. One is a curious tendency to "hold back" —to draw back before starting forward again, as it were; and also to linger on certain notes or tones, by repeating them before going on to another tone, thus almost impeding the onward course of the melody from time to time.[55] The other is a striking tendency to emphasize and dwell on scale-tones that are inconclusive or indecisive—the weak or passing tones, the ones that do not contribute to resolution or finality in the entire phrase or musical utterance, but rather to easy flow and facile continuity.[56] These qualities taken together give the purest Irish airs a peculiarly melodious, graceful softness of flow and outline; a sweetness and smooth ease that seem often on the point of slipping into diffuse weakness.

It is possible that the Hebridean style is the most archaic surviving in British folk music. By contrast with the symmetrical, highly organized tunes of Ireland and England, many of the Highland airs appear almost casually put together. The fundamental phrase-order patterns mentioned as characterizing the other two styles are not prominent at all in the Hebridean music. The Hebridean singers have a decided fondness for arranging tune-strains or phrases in groups of three—a habit not characteristic of the other two styles.[57] Also, the Hebridean-style repertory contains numerous airs which it is impossible to bisect. They do not fall into two equal-length halves any more than French folk tunes usually do, and for a similar reason: the lines of the songs in Highland and Hebrid repertories are interspersed with refrains and ejaculations, in such a way that the accompanying music sounds much more improvisational than the tunes of the English and Irish styles. Often it seems as if no clear ending-strain for a Highland tune can be discerned: as if another strain could be added, or one removed, without damaging what organization the entire melody has.

The frequent repetition of short units, or motives, also characterizes the Hebrid melodies. Likewise, the use of "gapped" scales, instead of full, heptatonic diatonic scales is very characteristic of Hebridean singing; and the gaps in these modes are not often filled in or slurred over by the use of passing-tones. The whole tonality of tunes in this style seems vaguer than that of the other styles: shifts from a minor-sounding tune-body to a major close, and *vice versa,* are not uncommon. Abrupt switches of register, with wide and frequent melodic leaps (of fifths, sixths and octaves) are quite prominent in this melodic style; yet here may also be perceived sometimes the peculiar "lingering" tendency just described for Irish-style music. In Hebridean tunes the melodic outline is apt to be relatively simple, lacking the florid multiplicity of notes which we often find in Irish music. The graceful and beautiful way in which Highland singers handle slides and short grace-notes has been eloquently remarked by Miss Broadwood.[58] But again, as in Irish tunes, we find, to some extent, the curious prominence given to indecisive tones in the scales; and in melodic idiom generally, the Hebridean style is much closer to the Irish than to the English.

In these three styles we find rendered the national and regional tune-repertories of British folk song singers—except for the sea shanties, which have developed in large measure still another style especially their own. But whatever may be the spread of one of these styles, or the prominence in any region or nation of one of the above-enumerated repertories, not one of these regions has a repertory consisting entirely of airs unknown elsewhere. All share to some extent in melodies known to all the others.

The tune-trading and mutual influence among the national repertories are bewildering—hard to describe, hard oftentimes to determine. It seems that in each of the above mentioned regional (or national) repertories we find certain tunes quite popular and known in many versions, which are peculiar to those parts and are not heard or recorded elsewhere. This, of course, is judging by the published collectanea, with all their acutely realized limitations. Thus, there are some tune-families that would seem peculiar to certain nationalities or regions of the British Isles.

Other tune-families show variant forms in more than one region— or perhaps in all parts. Thus, Highland and Lowland Scotland; England, Wales, Ireland and the Scottish Lowlands; Wales, Ireland, the Hebrides and the western Scottish Lowlands are seen to be bound up together, musically, in a network of melodies known in common. The music of the Isle of Man has very little peculiar to it, on the whole: outside of a very few airs, like the well-known "Mylecharane" [59] and some *carval* melodies, Manx folk music consists of versions of melodies known to Anglo-Scottish or Irish singers, or to both.

Now many of these tunes, as I said before, are apt to sound English in England, Irish in Ireland, etc. It is therefore often impossible to ascertain in which country the parent tune of a family was composed. When a tune-version travelled from one British region or nation to another, it was naturally re-created in the musical style of the region which adopted it. We can often reasonably infer that a given version of some widespread air is Irish or Scottish, for example; but we cannot therefore claim that the air itself was of Irish or Scots origin. The presence of Irish mannerisms in a melody current in midland England, then, indicates only that this version of the melody was presumably evolved in, and brought from Ireland; but it does not allow us to claim that the tune first arose there. Judging from the "traceability" of melodic style in the published records, tune-versions have travelled much and often between the countries of the British Isles. The creeping-in of Scottish- and Irish-style dance music on English country-dance accompaniments is a matter of record.[60] And many folk song tune-versions common in the English countryside are apparently just as well known in Ireland and northeastern Scotland—often quite thoroughly assimilated to the local melodic idiom.

The dominant tune-families of English folk song are about equally widespread elsewhere in the British islands, save for the Highlands and Western Isles of Scotland; so much the intensive collection of the last half-century or so has taught us. Conversely, it looks as though certain dominant Irish tune-families are now also at home in Great Britain. The realization of how untraceable these melodies actually are has finally halted the rather futile controversies over the claims of different lands to various internationally current melodies of merit.

To attempt a summing-up: the tune families dominant among English folk singers are likewise apparently dominant among the Irish and Lowland Scots. They form what may as well be called the *common* melodic repertory of the British Isles, and we expect to see their versions turning up everywhere and rather constantly in those lands—except in the Highlands and Hebrides, where they have not effected any wholesale penetration, apparently. Nor, on the other hand, does the Highland music seem to have affected the folk song airs of other British regions except (slightly) the Scottish Lowlands. With this exception, the melodic traffic of the various British nationalities and peoples seems to have been extensive. The *common repertory* is everywhere—versions of its tunes even occurring now and then in Highland music and among the airs sung to sea shanties. This *common repertory*, of course, consists of those prevalent tune-families that are the principal concern of the present essay. We must surmise that all the British nationalities have contributed something to this basic melodic fund. And the impressive community of traditional tune-repertory among most of the British peoples cuts right across distinctions of melodic style, as it also blurs the outlines of such exclusively national or regional tune-stocks as exist.

British folk tunes have been flowing across the Atlantic into North America for over three hundred years, presumably. Since members of all British peoples have migrated to this continent, and have undoubtedly brought over goodly shares of their old-world musical inheritance, we should expect to find a remarkable mixture of melodies from all these traditions in the folk song of this country. Likewise, if the foregoing analysis of the British music is at all correct, we should expect to find that versions of the airs composing the *common* repertory have been imported from all the countries of the British Isles, and have been conserved alongside each other in our own countryside. Moreover, we might assume—in view of the international travels of tunes and tune-versions among the British peoples—that tunes in the melodic style of one country did not necessarily reach this country direct from the land where that style is prevalent. As we have seen, there is reason to suppose that minglings of the national traditions were going on previous to any of the large-scale British migrations to America.

Since we may be sure that British folk music went right on developing during the period of colonization in America, and afterward, we may likewise assume that each group of British immigrants after the first great settlers' waves of the years before 1650 brought over some more newly evolved variant forms of the folk airs to add to the variety of our own tradition here. Also we can see, apparently, that some rather distinctive variant forms of widespread tunes evolved in the tradition of the American countryside.

Hence, the musical influences from the old countries must have come not all at once, but in a series of waves and impacts, each one probably adding some elements to the melodic culture implanted by the English migrations of the seventeenth century. Doubtless the most important of these fresh contributions were made by the Scotch-Irish migrations of the early eighteenth century, and the huge Gaelic Irish influx of the 1840's and 1850's. Folk melodies transplanted to America, meanwhile, have undoubtedly undergone continuous oral variation and development in their new homes, no matter at what period they were introduced.

If the preceding summary embodies an accurate enumeration of the main possibilities, we in America have to cope with a pretty complicated set of conditions in our efforts to discover approximately the true history of our individual folk songs and their music. We seem at present to have four ways of attacking the various problems: (*1*) by identifying widely current tunes in all their detectable versions; (*2*) by trying to determine (if possible) the national styles to which tune-versions current in America seem to have the closest affinity; (*3*) by studying together the texts and tunes of folk song versions in which appear a persistent association of a version of some song with a version of a widespread tune; and (*4*) by trying to plot the distribution of these close associations of particular text-versions with particular tune-versions, so that their area of currency may be correlated with regions of settlement and routes of settlers' migrations in this country. Obviously, these approaches are all to some extent interdependent.

However, the situation, as a whole, of British music current in America is qualified by several outstanding facts which must be recognized if we want to appreciate properly the relations between old-world and new-world folk song records. These facts may be set forth approximately thus:

1. The Scottish Gaelic tune-repertory of the Highlands and Western Isles has apparently not survived to any extent among English-language folk singers in America. I do not know what may be preserved among the Gaels of Nova Scotia; but it is obvious that the tune-families of the Highlands have had but little currency or influence over North America as a whole. Tunes in this style are of exceedingly rare occurrence.[61]

2. The same statement may be made about a number of the outstanding tunes peculiar to the Irish repertory. Perhaps their association with songs in Gaelic somehow inhibited their spread outside Ireland. There are indications that some of these distinctively Irish airs have been preserved among members of Irish colonies in our cities; but since no sizable attempt to investigate them has ever been made, nothing more can be said about them at present. However, in our countryside, very few melodies of exclusively Irish style and currency are found. If imported, they have not survived.

3. The *common repertory*—that limited number of internationally known tune-families to whose variants are sung the majority of our folk song texts—is dominant in our own countryside, as it is in the British Isles. This is a fact which every successive publication of Anglo-American folk song music simply confirms anew. The different British colonists have apparently succeeded in bringing over (at various times, no doubt) the greater number of the prevailing versions of these tunes, and have preserved them here in forms as clearly recognizable as those we see in old-country collections. It might be plausibly argued, in fact, that here in the folk song of America the common repertory is even more important than it is in its original homelands. On the whole, the traditional divergences of its component tune-versions are less wide than might have been expected, considering the vast reaches of the territory the versions were to cover, and the separation of early pioneering settlements.

4. There appear to be some rather considerable differences in the relative popularity of versions of these common tunes, between the old-country traditions and those of our country. Some of these differences are seemingly due to special relations between folk dance and folk song airs in our countryside: in the way certain dance- or march-versions of common tunes have been converted to the uses of song by American folk artists. This is a matter of such complication that it deserves separate treatment; there is no space for further discussion here.

Another source of difference between British and American repertories, as regards prevalent tunes, is the fact that certain versions that are widely or universally known to our folk singers appear but very little in British collections. For instance, one tune-version which in America is known all over the southern and many midwestern states has been recorded only a few times in Britain—and the recordings are all from the northeast of Scotland. In another instance, a tune-version exceedingly common in our tradition, to both ballads and lyric songs, has been recorded only once or twice in Lowland Scotland, and two or three times in the Isle of Man. The converse of this proposition is also true: American records fail to show certain versions broadcast in the folk music of Great Britain. In cases like these, one hardly knows how to interpret the available evidence. Perhaps certain little-known versions in the old country have taken on a new lease of life, and experienced an upsurge of popularity over here. On the other hand, they may be much more widely known in British regions than the published material indicates: collectors may simply have passed them by. But if they were actually very well known in Britain, it is hard to see how all collectors except those in one or two districts could possibly have missed them. After all, a purely local version of any well-known air in British-American tradition occurs very rarely indeed.

5. In the course of its further traditional development in this country, the common repertory would appear to have thrown off very widely divergent forms, to have had its component tunes mingled to some extent, and to have produced its crop of composite, indeterminate and nondescript melodies, just as I have presumed that it did in the British Isles. The character and occurrence of these tunes—non-allocable, yet definitely made out of familiar elements—are precisely like the manifestations of the airs of similar character in the old country, as I have described them above. Among the most important examples of this sort of air in the American tradition are the tunes of a number of white folk spirituals.[62] Another group of examples is

furnished by many of the tunes developed among the members of the religious sect known as the Shakers.[63]

6. The large mass of folk tunes sung by North American Negroes appears, on the whole, to be an independent creation by that people. The influence of imported European (mostly British) folk music is plainly discernible in Negro folk melody, and Negro repertories are shot through with versions of the principal British folk airs and other popular tunes; yet we cannot help recognizing in the music of this people a fund of song tunes generally distinct from that current among the whites.

7. As regards the association of texts of individual folk songs with certain tunes and tune-versions, we observe in the British and Anglo-American records both correspondences and differences which are alike interesting and striking. Many songs have been collected in America joined to the same tunes (in the same variant forms) to which they have been widely sung in British folk singing. On the other hand, we have in our rural traditions some widespread ballads and songs that show persistent musical associations which do not turn up in the British Isles at all. It is impossible to guess the age of these tune-text combinations; but some of them are certainly known almost everywhere in our countryside. There are three possible explanations for these phenomena: First, they may reflect the singing of some region not thoroughly explored by British collectors—hence, similar tune-text examples have been overlooked in the old country. Or, second, they may represent the junction of an English song with an air from Germany, or some other non-British homeland. Or, third, they may be the products of American tradition: an association, unmade before, between a British song and tune. What prevents us from making a clear decision one way or the other is the fact that, although different versions of a folk song may be sung to quite different melodies, these melodies are almost always forms of the often used and widely known airs of the *common repertory*. This means that when singers in the past have changed tunes for their songs, they generally shifted from one old stock melody to another—not to some newly introduced air.

8. Among the tunes sung in the eighteenth-century ballad operas, and to the broadside ballad airs of the seventeenth (and perhaps the sixteenth) century—e.g., those tunes which appear in the first (1650) edition of *The Dancing Master* and in other early sources—we find every so often a version of some melody which still has traditional cur-

rency among our folk artists. Nevertheless, the fact stands out that most of the known popular broadside ballad tunes of the seventeenth century bear no relation whatever to the melodies of the British *common repertory*. At present we do not know enough to attempt an interpretation of this fact. Are most of the tunes in our common repertory of more recent composition or development than the older dance and broadside airs? Or are they older than the latter, on the whole, and characteristic of a conservative country tradition that resisted the introduction of newer tunes from the town, the center of distribution for broadside verse? Answers to such questions, if they ever are attained, will have to await more exact organization of our knowledge of popular traditional music.

THE FOREGOING REMARKS have been assembled in order to provide a background to detailed studies of individual tune-families, which I hope will follow. They have been designed to make as many "blanket" and generalizing statements as possible, and thus to avoid repeated long explanations in those projected studies. Also they have been set down as an attempt to outline—however crudely—a picture of a tradition that is certainly one of the most glorious artistic achievements of the peoples of British descent. The general theory of tune-family growth that I have advanced may or may not be vindicated in the minds of other students by the evidence I hope to bring forward. But whether it be right or wrong, my theory (or any other) can do nothing either to enhance or diminish the nobility of this folk musical tradition.

In closing, one more generalization may be set down. One thing in this essay cannot escape notice: namely, the remoteness of the ideas expressed here from the views of those who insist that all folk tunes must originally have been the compositions of trained musicians, and must at first have been current in cultivated circles before they "sank" to a lower social level and were adopted by the uneducated mass of the people.[64] Naturally, this is no place for a detailed discussion of such a view—which, for that matter, has never figured to any extent in the writings of students of Anglo-American folk music.[65] However, a few statements about the applicability of this theory may not be out of order here.

There exist published British folk tune items which are unmistakably re-created versions of song airs by known musicians of the past.

One very typical example is the air in the *Journal of the Folk Song Society*, 1, No. 2 (1900), p. 49, to "The Plains of Waterloo." This tune, though simplified and "squared off" to accommodate a characteristic broadside stanza of four lines of even length, is obviously made up out of the first two verse-lines and the last two chorus-lines of "Rule Britannia." However, the air is a *hapax legomenon:* nothing like it has appeared elsewhere in our published folk musical records. And this lone appearance is characteristic of almost all such pieces, which are, moreover, exceedingly rare.

A somewhat different, but equally representative, case is furnished by sets of a tune sung on both sides of the Atlantic to "Sovay, Sovay" —the ballad of the girl who manages to test her truelove's devotion by robbing him in man's disguise.[66] These sets appear to have developed in several different directions and, though apparently interrelated, they differ puzzlingly. However, some of them look as though they might be derived from the melody composed by Robert Jones for "My mistress sings no other song," and found in his *First Book of Airs* (1600).[67] If this be indeed the case, the folk derivatives have not only changed in a striking manner, but they also appear to have been very much attracted to forms of the widespread air commonly sung to the ballad of "Young Beichan" (Child No. 53). In other words, we cannot tell whether the "Sovay" tunes are diversely re-created forms of Jones's air, of which some sets are partly assimilated to the common "Young Beichan" tune; or whether the dateless "Beichan" tune has had some of its versions influenced by traditional memories (or renditions) of the Jones air. In the long run, the two possibilities seem to amount to practically the same thing anyway. And the examples just cited illustrate perfectly, in my opinion, the character of the influence that art music has exerted on folk music in our British traditions. Apparently a vigorous folk music tradition can absorb and assimilate outside influences; but these influences do not necessarily arrest the development of the tradition.

I should certainly be the last to deny the influence of art music on our folk tunes. As Marius Bareau has recently put it, "Folk culture is alive and grasping. It feeds on everything within reach, and often assimilates its material beyond recognition." [68] But I should like to point out that any theory that holds our folk tunes, *as organized, individual pieces of music,* to be merely borrowed court or theater tunes of the past, signally fails to solve one problem or answer one question of importance raised by our recorded melodic versions. Anyone who held such a theory, moreover, would find the burden of proof weighing heavily upon him. The fact is that thus far not a single well-known air of our *common* (i.e. dominating) repertory has ever been traced definitely to any known composition of a trained musical artist.[69]

In such a richly developed and artistically re-created fund of melodies as this tradition possesses, the original authorship of any single tune is—as I said above—not only unknown, but also utterly unimportant. Any folk that can develop the possibilities of a few basic airs as have the peoples of the British Isles can take care of itself in matters of musical culture. It is itself in possession of a musical culture at once cumulative and powerful. It does not have to wait for educated composers to produce simple melodies which it can borrow. It can produce, out of its own funds and resources, its own simple melodies, and can develop them with amazing complexity and variety.[70] And this, I think, is what the untrained and unknown artists among the British folk have done in the past.[71]

9

✳✳✳✳✳✳✳✳✳✳✳✳✳✳✳✳✳✳✳✳✳

Professionalism and Amateurism
in the Study of Folk Music

CHARLES L. SEEGER

DISTINCTION between the professional and the amateur is commonly made, I believe, upon an economic basis. The professional cultivates a field as a vocation, a means of livelihood; the amateur, as an avocation, a hobby. Perhaps it is equally common to view the professional as a disciplined and the amateur as a comparatively undisciplined worker.

The distinction is a useful one, but does not always stand upon either count. We all know persons who do not earn a cent from their activity in a field of study but are well disciplined either by training or experience, or both. There are also persons without any discipline to speak of who make a living at a study. And some of the best disciplined obviously pursue scholarly work more with the air of a hobby than do some comparatively untrained workers.

There is a third, not so commonly held, but important, basis for the distinction between the professional and the amateur. This, too, has merit but does not always stand. It involves both etymological and methodological considerations. Derivation of the word "amateur" from the Latin *amare*, to love, has resulted in the curious situation in which cultivation of a field as a pastime presupposes love of it, whereas cultivation of it as a task may imply that love of it is irrelevant, if not dangerous. We all know of amateurs who are so enthralled by the object of their devotion that their activity is sometimes not quite rational. On the other hand, we all know professional workers who are themselves dry as dust and make everything they touch dry as dust. It is sometimes found that the discipline of study may shackle love of the field studied. Even though he begins with a warm love of a field and the objects in it, the worker who submits to the discipline of study must resist domination of emotional attachment simply because it imperils maintenance of the detachment necessary for objective analysis. In short, he must discipline his love. This does not necessarily mean that the love be diminished, but rather that it be raised to a higher level. Part of the love of the field can be transferred to the study. But love of the study and love of the field studied are two quite different things. Of course, one may enter the situation the other way around and transfer some of the love of study to the field studied. In either event, the ideal might be said to constitute a balance between the two. And some rare people achieve it, especially in the better established studies where agreement upon viewpoints, methods and aims is very general. Clearly, however, there is a difference between the natural and the social sciences in this respect. The emotional reaction of the student of the former group is of an order quite other than that of a student of the latter, especially in those branches of the social sciences that deal with the arts, where aesthetic factors are more highly developed. The love of the physical or natural scientist for the data he deals with would seem to be a more abstract nature, be these spiral nebulae, electrons, snakes, or nerve ganglia. It may be integrated with the precision, comprehensiveness, and orderliness of his methods of work in a mystical love of a cosmic whole. The social scientist or humanist may find the same generalized experience in his study but has in addition the love of particular things such as works of art, where personalized expression is highly emphasized. It is upon these grounds that some would withhold the designation "scientific" from the studies of the arts.

That there is some merit in this contention we must admit. And the situation in which we find ourselves with respect to the study of folk music gives evidence that the problem is a serious one, though it has not yet, so far as I know, been succinctly stated. I shall, therefore, try to do so here.

During the eighteenth and nineteenth centuries, the great scholarly disciplines were being established in the forms in which we know them today. Students were busy, among other things, with definitions of fields, viewpoints, data, methods and aims. Inevitably, a number of gaps were left uncultivated. One of these gaps comprised, as a sub-field, what we now refer to as the field of folk music. Two opposite approaches were made toward the filling of this gap. I shall label one the amateur and the other the professional.

The amateur approach had this in common with the physical and natural sciences: it began in the here and now of the student. This involved a logical progress from the most familiar to the least familiar. The word "folklore," coined by Thoms in 1846, was intended to designate a modest study of "popular antiquities," not, perhaps, to fill one of these gaps but to squat, as it were, upon a part of it, a vague area left untouched by the study of European history and various other studies, among them music, that were concerned, supposedly, with more important things.

Not being a professional folklorist, I am not going to attempt to deal with that study as a whole but only with the part of it that concerns music. Suffice it to say, the study of folk music has grown to some extent within the larger study of folklore, though only too often not very closely related to or governed by it. For it has involved or overlapped another study, music, in which most folklorists have not even been amateurs. On top of this mischance, the musicians who were called upon for help by the folklorists, or who wandered in of their own accord, were almost without exception not even amateurs in folklore. What a field for the tyro folk music has been—and still is!

The century of development that folklore has undergone has resulted, as we all know, in the raising of the level of this amateur or less than amateur approach. But it remains a fact that most of the work in folk music in the United States is either plain tyro or amateur, a meeting of popular but not of scholarly interest or need. The few jobs that have been out of this category are not so much the result of the improvement of the amateur approach as, rather, of the professional approach to the field by two other studies.

This second, or professional, approach perceives that the gap in which the music branch of folklore was active was originally created by the fences already erected by more solidly organized contiguous studies. The situation of the student of folk music has been very much like the situation one would find oneself in upon taking up residence in a walled town where all the houses were occupied but with some vacant lots in between. One would have to build upon a vacant lot whose boundaries were already defined by the fences of the built-up lots. The fences that enclosed the gap called "folk music" have been, mainly, those of anthropology (including ethnology, study of culture, etc.) and of musicology. These studies, belonging to the humanities or sciences of man, adopted the methods of the physical and natural sciences, but did not (in their modern form) begin with the here and now of the student, as did the amateur approach. To the contrary, anthropology established itself by studying the earliest available evidences of human life and society, and those most distant from the great cities and universities where most of the students lived. Musicology began by studying the music of the most ancient times and only in the twentieth century approached that of the most distant peoples. Thus, the gap above mentioned was left to form.

Little by little, the fences of both anthropology and musicology have been pushed nearer in time and space to the here and now of the student. In so doing, the fence of anthropology has completely enclosed the vacant lot occupied by the "squatter," folklore, and the musical member of his family. At the same time, a sizable portion of the lot has also been enclosed by the fences of musicology. This double fencing in of the area that we call folk music has involved no conflict between anthropology and musicology. It does, however, involve both in conflict with those musical members of the squatter's family who do not realize or who choose not to admit the possible change in the situation. The real situation now is that a good case can be made for the view that the professional study of folk music has set, as requirements for entry, competence in both anthropology and musicology.

I must hasten to say that there are some things to be said on the side of the musical members of the squatter's family. In the first place, the number of scholars in the United States who can meet the dual requirements of anthropology and musicology today can be counted on less than the fingers of one hand. They have produced little work. And little attention is paid to it. In the second place, the wave of popular and learned enthusiasm for folk music demands a wide cultivation of the field. In the third place, the squatters have developed during the last ten years some surprising new views that quite transform not only the traditional amateur but also the traditional professional approach to the study. And above all, they have provided us with perhaps nine-tenths of the data we have today. Without this, there might be no study!

Up to this point, I have considered the professional and the amateur as functioning only in the *study* of folk music. But how about the *field?* Is there not a distinction, there, homologous to the distinction we have made in the *study* of the field? I believe we must admit there is. We may find neither such large economic considerations nor such spectacular skills. But folk singers and players are not uncommon who have earned portions of their living through their art. Their training has not been as highly organized, but has been, in many instances we know of, deliberately sought and cultivated. There is a difference between the outstanding performers of a local community and the rank-and-file of the population. And it is generally recognized in the community. We should not ignore it even though the music performed by the outstanding performers is virtually the same as that performed by the rank-and-file. We must admit, I feel, that the outstanding performers have about them the essential qualities we have customarily found in "the professional" in scholarly life and upon various levels of music activity. In relation to these, the rank-and-file of the community where a folk culture can be said to thrive have similarly the essential qualities of those we have called "amateurs." *We cannot, therefore, class folk music, as a whole, as an amateur idiom.*

Now, another thing that makes the study of folk music an unusual problem for scholarship, is a situation in which the amateur and professional students of folk music study the amateur and professional performers in the field of folk music. But how about the students of folk music themselves? Are they amateurs or professionals in folk music? Frankly, the very large majority of them are amateurs, or not even that—mere tyros. The question naturally presents itself: are students of folk music—even if they have higher degrees in both anthropology and musicology—to be considered competent in the study of folk music if they are mere tyros or at best amateurs in folk music itself?

The point I raise here is a delicate one. I do not suggest that to be a competent student of folk music one must be a competent performer of folk music. I do suggest that a certain minimum of competence in performance *of* folk music is necessary for the evaluation of the knowledge *about* the idiom that is the essential stuff of the study. For, to possess the qualifications in musicology above referred to, means that the student must have a minimum competence in the fine art of music, i.e. concert music, necessary for the evaluation of the knowledge about that idiom, in terms of which modern musicology is organized. The crux of the predicament may be stated more or less as follows.

The fine art of music, upon a technical competence in which modern musicology, as I have said, is formally organized, is one of four main classes of music idiom: primitive art, fine art, folk art and popular art. The modern fine art of music is a predominantly written tradition, cultivated *by* a special class of professionals *for* sections of a community that either make no music themselves or make very little—and that in an idiom other than that of the fine art, which is by its nature beyond their technical competence. The fine art of music is, in the Occidental world, cosmopolitan in character.

Folk music, on the other hand, is a class of music idiom without formal or informal integration with musicology. Indeed, in the cultivation of the fine art the embryo musicologist, along with others of the more highly educated classes in the Occidental world, is expressly steered away from folk music both technically and in respect to content. For the idiom of folk music is in many ways technically opposite to fine-art music though in others complementary. Folk music is primarily an oral tradition, cultivated by people who make it for themselves. It is technically within reach of the vast majority of a community, though, as I have said, exceptionally talented individuals can give better presentations of individual items of repertory than can the average member of the community. Furthermore, folk music, in the Occidental world, is regional and even local in character.

The functioning of the written tradition of the fine art of music in a culture differs radically from the functioning of the oral tradition of folk music in the same culture. The fine art is an activity of from two to five per cent of our population; folk music of the vast majority. The factor of the composer, so important in the fine art, is practically negligible in folk music. The inviolability of the composer's text, so important in the fine art, is a nonexistent consideration in folk music. The individuality of the composer's expression in the former contrasts with the character of the most typical expression of the latter where, after sufficient passage from ear to mouth (or hand) the marks or even traces of individual expression have worn off, even as a jagged piece of stone is smoothed down to a rounded pebble by sufficient grinding in the bed of a running stream.

In the United States, as in other areas, the character of voice used in singing folk music and the type of instruments and the manner of playing them differ radically from the character of voice and the types of instruments and the manners of playing them employed in fine-art music. The handling of tonal and rhythmic functions differs radically in the two idioms. There are different conceptions of tempo, beat or pulse, accent, inflections and nuances of many kinds. There are radically different attitudes toward dynamics and their change—gradual or sudden—as there are also regarding changes in tempo.

For a person trained in the fine art from an early age, as are practically all musicologists, regularly for twenty or thirty years, it is practically impossible to turn the music-making apparatus sufficiently upside down to handle folk music in any but an amateur way. And even to do that involves a Copernican twist of no mean proportions, as well in the music-making apparatus as in the head and heart. One need not unduly censure the student for ineptness here, but one cannot help surmising that an inability even to observe certain data, or an actual hostility towards them, may be a result of ineptness, on the part of the student, in the idiom studied.

Perhaps I have said enough to indicate my conviction that though our fine and folk arts of music are not exactly two languages foreign to another, they are not interchangeable in technical or critical detail, nor can the student trip from one to the other on one passport. Although either one can and does borrow incessantly from the other and although hybrids of the two and of both of them with popular music are freely and easily developed, they exist side-by-side in our culture as more or less autonomous domains, each with its technical and critical integrity. From the point of view of style, our folk art is far more established than our fine art. Its values undergo change, as do the values of the fine art, but not so rapidly nor so extensively. It is a question whether even upon the most abstract level their values could be compared. There are two distinct sets of criteria and the values that can be asserted upon their evidence are not interchangeable. There is no comparing a folk song with a symphony. One may prefer one to the other, but at least for the present it would appear they are critically incommensurable. Their social functions are utterly diverse and their very natures also. There is, for example, only one authentic version of most symphonies. But no well-distributed folk song has any one authentic version or any dozen to which another equally authentic one or dozen may or may not exist, for all we know.

With the prejudices and resistances bred into a professional musicologist by years of training in and association with the fine art of music, it is not to be wondered that some comparatively untrained amateur can get at the insides of a folk music situation better than he. I am thinking especially of the terrific jolt received by all of our musical idioms by the advent of the phonograph disc, the radio, and the sound-film. Concert music, certainly, is reaching an audience never contemplated by a master before 1900. Folk music is recapturing an audience—that of the city—that it lost in the decades before 1900. Professional students with the qualifications required by anthropology and musicology will perhaps hesitate to speculate upon what the future will bring. But the amateurs—they are taking to wings! Starting with their here and now, with a minimum of historical knowledge, they are doing some prediction and getting at least a momentary success. The situation is not unlike that in a number of other studies, some of them of more venerable academic standing. I ran into the following passage the other day in a textbook on astronomy by Russell, Dugan and Stewart: "For the advanced student there is no field in which it is possible sooner to get out to the front line of scientific advance and to learn how territory is being won in a very active sector. Indeed, the number of objects that will repay observation is so great, and the opportunities for elementary calculation are so considerable, that undergraduate students, and amateurs without university training, have made and are making genuine contributions to the advance of astronomical knowledge." This can, in substance, be said as well for the study of folk music today.

As I see the immediate future, the study of folk music in the United States, as perhaps throughout the world, is entering a lusty teen-age. It will not be, because it cannot be, a well-integrated or organized phase. There will be a diversity of standards. There will be some awfully sweet prettifying for city people, a lot of slicking down of good folk stuff in radio stations and some terrible "folk symphonies." Out of it will come, I feel sure, a more unified continental music culture for North America. The professional must unceasingly lash the amateur for sloppy field work, sloppier transcription, lack of documentation, secrecy, preoccupation with the quaint and failure to deposit collectanea in permanent archives. But the amateur has a task also— to goad the professional out of too great preoccupation with the archaic and into a willingness to face the present and future.

And some Fate or Fury should fill all, professional and amateur alike, who have asserted or try to assert property rights over the genuine folk stuff they may have collected, with a decent sense of shame. Assertion of property rights in folk music must somehow be stopped.

There should be a maximum charge of a dollar or so for republication of transcriptions of collected material or, better still, complete freedom to republish providing only credit is given. Genuine folk music belongs to the whole people, and no one, even if he has paid fifty cents or five dollars to an informant for the privilege of recording or notating it, has any right whatever to stand between that singer and the people to which he and his music belong. Of course, if the material is not clearly of the oral tradition, this exhortation would be modified. But then, the material should not be either held or presented by the collector *qua* folk music.

I have offered the foregoing analysis of the situation in the study of folk music in the United States today with the sole purpose of outlining some norms in the relationship between the amateur and professional approaches to the study. I hope I have given the impression that while both have their drawbacks, both are essential to the well-being and present progress of the study, though it is the latter that I expect will and should be increasingly emphasized in the coming years. Before I close, however, I should touch upon one prime factor that has been mentioned only in passing. That is the factor of personality of the individual student. Here again, I am not an expert and cannot venture any definite integration of this factor with those of whose normal adjustment I have been speaking. Nevertheless, I must state very clearly that every one of these adjustments must be reconsidered in each case where the factor of personality enters. The science of personality being a very young study, most of us, rank amateurs in it, are faced with the necessity of making these adjustments with little or no expert guidance, mostly with only the common sense of our personal experience. For example: suppose one is faced with decision which of two applicants for a folk music job to support—one a comparative amateur, the other, a professionally trained student. One might cast one's vote in either direction depending upon the nature of the job and the nature of the personalities involved—and this, in clear view of a conviction definitely weighted in favor of more professionalism in the study. Some professionals are absolutely unfit for a field collection project. They would turn informants into stony-eyed statues. On the other hand, no amateur should normally have precedence over a trained worker in respect to a transcription, editing or archive project. But economic considerations, adaptability to organizational procedures, freedom from predatory attitude toward the materials—in short, integrity of character—might weigh heavily even in those situations.

Any one, two or more of a number of personality factors might, then, upset any of the norms I have proposed. But only in a particular case. In general, I support them as stated.

✳✳✳✳✳✳✳✳✳✳✳✳✳✳✳✳✳✳✳✳✳

The Meter of the Popular Ballad

GEORGE R. STEWART, Jr.

IN the history of English metrics the verse of the popular ballad occupies a strategic position. From it one may look backward toward Anglo-Saxon verse, and forward toward many developments of modern times. This investigation has been conceived in the belief that solution of some problems of ballad metrics not only will be of value in connection with the ballads, but also will open a new line of approach for the study of other verse, both more ancient and more modern. The principles here worked out will be found applicable, I believe, to popular verse in general; it is impossible, however, to cover the whole field, and the present investigation has accordingly been confined to the material in Child's *English and Scottish Popular Ballads,* as the best-known, most readily available, and on the whole most authoritative collection. At the same time no effort has been made to scrutinize very carefully the canon. The battle of the ballads is not our battle. Trojan and Tyrian are alike to the metrist. Be a poem Christmas carol, song, border ballad, minstrel ballad, or ballad *par excellence,* there is no necessary peculiarity of its meter, and the evidence here presented will go to show that as a whole Child's material is indeed reducible to a single metrical norm. The few exceptional cases will be pointed out in their places, but in general examples can be drawn indiscriminately from any of the different types.

The lack of a thorough-going study of ballad metrics is due, I believe, not so much to failure to recognize its importance, as to realization of the peculiar difficulties and even apparent impossibility of arriving at any scholarly conclusion upon the subject. Since they affect directly the method of investigation, these difficulties must be briefly capitulated. (*1*) There is little possibility of establishing any chronological development of ballad metrics because, except in rare instances, ballads have no date. The earliest text of "Hind Horn," for example, is of the nineteenth century, but no one doubts that the ballad originated at a much earlier period. (*2*) Ballads have no certain text. Since oral transmission is a *sine qua non* of ballad existence, there is always the chance that the memory of the last transmitter played him false sufficiently to distort the metrical form. To this must frequently be added errors and conscious revision on the part of transcribers. (*3*) Ballads are primarily songs. As such their metrical structure is involved with the melody, and sometimes can hardly be said to exist without it.

These difficulties in the way of scientific analysis require certain adaptations of method. Through lack of historical evidence conclusions as to the relation of different ballad forms must rest primarily upon a descriptive, not a genetic, basis. Confusions, moreover, resulting from textual and musical variation necessitate a method of analysis, quantitative rather than qualitative, gross rather than minute. No single exception can be permitted either to prove or to disprove a general tendency; in the ballads we are dealing with primitive not sophisticated art, and it is accordingly impossible to expect or to demand a metrical structure linguistically perfect. In doubtful cases, therefore, the present study bases conclusions upon numerical results obtained by actual count. By consistently applying methods of counting the subjective factor is reduced to a minimum, and the strength of the metrical tendency is mathematically expressed.

Of these three primary difficulties the relation of meter and music is, however, the only serious one. No one engaged in study of ballad form can fail to realize that his problems are often merely the result of hair-splitting attempts to translate into metrical terms a quite obvious musical situation. It might be affirmed in fact that, properly speaking, ballads have no meter, and that a study of their structure means only the analysis of the tune to which they are indissolubly linked. If this be so, there is nothing for it but to turn over the whole field to the musician. But is not this too extreme a position? Ballads are song, but they are also verse, in most cases quite obviously. We cannot, therefore, surrender the field to the musician, who is, indeed, much more interested in advances upon other provinces. Ballad metrics forms in fact a no-man's land between the two fields; it is a subject of a kind which scholarship is often reluctant to enter. But if we are ever to know anything of ballad structure, it will not be by a begging of the question which passes over to another field what is on its very face largely a metrical subject.

A study of ballad metrics thus steers a difficult course between the Charybdis of too much, and the Scylla of too little, deference to ballad music. The present study, however, being metrical rather than musical, bases its conclusions primarily upon metrical (that is, linguistic) evidence. The airs, when available, have been studied, but music has been actually used only for three comparatively restricted purposes: (*1*) as analogy, to demonstrate the metrical structure more strikingly; (*2*) as corroborative evidence for points already established primarily upon a linguistic basis; (*3*) as evidence of relation to other forms of forms too complicated to maintain a consistent linguistic structure.

The actual study of ballad verse can best begin with its commonest, and, we may also say, its simplest form—the so-called septenary, or "ballad meter" *par excellence*. The crux of the whole subject, however, is presented by the fact that the apparent septenary of the ballads does not ordinarily represent that form as conceived by modern metrists, and written by most modern poets. This later septenary is a line of seven units (call them feet, stresses, or what you will) usually opening with an unstressed syllable and progressing to a masculine rhyme through an alternation of one (or two) unstressed and one stressed syllable. The fourteen syllable type of this line may be shown: [1]

$$\cup\acute{\cup}\cup\acute{\cup}\cup\acute{\cup}\cup\acute{\cup}\,\|\,\cup\acute{\cup}\cup\acute{\cup}\cup\acute{\cup}$$

The fundamental fact, however, in the structure of the ballad is, that the seven stresses of its line tend to be alternately strong and weak:

$$\cup\acute{\cup}\cup\grave{\cup}\cup\acute{\cup}\cup-\,\|\,\cup\acute{\cup}\cup\grave{\cup}\cup\acute{\cup}$$

In other words the ballad line consists not of seven simple, but of four complex units. The structure, therefore, can best be termed *dipodic*, and the units *dipods*. In the type of verse under consideration the complete dipod consists of two half-feet, each characteristically of two syllables. Beginning at the primary stress, the metrical unit therefore is composed of four syllables which may be represented:

$$|-\cup-\cup$$

The rhyme usually cuts off the line at the fourth syllable of primary stress.

The first problem is to demonstrate the truth of this hypothesis that the ordinary ballad line is composed of four dipods, and not of seven simple feet. As before stated, the method of investigation, being quantitative rather than qualitative, cannot be expected to arrive at any absolute conclusion; the structure of the ballads, owing to their primitive nature and their frequent dependence upon musical support, must always display general tendencies instead of universal rules. A method for the testing of dipodic structure in verse has already been proposed,[2] and it will not be necessary here to repeat the somewhat lengthy discussion of the question. The method employed is based upon the fact that in the long run the accented syllables of nouns, adjectives, and adverbs comprise the stronger stresses, while secondarily accented syllables, together with prepositions, conjunctions, auxiliary verbs, and copulas, are of distinctly weak stress. Accordingly, if our dipod is a reality, the first position (primary stress) should be filled by a much larger proportion of syllables of the first group than of the second, while the situation should be reversed for the third position (secondary stress). The figure called here the Dipodic Index[3] represents merely the simplification and summation of all these factors. Its value is of course comparative, but in general I should say that an index figure of above 35 shows what can be recognized by the ear as dipodic movement, while a value approaching even 20 represents a syllabic arrangement too marked to be the work of chance.

The dipodic indices of the following ballads[4] may be offered as examples:

Tam Lin (A)[5]	64
Sir Patrick Spens (A)	60
Brown Adam (A)	47
Little Gest of Robin Hood	43
Lass of Roch Royal (A)	41
Knight and Shepherd's Daughter (D)	39
Wife of Usher's Well (A)	36
Lady Isabel and the Elf Knight (H)	33
Fair Annie (E)	30
Fair Annie (A)	27
Battle of Philipshaugh	21
Young Johnstone (A)	18
Battle of Harlaw	16

In contrast we may list the indices of some septenary poems composed

in literary fashion without musical association, or conscious effort for
dipodic effect: [6]

Ormulum	—9
Chapman's *Iliad*	—23
Universal Prayer (Pope)	—14
Ancient Mariner (Coleridge)	—10
Village Blacksmith (Longfellow)	5

In view of the striking contrast of the two groups of poems, I believe
that, even if further evidence were lacking, we should be justified in
stating the dipodic structure to be a pervasive tendency in the best
type of "septenary" ballad.

Corroborative evidence, however, is not wanting, of which the
most readily presented is that of the traditional ballad tunes. The
musical unit corresponding most aptly to this type of dipodic foot is
the common bar of four-four time:

The analogy is close; the four notes, and a division into halves marked
by primary and secondary accent correspond to the four syllables of
the dipod similarly arranged. Keeping in mind this analogy, we find
the dipodic structure of the ballads corroborated by the fact that they
are on the whole most frequently linked with four-four time. If their
rhythm had not been dipodic, the musical transcriber would have found
two bars of two-four time equally as useful as the single bar shown
above. When two-four is used, however, the notes are also halved, so
that the resulting measure:

is also analogous to dipodic structure. Tunes in two-two and six-eight
times show similar adaptations, and even the not uncommon use of
three-four (or three-two) time leads generally to the same conclusion.
In this last case the measure is usually composed of four notes of some
such arrangement as:

Here are still four syllables sung to the measure and four measures to the line, so that the essential characteristics of the ballad meter are preserved. Thus, if the tunes are of any value for evidence, we must grant that this evidence argues strongly in favor of the dipodic structure of ballad verse.[7]

More support for the point in question may be gained from the fact that in this verse secondarily stressed syllables are sometimes omitted (metrical pause). Syllables of primary stress, however, are not so omitted. We have, for examples:

> Lord Thomas and Fair Annet
>   Sate a' day on a hill
>   (Lord Thomas and Fair Annet-A)

> But now I have it reapen,
>   And some laid on my wain
>   (The Carnel and the Crane)

> Chiel Wyat and Lord Ingram
>   Was baith born in one hall
>   (Lord Ingram and Chiel Wyat-A)

> Is that my father Philip,
>   Or is't my brother John?
>   (Sweet William's Ghost)

Here the structure is that of the ballad "septenarius" except for the omission of the second syllable of secondary stress:

$$\cup\,|\,{-}\cup{-}\cup\,|\,{-}\cup\wedge\cup\,|\,{-}\cup{-}\cup\,|\,{-}$$

This is a common situation observable in a large number of ballads.[8] Sometimes a secondarily stressed syllable is omitted even when not in conjunction with the ordinary caesura, as in *Edward* (A):

> What bluid's that on thy coat lap,
>   Son Davie, son Davie?

$$\cup\,|\,{-}\cup{-}\cup\,|\,{-}\cup\wedge\cup\,|\,{-}\cup\wedge\cup\,|\,{-}\cup$$

In general the evidence of this omission of syllables goes to show that the structure of the verse rests fundamentally upon the four primarily stressed syllables; these cannot well be omitted, whereas omission of secondarily stressed syllables can be compensated by a pause which does not break up the verse. We thus find here again a basic principle of dipodic verse—the maintenance of distinction between the primarily and secondarily stressed syllables.

As another corroboration we may take one of the very frequent metrical situations in this type of ballad—the apparent inversion of stress just before the caesura. In the 22 lines of *Patrick Spens* (A) this is the case three times; in the 84 lines of *Tam Lin* (A) there are 20 examples, e.g.:[9]

> Sir Patrick Spence is the best sailor
> That sails upon the se.

> But the night is Hallowe'en, lady,
> The morn is Hallowday.

> Roxburgh he was my grandfather.
> Took me with him to bide.

The most obvious explanation here would be that under the influence of the music the accent was fairly evenly distributed between the two syllables with that upon the second slightly predominating. If this be the case, it harmonizes with the dipodic theory, for the doubtfully distributed stresses upon the final word would render both subordinate to the naturally stressed syllable preceding. Some additional support for this explanation may be drawn from the fact that occasionally the ballads will even rhyme upon such ordinarily unaccented syllables.[10] If it seems incredible, however, that such a ballad as *Tam Lin* should violate one of the most deeply seated characteristics of English pronunciation in nearly one-fourth of its lines, one may accept another explanation. This also, however, rests firmly upon a dipodic basis. The situation in question may represent a dipodic foot with omission of the first unstressed syllable ($\acute{-}\grave{-}\smile$)[11]—a very common type of foot (see below). The relation between the two stressed syllables would naturally be as represented, since the first being preceded by weakly stressed syllables would receive almost by rhythmical necessity a very strong stress. This stress relation is also rendered likely by the character of the words composing it; these are usually either (*1*) an adjective and a dissyllabic noun, or (*2*) a noun or an adjective, and a dissyllabic vocative. In the former case the adjective is, I should say, somewhat more likely to be the important component: thus in the following stanza the contrast of "first" and "second" throws the strongest stress upon these adjectives:

> An she gid by the first table,
> An leugh amo them a';
> But ere she reachd the second table
> She let the tears down fa.
> (Fair Annie-E)

In a similar manner the numerous epithets of *father*, *lady* and *Janet* of "Tam Lin" are repeated unemphatically, and stand subordinate to the words which they follow. Thus either hypothesis in explanation of the so-called "reversal of accent" counts in favor of dipodic structure.[12]

One of the most striking pieces of corroborative evidence in the present connection is to be found in the characteristic ballad manner of word repetition:

> They hadna been a month, a month
> In Norraway but three.
> (Sir Patrick Spens-G)

> O, bonny, bonny sang the bird
> Sat on the coil of hay.
> (Sweet William's Ghost-F)

> She had na pu'd a nut, a nut,
> A nut but barely ane.
> (Hind Etin-B)

> "An askin, an askin, dear father,
> An askin I'll ask thee."
> (Lord Thomas and Fair Annet-I)

> O huly, huly rose she up,
> And huly she put on,
> And huly, huly she put on
> The silks of crimson.
> (The Lass of Roch Royal-A)

The significant fact is that the first stressed syllable in each such series falls in the position of primary stress; this is an almost invariable rule.[13] Obviously a phenomenon repeated so frequently and always in the same way cannot be the result of chance. It is plain, moreover, that when words are thus repeated the first only is of real importance, while the second follows merely as an echo or refrain, of metrical but scarcely of logical value. The third of the series, however, tends to collect the value of both the preceding, and takes a new start with redoubled emphasis. Finally, then, we have this invariable arrangement of repeated words as an interesting confirmation of the dipodic structure.[14]

A special case of the septenary ballad occurs when trisyllabic substitution is frequently used. In the texts so far considered the lines have rarely more than fourteen syllables; in "Sir Patrick Spens" (A) only 7% of the half-feet are trisyllabic, and in "Tam Lin" (A) only 6%. In other ballads the proportion is much higher: thus, "Lord Lovel" (A) 34% and "Lord Thomas and Fair Annet" (D) 47%. The dipodic indices of such ballads may, nevertheless, remain high:

Lord Lovel (A)	17
Lord Thomas and Fair Annet (D)	45

The actual relation between the two types of septenary ballad may be shown best by musical analogy. The non-trisyllabic usually corresponds, as we have seen, to music of four-four (i.e., twice two) time; the trisyllabic, on the other hand, carries with it the idea of three as well as two, showing thus that it is the result of building verse against a background of six-eight (i.e., twice three) time. The two- and three-syllable feet thus represent the notations respectively of

$$\text{♩♪} \quad \text{and} \quad \text{♪♪♪}$$

Half-measures of two and three elements mingle much more readily in songs of six-eight than of four-four time. Both are, however, march time, and so offer no fundamental difference for popular music. It is thus easy to find the same ballad with a tune now of the one type, now of the other.[15] From the more strictly metrical point of view, appeal to the ear in reading without music, the two types of ballad show much greater difference. Such a loose usage of trisyllabic feet demands that the proportion of strongly stressed syllables must decrease from one in four, and approach one in five or six. This, however, is a difficult matter in English with its large number of monosyllabic nouns, adjectives, and verbs. At the same time, to an even greater degree, the dipodic effect upon the ear is lost by the necessity of minor variations of stress produced within the dipods. Dipodic rhythm is necessarily complicated, and any additional complication renders it so confusing to the ear that even the primary effect tends to be lost.[16] Although the secondary metrical differences are thus frequently important, nevertheless underlying identity between these two types of ballad meter is sufficiently established by musical analogy, by the test of the dipodic index, and by the general nature of the septenary line occurring in both. They are thus fundamentally the same metrical form; the trisyllabic variety can be considered simply as a special case of the more common type.

While it has thus been possible to establish the dipodic nature of certain ballads, the question remains as to whether this is true of all the Child selections of the septenary type. The answer must be in the negative. We have as instances of low dipodic index:

| James Harris (A) | 6 |
| The King's Disguise | —28 |

Examples of this group are, however, relatively rare. Comparison of these ballads, moreover, with those of highest dipodic index will leave little real doubt as to which represents the truer ballad style. "Tam Lin" and "Sir Patrick Spens" are members of the ballad aristocracy, while "James Harris" (A) and "The King's Disguise" both show the style of the broadside. The principal reason for the occurrence of these comparatively few nondipodic texts may be deduced, I believe, without great difficulty. To regard them as the more recent form and the dipodic as the older would be easy, but fallacious. For one reason, we do not know ballad dates definitely enough to make possible any sound conclusions, and at the same time some ballads which would seem to be of late composition (such as "Philipshaugh") are rather strongly dipodic. A relationship which may be more surely argued is that the dipodic type represents the more primitive ballad, and the other a metrical form farther from its origin. Thus while the typical versions of dipodic ballads have usually been transcribed directly from the words of the singers themselves, "The King's Disguise" is the product of the printing-press perhaps as late as the eighteenth century, and seemed to Ritson "to have been written by some miserable retainer to the press." Similarly "James Harris" (A) is from a broadside text so sophisticated as to entitle itself "A Warning to Married Women." The explanation of the failure of these less primitive ballads to be dipodic is almost certainly to be found in their relation to music. The more primitive were sung; the others probably were not. The connection

between dipodic verse and music is always very close; in fact for anything but song-verse dipodic rhythm is probably a recent artistic inno-
vation. The reason for this is that, except for a skilful conscious artist,
such complicated structure is too difficult to be maintained without the
constant aid of a musical air. Since the ballads are primarily songs, we
may assume that some kind of a tune developed along with the text.
The tune itself was ordinarily the accompaniment of marching, dancing,
or some kind of bodily movement, and accordingly, to mark the components of such movement, the music was in four-four, or six-eight, that
is, dipodic time. The words, developing along with the tune, managed
to represent a more or less rough approximation of this fourfold
rhythm. On the other hand, when ballads were composed without the
aid of the tune such dipodic movement was too subtle to be preserved.
One may conclude, therefore, that the dipodic ballad represents verse
sung originally to four-four or six-eight time, and maintaining in its
text this dipodic rhythm; the non-dipodic ballad, on the other hand,
shows the divorcement of the ballad text from the air, and the consequent absence of dipodic structure.[17]

Next to the "septenary" type the most used ballad form is an
apparent stanza of four four-stress lines with rhyme *abcb;* this is very
common, occurring in more than fifty ballads. A few examples will
illustrate the type:

> Then ffarewell hart, and farewell hand
> And ffarwell all good companye!
> That woman shall neuer beare a sonne
> Shall know soe much of your priuitye.
> (Northumberland betrayed by Douglas)

> When Johnë wakend out of his dream,
> I wate a dreiry man was he:
> 'Is thou gane now, Dickie, than?
> The shame gae in thy company!
> (Dick o the Cow)

At first glance this seems totally unrelated to the type of verse just
considered; observation of a few facts will, however, enable anyone to
deduce the really close and simple relation. In the first place, the line
unit, as in the septenary, must be measured between rhymes; this yields
what is apparently a pair of eight-foot lines. In the second place it will
be observed that in the examples the rhyme is upon syllables of weak

stress. This yields the clue to the solution—the "four-foot quatrain" is really a dipodic couplet differing from the septenary only in that its line is not cut off by rhyme at the primary stress, but is extended to the secondary stress of the last foot, thus being lengthened by two syllables. The "septenary" represents the line:

$$\smile|-\smile-\smile|-\smile-||\smile|-\smile-\smile|-$$

the other:

$$\smile|-\smile-\smile|-\smile-||\smile|-\smile-\smile|-\smile-^{18}$$

Since the theoretical relation between the two lines is so close, it is to be hoped that the writer (as well as the reader) can be spared the necessity of again taking up the dipodic question from the beginning. If the theory as regards rhyme can be proved independently, the rest of the relation of the two forms can be considered to follow.

Fortunately the problem of rhyme yields readily a direct method of approach. The following tables show the nature of the syllables which carry the rhyme in the two types of ballad, as well as in two literary poems. The general principle of counting is the same as that used for determining the dipodic index.

	Rhymes on—		
"QUATRAIN" TYPE:	*Strong syl.*	*Neutral syl.*	*Weak syl.*
Bonnie Lass of Anglesey (A)	0%	22%	78%
Young Beichan (A)	41	28	30
The Bold Pedlar	33	44	23
Lord of Lorn (A)	45	32	23
Johnnie Armstrong (A)	44	38	18
Bothwell Brig	34	34	32
Northumberland betrayed etc.	21	38	41
Kemp Owen (A)	39	22	39
Average	36	33	41
"SEPTENARY" TYPE:			
Sir Patrick Spens (A)	86%	14%	0%
Tam Lin (A)	66	31	3
The Wife of Usher's Well (A)	75	21	4
James Harris (A)	62	38	0
Average	72	26	2
LITERARY VERSE:			
The Universal Prayer (Pope)	57%	43%	0%
Mandalay (Kipling)	74	18	8

The results of counting as expressed in the foregoing tables show striking contrast between the nature of the rhyming syllables in the two types of ballad. The evidence of the literary poems shows also that secondary stress rhyme is in itself unusual and not part of the ordinary nature of English verse. A comparison in greater detail will be instructive at least in the case of the two extremes of ballad type. "Sir Patrick Spens" (A), a fine "septenary" ballad, has twenty-two rhymes; of these, one is on an adjective, two on adverbs, three on verbs, and sixteen on the accented syllables of nouns. "The Bonnie Lass of Anglesey" (A), on the other hand, has only one rhyme upon an important verb, and none at all on the primarily accented syllable of adjectives, adverbs, or nouns; of its fourteen rhymes two are on pronouns, three on copulas, and eight on secondarily accented syllables of trisyllabic words. The contrast of the two poems in this respect is in fact practically complete. The situation is less marked in other examples, but this is only to be expected in view of the general nature of ballad metrics. There need be no hesitation, however, in declaring that in the one type appears a marked tendency toward rhyming on weak syllables, while in the other there is no such tendency.[19]

As before, corroborating evidence can be drawn from the ballad tunes. Both types fit readily into the same musical structures. The only difference is in the fourth bar (that which connects the two half-lines), and in the corresponding case of the last bar. In the septenarius type the fourth bar is usually:

$$| \; \flat \times \flat \; |$$

that is, a period of rest is admitted between the two lines. In ballads of secondary stress rhyme, however, the music runs through:

$$| \; \flat \flat \flat \flat \; |$$

The fourteen syllables of the one line and the sixteen of the other thus fit into the same period of musical time. Both are thus basically the same, and in their structure strictly defined are metrically identical, that is, both are four-foot dipodic lines.[20]

In the types of ballad so far considered the dipod consists characteristically of four syllables; in the remaining texts we must take account of other linguistic arrangements metrically equivalent. The number of syllables may be decreased from four to three or two, or, on the other hand, increased to six, or even more. This increase in the number of syllables involves a comparatively complex process; accordingly, it will be better to consider first those dipods in which the number of syllables is reduced.

Before attempting to observe their actual occurrence in verse, the nature of the two- and three-syllable dipods can best be demonstrated by musical analogy. Metrically the process consists in "pinching out" either or both unstressed syllables; musically this is represented by the substitution of one half-note for two quarters. The feet thus formed can be represented in metrical and in the commonest corresponding musical notation as follows:

$$\frac{4}{4} | \; \text{♩♩♩} \; |$$
$$\frac{4}{4} | \; \text{♩♩♩} \; |$$
$$\frac{4}{4} | \; \text{♩♩} \; |$$

Each of these musical units is, of course, the equivalent of any measure in four-four time. In a similar manner all the dipods, whether of four, three or two syllables, are equivalent and may be mingled readily in the same line.

A mixed type of verse offers the best approach to the study of the trisyllabic dipod. Starting with ballads in which the four-syllable feet greatly predominate, we may trace a progression which ends finally in a few texts composed entirely of the trisyllabic type. As a beginning we may quote the first three stanzas of "Lamkin" (A), noticing the remarkable situation there displayed:

> It's Lamkin was a mason good as ever built wi stane
> He built Lord Wearie's castle, but payment got he nane.
>
> "O pay me, Lord Wearie, come pay me my fee."
> "I canna pay you, Lamkin, for I maun gang oer the sea."
>
> "O pay me now, Lord Wearie, come, pay me out o hand."
> "I canna pay you, Lamkin, unless I sell my land."

In these lines the first and third stanzas are quite passably of the four-syllable dipodic type, even to the omission of secondarily stressed syllables before the cæsura. On the other hand, the first line of the second couplet is trisyllabic although it rhymes with a line of the other type. In addition, as if to show that the trisyllabic line was not a negligence, the first line of the third couplet is nearly an echo, though it inserts just the proper syllables to make the structure surely dipodic. Farther on the mingling of three- and four-syllable feet becomes even more complex. As far as couplet No. 13 the movement is generally dipodic; then we have suddenly:

> Then Lamkin he rocked, and the fause nourice sang,
> Till frae ilkae bore o the cradle the red blood out sprang,

where all except the first half of the second line appears trisyllabic, and where this one half-line is not only dipodic but even goes so far as to admit a trisyllabic substitution within the dipodic foot. From couplets No. 13 to No. 17 this seemingly mixed movement continues; [21] at couplet No. 18 the dipodic structure reappears, and continues to No. 23; thence to the end three-syllable feet appear frequently.

If this anomalous mingling of meters occurred only in one version of a single ballad we might be justified in throwing its evidence out of court upon the general grounds of the untrustworthiness of ballad texts for minute metrical analysis. The same situation, however, appears not only in the other texts of "Lamkin," but also in a number of other ballads. The first couplet of the B-text, for example is in wording closely analogous to the couplet already quoted; except that in this case the "mixed" structure appears:

> Balankin was as gude a mason as eer picked a stane;
> He built up Prime Castle, but payment gat nane.

Since this seemingly incongruous structure appears as a characteristic practice in the texts of at least ten ballads, it cannot be dismissed, but must be explained. No one, I think, will explain the structure of the meter as an actual combination of four-syllable dipodic with simple trisyllabic rhythm. One trial at reading "Lamkin" as an attempt at mingling these two rhythms is sufficient to demonstrate its impossibility.[22] The meter then must be either all trisyllabic or all dipodic. With the dipodic feet so greatly in preponderance, however, the overwhelming difficulties in the way of making the tail wag the dog will, I believe, render the attempt obviously impractical. Accordingly, by this *reductio ad absurdam*, we arrive at the conclusion that the verse of "Lamkin" must be dipodic throughout.

It is not necessary, however, to rest this conclusion on such negative evidence alone. "Lamkin" and its related ballads actually read well as dipodic verse; in fact, to me at least, there is no meter in them at all by any other method of reading. The advantages of dipodic rendering can often be seen in the inspection of the text itself; such feet as

and the fause nourice sang

and

the red blood out sprang

can certainly be read as trisyllabic verse, i.e.:

$$(\smile)\smile|{-}\smile\smile|{-}$$

With equal certainty, however, the meaning is more fully brought out if a dipodic interpretation is used to allow a more natural stress upon *nourice* and *blood:*

$$(\smile)\smile|{-}{-}\smile|{-}$$

The objection may be raised that this structure produces difficulties by frequently demanding a secondary stress where it does not occur naturally. If we quote for instance the whole line reproduced above only in part, we see that a secondary stress is called for upon the second syllable of "Lamkin," or else upon the unemphatic pronoun *he:*

Then Lamkin he rocked, and the fause nourice sang.

To this the only reply must be that ballad metrics is not an exact science. If in couplets No. 8 to No. 11 the accent upon "Lamkin" must undoubtedly be entirely reversed (as shown by the rhyme) no one can be greatly shocked when the same word suffers a comparatively slight modification a few lines farther on.

In "Lamkin" (A), as we have seen, the four-syllable type of dipodic foot greatly predominated. It is possible, however, to establish a progression leading finally to a few ballads in which all the feet are trisyllabic. In "Lamkin" (B) the two types of foot are fairly well balanced; the same is true of "The Bonny Earl of Murray" (A), and (allowing for some dipodic feet of two syllables) of the B-version of the same ballad, and of both texts of "Willie Makintosh." Passing, however, to "The Death of Queen Jane" (B), we find the situation of "Lamkin" (A) approximately reversed; less than one foot in four is of the four-syllable type. Nevertheless the dipodic structure is still certain, since on any other basis it would be impossible to handle metrically such a couplet as:

At this bonie babie's christning there was meikle joy and mirth,
But bonnie Queen Jeanie lies cold in the earth.

Progressing farther in the same direction, we may notice a group in which four-syllable feet are rare, perhaps as in "Bonnie Annie" (A) represented by only two or three indubitable examples (see couplet No. 9). Finally, we come to a group of about fifteen texts (representing six different ballads) in which there is no absolutely certain case of a foot of four syllables. Since the evidence of the tunes is inconclusive, these texts might, if they stood alone, be considered ordinary trisyllabic verse. They do not, however, stand alone. With one exception all have closely related versions in which undoubted four-syllable feet occur, sometimes with considerable frequency. Accordingly, it would seem justifiable to consider these last texts merely as the terminus toward which the dipodic verse of the transition ballads has been working.[23]

In addition to the argument from transitional texts the actual linguistic structure of these "trisyllabic" ballads may be regarded as confirming their dipodic structure. For example, in "Bonnie James Campbell," which alone has no four-syllable foot in any version, it is *possible* to read as ordinary trisyllabic verse such lines as:

> Hame came horse, hame came sadle, but neer hame cam he,

and

> And doun cam his sweet sisters, greeting sae sair.

On the other hand, the dipodic structure brings out a much fuller meaning to the text, and a much better movement to the verse:

$$\text{—◡} | \text{——◡} | \text{—◡∧◡} | \text{——◡} | \text{—}$$

and

$$\text{◡} | \text{——◡} | \text{——◡} | \text{—◡—} | \text{—}^{24}$$

That a dipodic rendering thus turns geese to swans, must certainly be considered strong evidence of its reality.

The result of this investigation is to justify the general conclusion that the apparently "anapestic" ballads are connected by unbroken transition with the dipodic verse of four syllables to the foot. The trisyllabic ballads (with only one exception) show versions with feet of four syllables. Nowhere, therefore, can a line be drawn, and the only conclusion must be that the two types are fundamentally the same in structure, that is, that both represent a line of four dipodic feet, varying only in syllabic arrangement.

After study of the three-syllable dipod that of two syllables offers little difficulty, and may be quickly dismissed. The essential nature of the three-syllable type we found to be the pinching-out of one unstressed syllable so that two important syllables were placed together; the two-syllable dipod merely carries this process one step further by dropping both the unstressed syllables. As a result, three important syllables stand consecutively. Obviously, continuous verse cannot be written in this manner; even English has a certain number of necessarily light syllables. Such a chanting effect can of course be imposed upon verse by the aid of music. That this is not the case in any ballads, however, is good evidence that the music does not entirely dominate their metrical structure. We must consider, therefore, the two-syllable dipod as an only occasional variant to that found in verse prevailingly of three- and four-syllable feet. We need do no more than point out some examples, and comment briefly upon them.

The two-syllable dipod occurs occasionally in a considerable number of ballad texts; its close relationship to the trisyllabic type is shown by the fact that it appears almost always in conjunction with the latter. It can be best observed probably in "Willie Mackintosh" (B), "The Bonny Earl of Murray" (B), and "Our Goodman" (A). When most effectively used it is not dependent upon musical support, but represents actual linguistic structure:

> Head me, hang me
> That sall never fear me;
> I'll burn Auchindown
> Before the life leaves me.
> (Willie Mackintosh)

$$|--|--|-\smile-\smile|--$$
$$|--|-\smile-\smile|-\smile-|--$$

Her corn grows ripe, her meadows grow green,
But in bonny Dinnibristle I darena be seen.
(The Bonny Earl of Murray-B)

> Poor blind body,
> And blinder mat ye be!
> (Our Goodman-A)

He neither shall be christened in white wine nor red,
But with fair spring water, with which we were christened.
(The Cherry-Tree Carol-B)

In texts of this type one should note particularly the often intimate mingling of dipods of two, three, and four syllables. This is a degree of metrical intricacy not attained in literary verse until the present generation. As with all usages in ballad metrics, the technique of the dissyllabic foot is at times not linguistically established, but depends frankly upon musical support, or, what is essentially the same, upon an already established metrical rhythm in the mind of the reader. In the following examples secondary metrical stress is demanded upon syllables naturally unstressed:

> He's ben and ben, and ben to his bed.
> (The Bonny Earl of Murray-B)

> Lamkin rocked, and fausse nourice sang.
> (Lamkin-M)

In view of the nature of ballad metrics this situation is only to be expected; in fact its absence would be more peculiar than its occurrence.

In general the dissyllabic dipod is not very widespread or characteristic in ballad metrics.[25] It affects, however, the metrical interpretation of a dozen or more texts, and at the same time an establishment of its usage is necessary for the study by analogy of the more complex forms of the dipodic foot.[26]

Having confined our discussion of the dipod in ballad verse thus far to feet consisting of four syllables or less, we must now proceed to the more complicated subject of feet with five, six, or even more syllables. A large number of ballad texts demand the existence of feet of this latter type; otherwise it is impossible to read them metrically.

Since metrical notation has not reached a sufficiently high degree of complexity, we must depend upon musical analogy for the first demonstration of the more complicated dipods. Note has already been made upon the analogy of the four-syllable dipod with the musical measure:

For greater simplicity it is more convenient to consider only half of this foot, which would yield the musical analogy of two quarter notes in four-four time:

$$\text{♩♩}$$

The musical equivalents are, of course, many, but of those which consist of three or four notes the simplest are the following:

$$\text{♩♪♪, ♪♪♩, ♪♪♪♪}$$

These three musical expressions correspond to the three ordinary ways of forming the polysyllabic dipodic *half*-foot. The whole dipod may be composed, generally, speaking, of any combination of these half-feet with one another or with the simpler dipodic forms. The situation will become the clearer with further explanation.

The simplest case of the polysyllabic dipod may in a certain sense be said to occur with any trisyllabic substitution. Thus in even the best dipodic ballad text there is now and then a dipodic foot of five syllables:

> And she has broded her yellow hair
> A little aboon her bree.
> (Tam Lin-A)

$$\smile|{-}\smile{-}\smile\smile|{-}\smile{-}||\smile|{-}\smile{-}\smile|{-}$$

> O say na sae, my master deir,
> For I feir a deadlie storme.
> (Sir Patrick Spens-A)

Cases of this sort, however, come within the general limitations of the metrical theory of trisyllabic substitution; at the same time the two unstressed syllables are equally unemphatic and so generally present no new stress relation. Accordingly they may ordinarily be disregarded. The difference between trisyllabic substitution and the real trisyllabic half-foot can be seen by comparison of examples. Although the number of syllables in each of the two following lines is the same, the metrical movements are distinctly different:

> "Come riddle my riddle, dear mother" he said,
> "And riddle us both as one."
> (Lord Thomas and Fair Annet-D)

I heard a cow low, a bonnie cow low,
An a cow low down in yon glen.
(The Queen of Elfland's Nourice)

As Child, in one of his few metrical observations, remarks of the latter ballad, it "forces you to chant and will not be read." This chanting effect is due to the fact that the line has not only more than fourteen syllables, but also more than the ordinary number of stresses, that is, the extra syllables are frequently important. On the other hand, the extra syllables of the first quotation are entirely unemphatic (unaccented syllables of dissyllabic words and pronouns). It is therefore possible to represent the structure of the first line by the ordinary four-foot scheme:

$$\cup|-\cup\cup-\cup\cup|-\cup\cup||-\cup\cup-\cup|-.$$

Although a closely similar scheme might satisfy a theoretical "scansion" for the second line also, this would class articles, and nouns equally as unstressed syllables, and would fail utterly to represent the chanting effect. Obviously in this kind of ballad meter some factor as yet unconsidered is at work.

For the simplest working of this new factor we must turn to such a text as "The Gay Goshawk" (B). Here occurs frequently the half-line:

Here is a gift, and a very rare gift

in which the two words *very rare* approach the trisyllabic type of half-foot represented by the musical structure:

♪♪♩

In the same ballad also we find inserted in the regular dipodic ballad structure a full four-syllable half-foot:

Out then spak a pretty little bird . . . .
And thrice he has kissed her cherry, cherry cheek . . . .
With one side of the bonny beaten gold . . . .
With one side of the beaten gold,
    And another of the silver clear.

There are even lines in which two such half-feet occur:

Where will I get a boy, and a pretty little boy.

It is clear that, musically at least, these situations represent the substitution of four eighth for two quarter notes, or at least something closely analogous to it. Thus the transliteration of the first quoted line might be:

Numerous other ballads show feet of the same structure.[27]

This type of half-foot has, however, metrical as well as musical basis. It does not depend upon the tune, but, at least when its occurrence is not too frequent, can be felt in the linguistic structure of the text. This can be perceived by observing that the four-syllable half-feet consist usually of stereotyped constructions which yield particularly to rapid pronunciation. (*1*) The commonest is a repeated adjective with short vowel such as the "cherry, cherry cheek" already quoted. "Bonnie" is very frequently so used, as in "The Broom of Cowdenknowes," and in the recurring line of "Geordie":

> O where will I get a bonny, bonny boy.

In the G-text of this latter ballad occurs also the interesting case:

> When she cam to the canny Cannygate.

Here desire to emphasize the proper metrical structure has led to the use of a meaningless adjective (as applied to a gate), and has changed *Canongate* to *Cannygate*. (*2*) Another common construction is the combination of two adjectives generally of short vowels and of conventionalized usage. Frequently alliteration is called in to aid, as in the *bonny beaten gold* already quoted. Of these combinations *pretty little* is practically stereotyped. (*3*) In other cases the four-syllable half-foot departs from these conventionalized arrangements, and depends merely upon any group of words which flows easily from the tongue. On account of this care in selection of syllables, their extra number within moderate limits does not tend to break down the primary structure of the verse.

In a limited number of ballad texts, however, the polysyllabic type of dipod predominates: in these cases certain secondary factors operate to disrupt the original metrical form, and thus to produce what is practically a new structure. One case of this sort has been observed in "The Queen of Elfland's Nourice," and others can be illustrated:

> Over night they carded for our English mens coates;
> They fished before their netts were spunn;

A white for sixpence, a red for two groates;
  Now wisdome wold haue stayed till they had been woone.
    (Mussellburgh Field)

It fell upon a time, when the proud king of France
  Went a hunting for five months and more,
That his dochter fell in love with Thomas of Winesberrie
From Scotland newly come oer. (Willie o Winsbury-н)

"And are ye come at last? and do I hold ye fast?
  And is my Johny true?"
"I hae nae time to tell, but sae lang's I like mysell
  Sae lang will I love you." (The Grey Cock)

The lady looked over her own castle-wa,
  And oh, but she looked weary
And there she espied the gleyed Argyle,
  Come to plunder the bonny house of Airly.
    (The Bonnie House of Airlie-в)

While musically such lines can be held within the ordinary bonds of
four measures of four-four time, from a metrical point of view the occurrence of so many polysyllabic dipods really breaks down the original
structure so that three- or four-syllable half-feet really become dipods in
their own right. For example, the first line quoted above might be
transliterated into music thus:

This would represent legitimate musical usage, although for practical
purposes in singing eight measures of four-four time could have been
used equally as well as four. On the other hand, to attempt to represent
the line as only four metrical feet leads to absurdity. It would suppose a
linguistic structure:

where the numbers represent the relative degree of stress necessary
to maintain this arrangement. This presumes *four* consistently used
gradations of stress—a complexity of which the language has never

yet shown itself capable. What actually occurs is, of course, that the first and second degrees of stress (as represented above) fall together so that the metrical structure becomes:

$$-\cup|--|-\cup-\cup|-\cup-|-\wedge\cup|-\cup-\cup|--|-$$

We are now in a position to scan also the line already quoted from "The Queen of Elfland's Nourice." In this case there are no four-syllable half-feet, but the original dipod is equally well broken by those of three syllables. The chanting effect is in reality the result of numerous strongly stressed words forming trisyllabic or dissyllabic dipods in the place of the original structure:

$$\cup|-\cup-|-\wedge\cup|-\cup-|-||-\cup-|--|-\cup-|-^{28}$$

The frequent occurrence of polysyllabic dipods has thus two concomitant effects—seven, or better (allowing for rest at the end of the line) eight, dipods take the place of four, and at the same time the actual structure of the feet returns to the simpler forms. The piling-up of syllables in the foot has proceeded until too high a degree of complexity has been reached; linguistic necessity then reasserts itself, and the expanded feet break into their component halves.

The only other ballad form which can be said to represent a change in the structure of the foot is that represented by the complex stanza [29] of "The Twa Sisters," the closely related stanza of "The Cruel Mother" (F), and probably that of "The Maid and the Palmer." This is so highly complicated that no one could attempt to relate its structure to that of the other ballads by purely metrical means. Music, however, shows the relationship. In this case the tune (as given by Child) is taken from the Abbotsford manuscript and, like other tunes from the same source, is rather inaccurate. The time is three-four; if this is changed to six-four, however, the whole complicated stanza falls into the normal ballad form of a four-foot couplet.[30] In other words, the two quarter notes of the usual half-measure of ballad music becomes when most fully expanded:

This is, of course, too high a degree of complexity to have reality in linguistic structure, and therefore does not actually represent any metrical conception. It is interesting, nevertheless, in showing that at least a theoretical relation may be established all the way from the simplest to the most complex ballad form.

THE PRESENT STUDY is too general to permit of considering minor variation. There are many single ballads which with their different texts would furnish material for pages of discussion; this would tend, however, to become for the most part mere description, not very valuable from a strictly metrical point of view. More applicable to the present subject would be the study of the metrical significance of ballad refrains, and of the various methods of stanza formation. In general, however, matters of refrain and stanza will be found to offer no real difficulty, if the fundamental principles of ballad metrics are grasped.

These fundamental principles it has been the purpose of this study to demonstrate, and we are now, I believe, in a position to present the conclusions as to the general nature of English popular meter as represented by the Child collection:

1. The meter of the ballads is fundamentally a four-foot dipodic line. In the less popular texts the dipodic structure may be lost.

2. The rhyme is usually upon a primary stress, but in a considerable number of cases the line is apparently lengthened by the occurrence of secondary stress rhyme.

3. The number of syllables in the foot is most often four. This may be decreased to three or two, and under certain circumstances increased to five or six without loss of the original dipodic structure.

4. When the number of syllables to the foot is frequently more than four and when more than the usual number of stresses is logically demanded, the linguistic complexity becomes too great, and the original dipodic structure is disrupted with the accompanying development of a secondary dipodism.

5. In its simpler forms ballad verse is founded upon linguistic principles, but in its more complex developments is dependent largely upon musical support.

As a final word this inherent unity of ballad metrical form should be stressed. There is indeed no real possibility on the basis of metrical structure of separating the ballads into various types. This may be useful in some cases, but usually the supposed types will be found to shade into one another so gradually that no line can be drawn between them. The different ballad forms are not separate species, but only varieties of the same metrical norm—the line of four dipodic feet.

iii

****

THE BALLAD

&

ITS LITERARY TRADITION

✳✳✳✳✳✳✳✳✳✳✳✳✳✳✳✳✳✳✳✳✳

Ballad Source Study:

Child Ballad No. 4 as Exemplar

HOLGER OLOF NYGARD

TRADITIONAL ballads have interested people in many different ways, and this interest has variously obscured, as well as enriched, our understanding of ballads. One activity, certainly, the hunting of sources, has been relatively fruitless. We are all led by natural curiosity to wonder how this or that song originated, and in response to this natural interest, vast amounts of energy and argument have been expended in efforts to trace the different ballads to their root ideas, with varying success.

The question of origin may indeed not always be difficult to answer. The general impression is that historical ballads are, after all, history; they are songs that identify time, place, and person. The inference is therefore that these songs originated after the events they describe. By such reasoning the ballad of "The Death of Queen Jane" (Child, No. 170) originated not long after Jane Seymour gave birth to Prince Edward in October 1537; "Thomas Cromwell" (No. 171) arose from events of the summer of 1540; "Musselburgh Field" (No. 172) celebrated the victory of the English over the Scots in the battle of 1547. With the well-known "Mary Hamilton" (No. 173) we are on less firm ground, for despite the air of historicity about the song, there is no certainty as to the identity of the four Maries or the truth of the incident. Attempts have been made to underwrite the historical origin of the piece, notably by C. K. Sharpe and J. W. Courthope. But is the historical event necessarily the genesis of a song so traditional in outline and so classic in content? Is it not as conceivable that the historic event has merely reinvested a song of earlier date with new vigor through an adventitious historical applicability? A notorious event is able to give new life, another habitation and name, to the narrative which has passed current in tradition—much as anecdotes gravitate to the famous. Certainly some ballads are so lacking in circumstantial detail, so fraught with commonplace event and phrasing, that one must recognize the possibility that the single ballad often no better describes one historical event than another. The Scottish bride-stealing ballads may be taken as cases in point.

Robin Hood, who figures large in English balladry, has been fair game for those who have seen history between the lines. After it had become unpopular to identify him as the Earl of Nottingham or as Robin Fitzooth, a more subtle historical approach was called for. The Gomme school chose to interpret ballads as history obscured, even as anthropologists like Andrew Lang prized the ballads for their obscured anthropological record. It may be illuminating and rewarding for us to think that the Robin Hood songs reflect social and cultural tensions between the lowly and aristocratic, between the English community and the Norman master, but the idea remains no more than an hypothesis. Robin Hood, insecure in the annals of history (despite the longish entry in the *Dictionary of National Biography*, and despite the recent effort to identify our ballad hero with the Robert Hood in the Wakefield Manor Court Rolls),[1] can be interpreted as no more than a comment on historical event; where he came from, what he was originally, and what gave the tradition such vitality remain as puzzles for ballad scholars.

If the attributed historical origins of a great many historical ballads are open to question, then certainly the beginnings of the nonhistorical material in folksong are shrouded in far greater mystery. Yet it is noteworthy that the ballads that have received the greatest attention as regards source are not the historical or quasi-historical songs, but precisely those that have been recognized by Child, Grundtvig, and others as old and international, those which Child honored with an early place in his collection. In dealing with the most ancient of ballads and those that least reflect time and place, source studies have the greatest room for speculation, and for error.

Source studies deserve scrutiny, for they reveal patterns of approach and thought that might well be noted for their inherent virtues or dangers. These patterns are in themselves a chapter in the history of ballad scholarship. By way of contribution to that chapter I propose to review the various attempts that have been made to explain away, to lay the ghosts of "Lady Isabel and the Elf-knight" (Child, No. 4), the ballad which more than any other has led scholars to exercise their learning and ingenuity in this direction.

During the past century many assertions and theories of origin for "Lady Isabel and the Elf-knight" and its continental analogues have been promulgated. Some have been highly provincial, innocently narrow in view, rather falling into the classification of local antiquarian misinformation, and not deserving of the term "theory" at all; others have been rational and informed, even super-rational and symbolic in essence, partaking of a rationale beyond reason itself. The contributions have for the most part been made by men prominent in ballad scholarship who have all been motivated by the same desire: to demonstrate the ballad's antecedents, to reduce the ballad to its source or germinal idea.

The narrowly provincial interpretations of the events described in the ballad need hardly concern us here (save for the amusement they afford in their quaintness); for they are nothing more than local custom foisted upon the song or, perhaps more properly, legends that the song has foisted upon the locality. Robert Chambers reported how in Ayrshire the country people pointed to "a tall rocky eminence called Gamesloup, overhanging the sea," where it is said the false Sir John "was in the habit of drowning his wives, and where he was finally drowned himself." These people who look upon the ballad as a representation of fact "further affirm that May Collean was a daughter of the family of Kennedy of Colzean."[2] The Scots of Ayrshire, not unlike ballad singers elsewhere, made the ballad vividly their own by framing the narrative as if the event did indeed happen "in these very parts."

Svend Grundtvig, in his informative Headnote to *Kvindemorderen*, the Danish form of the ballad (*Danmarks gamle Folkeviser*, No. 183), gave little attention to the question of origin, for he found the matter beyond demonstration; but he tentatively suggested that to his mind some obscured elf song ("fordunklet Elvevise") lay behind the narrative.[3] His suggestion was in great part predetermined by his belief, also held with reservations, that the ballad may have originated in the Scandinavian North, for he would read the names of the villain of the ballad as deviations from a Danish name. Grundtvig would have been hard put, however, to explain why this elf destroyed his victims, for elves in Scandinavian lore are not predatory and murderous; and Grundtvig's critics have not missed the opportunity of raising this question.[4] The villain in the Scandinavian variants is nowhere identified as an elf; he is called an elf only in British variant A.

As a possible elf story suggested itself to the Dane Grundtvig, so a possible merman story suggested itself to the German Franz Böhme,[5] for mermen are as characteristically North German as elves are Scandinavian. Rivers and seas are a constant feature in the ballad, and the villain of the piece drowns his victims in the variants of France, England, and Poland. Child, in his first collection of ballads, following J. H. Dixon, has espoused this theory: "The Merman or Nix may be easily recognized." [6] But he quite dropped the idea for the 1882 edition after having been soundly twitted by Grundtvig for suggesting that the heroine escapes from the merman by pushing him into the sea and so bringing about his death through drowning. This would make the ballad a variant of the "Wise Men of Gotham" who tried to drown the eel.

There is insufficient reason for giving credence to either the obscured and distorted elf-tale or the submerged merman-tale. They are both shots in the dark, and we remain, and probably will remain, ignorant of how far off the mark they in fact are.

The association of "Lady Isabel and the Elf-knight" with the Bluebeard tale leads us to apparently firmer ground, for here we may consult the evidence and reach conclusions not entirely built on faith. Goethe was the first to make the association, and a number of scholars have followed his example, including Ludwig Uhland, Franz Böhme, and Lutz Mackensen. It is not unusual to find references in German scholarship to the *Blaubartlied*, suggesting that the association is sound and proven. But, in point of fact, the association is all too readily made; the tale and ballad in all their multiple forms are distinct and separate in their histories, as far as the records dating from as far back as the mid-sixteenth century will permit us to judge. Ballad and tale do share a narrative idea: a man or demon murders a number of women and is in turn destroyed by one too clever for him. The startling thing is not, however, the similar narrative idea (similar only if sketched in such a summary way), but the complete difference of treatment and interpretation of the narrative. There appear to be no details in the total body of variants of either ballad or tale that would render possible a demonstration of relationship. Each appears sufficient unto itself and will reveal no affinities with the other. If the doctrine of polygenesis of a narrative idea commands respect, its adherents might well cite this ballad and tale as instances.

Both Franz Böhme [7] and Paul Kretschmer [8] have considered the possible relationship. The variance of their opinions is good demonstration of the difficulties involved. Böhme thought that the ballad was originally an elf-song (here he disconcertingly follows Grundtvig), into which had been stuffed the Bluebeard story of multiple murders, a story with a historical basis. Kretschmer thought that the tale was originally about an otherworld demon, a tale into which was stuffed the ballad narrative of multiple murders, a ballad with a historical basis.

Both points of view are sheer speculation. Just as there are no discernibly valid reasons for arguing the precedence of one form over the other, or for admitting the relationship itself, for that matter, so there is no reason for believing either tale or ballad to be historical in its inception. Kretschmer thinks the ballad may have derived from some possible broadside account of actual murders such as were perpetrated by the Frenchman Comorre in the early thirteenth century, or by the more notorious Breton Gilles de Laval in the early fifteenth century. The point is not very well taken when one considers by how much both of these gentlemen antedated the printing of *fliegende Blätter*. But more significantly, Kretschmer failed to study the ballad's history closely and so recognize that it was not "einfach ein Lustmord" (simply a sex murder); its motifs point back to an earlier supernatural content. This oversight would render Kretschmer's position less secure than Böhme's. Böhme, who would give precedence to the ballad, saw the tale as a tradition possibly relating to Gilles de Laval, a supposition that Kretschmer flatly denied. It is to my mind reasonable to consider this historical attribution of source made by both Böhme and Kretschmer as akin to the naïveté of the Scottish country people with their Gamesloup.

We move next to a study made about the time when the appearance of the copious *Handwörterbuch des deutschen Aberglaubens* focused attention upon superstitions. In 1929 Friedrich Holz [9] presented the theory that the germinal idea of the ballad was the medieval belief that maiden's blood cured leprosy. Holz cites tales which illustrate the superstition (Hartmann von Aue's *Der arme Heinrich* is the best known example), as well as cases from medical history that prove the wide currency of the belief and the respect with which it had on occasion been held by medical practitioners. But when we turn to the variants of the ballad the idea does not inspire us with confidence. There are streams of blood and springs of blood in Scandinavian and Dutch variants as well as the more usual streams of water. But no variant from these areas gives the slightest hint of what the villain does with the maids, aside from hanging or burying them. No statement is made of his using their blood. And no indication is to be found of ill health on his part. It is perfectly true that the villain seems motiveless in the older tradition (gold and robbery are a latter-day tradition in the ballad), but that is no reason for attributing to him the motive that Holz suggests. Only one single variant in the entire tradition of the song furnishes him support for his idea, a variant from Switzerland clearly removed from the center of the tradition. In this variant the knight promises to teach the maid the "Baderliedli" if she will come away with him. Holz interprets this song as a reference to a particular healing bath: "gemeint ist hier das Schongauerbad am Lindenberge." [10] His case is bolstered by the fact that this ballad from Aargau in Switzerland has a parallel folktale from the same district, a tale in which leprosy is cured by baths in the blood of maidens. Linking the entire European tradition of "Lady Isabel and the Elf-knight" with this superstition on the basis of the single folktale and variant is questionable method. The chain of causation moves in the opposite direction: a well known and much sung ballad, having reached the district of Aargau, has probably submitted to the influence of a local tradition. The song has been maintained in tradition over all Europe for centuries without the awareness on the part of singers of such a reasonable motive for what is, after all, an other than human villain. Holz' demonstration of origin is a forced argument.

The solar mythologists have had fair game with "Lady Isabel and the Elf-knight," with Léon Pineau [11] as spokesman. By a process of fabulous analogizing he identified the hero as the spirit of shadows, death, night, and winter, finally overcome by the warmth of summer. The murdered maids thus represent months of the year. Refrains from Scotland and Denmark are cited as final proof of the *ur*-meaning of the song: Scottish variant A has the refrain, "Aye as the gowans grow gay, / The first morning in May"; and Danish variant A, "Men linden groer." Such refrains are, of course, the most common of commonplaces in balladry and have less to do with the narratives they accompany than with the tunes. Andreas Heusler has fittingly pointed out that Pineau went so far as to date the Scandinavian ballads of magic and the supernatural much earlier than the Eddic poetry.[12] The solar mythologists of the school of Max Müller have long since been laughed out of court with their poetic subjugation to their simple formula of all imaginative creations that seem to stand outside history. I have no interest in belaboring a dead issue; I have touched upon Pineau's interpretation of the ballad only because it forcibly illustrates a common denominator among the source attributions, the tendency to write the ballad's early history not on its own terms but on terms dictated by something else.

Another theory of inception, not unlike Pineau's adventures of a soul among the masterpieces of folk poetry, is Paul de Keyser's [13] psychoanalytic interpretation of the morphology of the ballad. Unmindful of the fact of change in ballads as they pass through tradition, the oblivious of the national variants outside his native Holland, de Keyser points out how in the usual Dutch ballad, the brother of the main (in a passage of incremental repetition—itself a commonplace passage) gives his sister permission to follow Halewijn, the villain, provided she remain chaste. According to de Keyser, Halewijn is, in the singer's subconscious mind, the brother of the maid. The beheading of Halewijn by the maid is then interpreted as punishment by castration arising from the suppressed desires of the singer. The ballad is an expression of unconscious drives of sibling incest on the part of those who have given the song its narrative shape.

De Keyser's interpretation is not without its interest, and the reinterpretation of the events of the human scene by sexual symbol may not be without value, but does it in fact tell us what we wish to know about the origin of "Lady Isabel and the Elf-knight"? We must be prepared to rewrite the psychological correlatives with every major change that the ballad has undergone in its transmission. We cannot, for instance, be certain that the brother played a part in the ballad in its earliest form. Apart from the Dutch variants, the brother enters the ballad only in a minor tradition in Germany, and then quite differently, as the protector of the maid at the close of the narrative. One is also forced to observe that a psychological interpretation such as de Keyser's does not distinguish the song under consideration from a number of other songs that might be reduced to the same drives. "The Cruel Brother" (No. 11) is undoubtedly read by many as an exhibition of sibling love; psychological explication makes good sense of the ballad story. But the psychological analogizing of Halewijn by de Keyser does not enrich and support our understanding in the same way.

It must be admitted, of course, that de Keyser is not seeking the same kind of root that the literalists are attempting to find. De Keyser cannot help us determine an early from a late form of the same narrative, but that is precisely what a source study must do. In defense of the literalist it must be remembered that whoever first fashioned the ballad, despite his troubles and joys, confused Halewijn no more with the brother than with winter. To say that he did so unwittingly is to undertake a proof hardly feasible within the limitations of the pragmatic foundations of the psychoanalytic science.

These then are a goodly number of attempts to disclose the possible beginnings of one ballad. Their very number and the fundamental disagreements among them bring home to us the difficulty of the task. There is clearly room for more hypotheses, for none of the half-dozen so far reviewed has been widely accepted. But where so many have failed, there seems as little hope of success as in the turning of the sands of Egypt for the tomb of Sanakht.

We have not in fact finished the review of source hypotheses for "Lady Isabel and the Elf-knight"; one remains, which will occupy our attention at greater length if only because it has gained credence among scholars by its deceptive plausibility.

I call Sophus Bugge's [14] source theory deceptively plausible, for it makes its appeal to one's reason, is supported by a show of linguistic techniques, and is the address of a scholar to his problem. What is more, Bugge's conclusion has been accepted without questioning by George Doncieux, Knut Liestøl, W. J. Entwistle, and Marius Barbeau, to name a few.

Bugge argued as long ago as 1879 that "Lady Isabel and the Elf-knight" is derived from the Book of Judith in the Apocrypha, that heroine and villain are Judith and Holofernes. Child presents Bugge's argument very fairly in his Headnote to the ballad, without comment, although he did have misgivings. The forcefulness of Bugge's argument resides in the wealth of minute points he offers for the reader's consideration. In our bid for scepticism we shall consider the nature of the minutiae, the premises of his argument, and its mainstays.

Phrased in a general way the two narratives have a likeness: a man who stands in enmity to a woman is killed by her, and her method of killing him is by decapitation. But there are some major differences too: Holofernes does not intend to deprive Judith of her life, nor has he indulged in a series of murders. This multiple murder motif is the very heart of the ballad narrative, for it appears in all variants from all countries. It is difficult to conceive of the series of murders as absent from the ballad at its beginning. And Bugge would be hard put to explain how the supernatural element entered the ballad if the original was indeed a redaction of the Apocryphal tale.

Analysis of Bugge's argument reveals that it rests upon a number of assumptions that rather beg the question. He assumed, first, that any small detail in any of the many widespread variants from Iceland to Italy was "original" if it was in any way suggestive of a parallel with the Judith story.[15] He assumed, second, that an early German poem about Judith, another source of the ballad maker, is corrupt in its phrasing so that it differs from the ballad in the one significant instance in which the ballad shows a supposed direct borrowing from the poem. He assumed, third, that the ballad maker, in writing his ballad after the Vulgate account of Judith and Holofernes, misread and misinterpreted the Latin in such ways as account for particular details to be found in certain scattered variants of the ballad. He assumed, fourth, that the earliest form of the ballad, the original, differed greatly from the extant forms. This assumption looks innocent enough; we take the statement to be a truism. And yet a comparison of the national forms of the song during the last 400 years reveals an overall correspondence and consistency that do not permit us to think that prior to the mid-sixteenth century vast changes were being worked in the narrative outline. Fifth, he stretched the concept of parallels and echoes beyond the point permitted a careful student and one less enamored of the argument. And sixth and finally, he assumed that the name Holofernes is the root name from which the various names of the villain have arisen.

Let us look more closely at the arguments themselves. The High German poem from c.1200, which follows the Vulgate in its outline and major details, has a pair of lines that read: *du zûhiz wîblîchi / uñ slabranihichi*.[16] The lines are part of the angel's advice to Judith about dispatching Holofernes; they have been variously emended by editors, for they do not make good sense. Bugge translates these words as, "You draw it in a womanly fashion and strike. . . ." In one Danish variant we meet the lines: *Saa qwindelig hun det suerd uddrog, / saa mandelig hun til hannem hug.* These lines from Danish D are a commonplace in Danish balladry, a fact that Bugge does admit. But nevertheless he thinks a relationship with the old German poem is sufficiently clear to permit his making an editorial change in the text of the poem, thereby bringing it into conformity with the Scandinavian commonplace. He alters the poem to read, on the basis of what is in the Danish ballad: *sû zôhiz wîblîchi / undi sluoc mannlîchi*.[17] His procedure is a clear begging of the question; he has not demonstrated a similarity between poem and ballad, but has instead made one.

Bugge disarmingly suggests that some of the parallels he presents may be accidental agreements, but only after he has completed a lengthy barrage of citations that do not convince the reader. He does not recognize ballad commonplaces as such, but cites them as illustrations of how the ballad and the Apocryphal tale (also not devoid of traditional commonplaces) are related. In some Low German and Danish variants the principals ride for three days and three nights. The statement occurs in a great many ballads as a standard folksong description of a long ride. What is more, Grundtvig points out that the statement in the Danish variants has entered the ballad from *Den farlige Jomfru* (*DgF*, No. 184); the nature of commonplaces is that they do wander. The figure three bears no singular significance in balladry, for most multiple things tend to three. Yet Bugge finds the three day ride revealing, for did not Judith kill Holofernes on her fourth day at his camp?

Bugge disregards the changes incurred by traditional dissemination in the ballad. He draws his catalogue of parallels from any variant that suits his purpose. With him all motifs in the ballad are original which seem to echo the Judith story, and all other motifs are later interpolations and changes. In certain English variants the knight comes from the North; so must we infer that Holofernes did (Book of Judith, 16: 5)? The trait in the ballad is so distinctly confined to England (in a tradition that came from France, without mention of "North") that one can only assume that the North of the Outlandish Knight and the Assyria of Holofernes have nothing to do with one another. The same thing must be said of May Collin's (variant D) leaving her home at night, and Judith's doing the same thing. Holofernes' armies are to be seen as metamorphosed into the brothers, sisters, and followers of the villain found in certain variants. Surely such an interpretation takes advantage of the most fortuitous details. The Scandinavian picture of a wonderland to which the false knight will take the maiden and his offer in the English ballad of castles over which she shall rule as lady are cited as correspondences for Holofernes' promise to Judith that she shall be great in the house of Nebuchadnezzar and her name shall be known in all the land (11:21). But such offers of attractive bait are to be met with in any story in which a seduction or artful vanquishment of a woman by a man is attempted. In the Danish ballad the heroine binds the murderer's hands and feet; Bugge points out that in the German poem Judith's handmaid stands by to restrain Holofernes if he should awake while she is preparing to take his life. The passages are hardly correspondences. The closing stanza of the Icelandic ballad, in which the heroine is described as retiring to a nunnery, is a Scandinavian commonplace, not original with this ballad; Bugge believes the stanza to be an echo of Judith's living out the rest of her days as a chaste widow. One lone Swedish variant gives the villain sisters who cry out when they find him dead; this suggests to Bugge the lamentation of Holofernes' lieutenants. In one English variant (D), the maid and her parents journey to the seashore to behold the body of the murderer; Judith and the Jews journey to find the body of Holofernes after their victory at arms. Clearly such "parallels" do not convince. Bugge, searching about among the vast number of variants of the ballad that were available to him, has made a case by pointing out every fortuitous resemblance that a rich ballad tradition through the vagaries of oral transmission could provide. His method was not to sort out in the first place those things that could clearly be argued as original or old in the ballad's tradition. To him, that which seemed closest to the Apocrypha was original.

But now for the ballad maker's misreading of the Vulgate text. At no point is the phrasing of the ballad like that of the Book of Judith. The words of the one approach the words of the other most closely in the instances where the words do not mean the same thing. In the Scandinavian ballad the villain lifts the maid upon his horse and they ride away. Bugge suggests that this lifting is an echo of the verb "elevaverunt" in the description of Holofernes' men carrying Judith into his tent (10:20). He does not mention that lifting the maid upon the horse behind the rider is a commonplace in Scandinavian balladry. In the Dutch ballad the maid blew the horn like a man; Bugge compares this with "cum audissent viri vocem ejus" (13:14), believing that the ballad maker read "viri" as being in the genitive case. Bugge believes that the couplet from a High German variant, "Der Ulinger hat eilf junkfrawen gehangen, / Die zwölft hat er gefangen," is a rendering of "Dixit se incessurum fines meos et juvenes meos occisurum gladio, infantes meos dare in praedam, et virgines in captivitatem" (16: 6). Bugge believes further (although he admits the idea is daring) that a High German form of the ballad in which the murderer is bound and himself hanged may stem from a misreading of the Vulgate "accessit ad columnam, quae erat ad caput lectuli ejus, et pugionem ejus, qui in ea ligatus pendebat, exsolvit" (13: 8). He believes the misreading took place by a misplacement of modifier, as in "She loosened the knife, which belonged to him, that hung on supports." It is inconceivable how such an echo of the Vulgate (if we were to admit it as one) could remain intact through oral transmission of the ballad into Southern Germany and reveal itself in one isolated variant that is not in the usual stream of the tradition. These are instances of the ingeniously drawn parallels between ballad and source.

In the Apocryphal story an angel visits Judith to give her advice as to how to dispatch Holofernes. Bugge finds traces of the angel in two places in the tradition of the ballad: first, in the form of the white dove that warns the maid in the High German ballad that she is going to be killed, and second, in his reconstruction of the refrains of the Scandinavian variants. As others have pointed out, the talking dove is a commonplace in German ballad lore and folktales, and is, as best one can determine, a late entry into the tradition of the ballad. Bugge's reconstruction of the refrain is the epitome of ingenious argument. As he expends an entire page in the demonstration, and as it is his closing point, we shall examine it here. Danish A has as its Indstev (refrain following the first narrative line of a stanza) the following: "Men lienden groer," or, less frequently, "Men leinenn grodt." Danish B has the fuller "Se Vindelraad til edele Herre din!" Danish C has an Indstev much like Danish B, in which both the gentleman's and lady's names are mentioned: "Se Hollemen ind til Vendelraad!" Because Danish A has the same Efterstev (refrain following the second and last line of narrative text in the stanza) as has Danish C, Bugge believes that the Indstev of A should therefore be the same as that of C. "Men leinenn grodt" (the less usual form) is to his ear and understanding a corruption of the name of the maid as it is found in Danish B and C, Vindelraad, Vendelraad. He believes that "leinenn" in the Indstev represents the name of the maid, which originally must have been Lenel, Lennel, or Linnel. The "raad" (which "grodt" in A sug-

gests to him) was in his view not part of the original name. Lenel or
Linnel is, like Linnich of a Low German variant, the diminutive of
the name Helena to be found in one German variant. And so Bugge
reconstructs the Indstev for Danish A to read: "Se, Lennel, raad til
Hollevern aedele Herre din!" The Indstev in this form is then interpreted by Bugge as an admonition on the part of the angel to the
heroine that she should bear a weapon against the villain. The phrase
"raad til" is not as specific as Bugge would have it; the import of
Bugge's refrain might be, "Be advised regarding Hollevern your noble
lord." In terms of other Scandinavian ballads it would be very strange
if the refrain were as explicitly a part of the action of the ballad as
Bugge would make it. The B and C refrains are commonplaces that
suggest the dance motions that once accompanied the singing of the
Danish ballads. The A refrain as it appears in the Karen Brahe MS of
c.1550 is understandable as a commonplace statement about the natural
scene, much like the Scottish "Aye as the gowans grow gay."

But the reader will wonder how the name Hollevern entered the
reconstructed refrain. Bugge put it there. For he argues that the
mainstay of his source attribution is that the villain's various names
seem to have arisen from Hollevern, a name palpably suggestive of
Holofernes.

In early Scandinavian variants we meet such strikingly Germanic
names as Oldemor, Olmor, Romor, Hollemen, Ulver, Alemarken,
Rulleman, etc. The names in German variants are not unlike these:
Ulinger, Ulrich, Adelger, Alleger, Helsinger, Halsemann, Olingen,
Olbert, etc. Bugge thought that there was some obscured but ascertain-
able original form behind the series. He disagreed with Grundtvig's
choice of Oldemor. He decided that the original name must have been
Hollevern, Holevern, or Olevern. He explains that even before he
had any thought about the source of the ballad's theme, he had arrived
at the decision, from a comparison of the names, that the root form
was (H)ol(l)evern, although, as he admits, it appears nowhere un-
altered, "skjønt dette ingensteds uforandret foreligger." A counting
of the frequencies of the successive phonemes that make up the twenty-
one names Bugge had at his disposal gives us a choice among the following names: Olemor, Ulemor, Oleger, Uleger. Bugge suggests that
an original *v* had given way to *m*, *g*, and *b*, an idea that is hard to
accept without good reason. The *v* sound, which he argues for, appears
in but three names, Ulver, Halewijn, and the English Elf (a questionable member in this company). None of the names end in double

consonants as does his reconstructed name. The mainstay of his argument, as he calls the name derivation, is very insecure.

Bugge admits that the extant ballad is much different from his postulated original, that the ballad is but a wild shoot of the Judith story. But in making his case he has asked us to dismiss all our native caution and to stretch our credulity beyond reason. Andrew Lang's response was: "If so, the legend is *diablement changé en route.*"

In Hoffmann von Fallersleben's collection of Dutch ballads, which Bugge had to hand, appeared a nineteenth century broadside variant of Halewijn [18] that von Fallersleben cites as an example of the depths to which the folk poetry of the Netherlands has fallen. A third line has been fashioned for every stanza, usually by merely varying the substance of the second line. Two of the stanzas read:

> 34. Ik heb van 't leven hem beroofd,
> in mynen schoot heb ik zyn hoofd;
> hy is als Holofernes, my gelooft.

> 37. Zy reed dan voord als Judith wys,
> zoo recht nae haer vaders paleys,
> daer zy wierd ingehaeld met eer en prys.

The vague similarity of the story of Halewijn and the Judith-Holofernes narrative had not escaped notice before Bugge. This mention of the two principals from the story in the Apocrypha lends no support to Bugge's theory (he strangely makes no mention of this particular variant), for the names are clearly a late addition to the ballad. The names are both introduced in unballad-like similes and as part of a line filling process. Is it beyond the realm of probability that Bugge took his cue from this variant?

We have now come to the end of a lengthy list of source studies for "Lady Isabel and the Elf-knight." This ballad has been most richly endowed with sources, none of which can safely be accepted as valid, even though each is heralded by its author as a certitude. We may learn from the experience of others that the certitude is not with the findings, but with the preconceptions and determination brought to the problem. It has become apparent in the course of this paper that all the attributions of source considered have been fathered by world views, *Zeitgeist*, climates of opinion, attitudes, partialities, rather than by the evidence that the subject itself, the ballad, affords. The difficulty is undoubtedly in the paucity of information that the ballad does afford. But the facts and inferences that we may read in the variants of the ballad do provide strong grounds for doubting each suggested source. It would be singularly wrong-headed to neglect what the ballad record can offer as a guide and restraint. We are left with a handful of improbable possibilities as to the source of the ballad. And for these we may well be thankful, for their authors have trod the sands of surmise and have taught us how to avoid them, if we will but learn by example.

It is true that Bugge's argument, in its devious ingenuity in holding to the text, bears no outward mark of fashion, but nevertheless his position was much predetermined by other habits of thought. His addiction to Biblical parallels was noted by his Scandinavian colleagues. Grundtvig made a decidedly questioning appraisal of Bugge's theory in an addition to a letter to Child dated 29 January 1880. Child's reply gives a much clearer view of his judgment of Bugge than does the Headnote to "Lady Isabel," which was written two years later: [19]

> The very important article of Sophus Bugge, I have not had time to consider, but should imagine that it was a corollary to his other theories which are now making such a stir. He will expect a Bible story in many a ballad, I dare say, and such suggestions being infectious, and not to be demonstrably refuted, many minds will be ready to follow him to any length.[20]

When Léon Pineau presented his theory of origin, he had this to say of Bugge: "Nous ne croyons pas qu'il se trouve encore quelqu'un pour défendre cette théorie." [21] But his countryman, George Doncieux, defended the theory six years after Pineau's words appeared in print. A number of scholars have accepted Bugge's demonstration (possibly for lack of a better theory); the late W. J. Entwistle on six different occasions in his *European Balladry* identifies the source of "Halewijn" as the Book of Judith, and the identification has spread to other general accounts of balladry as well as to specific accounts of this ballad. A certain scepticism is a salutary thing in these matters, on the part of investigators and their readers alike.

It may be gratifying for us to know that some ballads do have identifiable sources. That "Lady Isabel" is so unattached, as it were, should not disturb us, for the ballad is still with us in all its multifarious variety. We still have the adventure of Lady Isabel with an elf-knight as full of mystery as ever.

＊＊＊＊＊＊＊＊＊＊＊＊＊＊＊＊＊＊＊

Lambkin: A Study in Evolution

ANNE G. GILCHRIST

AS the main purpose of this study of "Lambkin" is to trace its development along two different streams of tradition, it may be well to preface the discussion of the ballad by printing a version from each form, also some "Lambkin" tunes, all from hitherto unpublished manuscripts or scarce collections. As a label for each of these traditional forms may be useful, I shall distinguish the first as "Lambkin, the Wronged Mason" and the second as "Longkin, the Border Ruffian"—the first being the Scottish, the second the Northumbrian, form.

FORM I: The Wronged Mason

FIRST TUNE [1]

1. It's Lam-kin was a ma-son good, And ev-er built wi' stane; He built Lord Wea-rie's cas-tle But.. pay-ment gat he nane.

SECOND TUNE [2]

1. A bet-ter ma-son than Lam-mi-kin ne'er build-ed wi' the stane; He build-ed Earl Rob-ert's house, But wa-ges he gat nane. Come

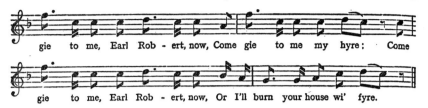

gie   to me,   Earl Rob - ert, now,   Come   gie   to me   my   hyre: Come

gie   to me,   Earl Rob - ert, now,   Or I'll burn   your house wi'   fyre.

GIL MORRICE [3]

LAMMAKIN [4]

A Fifeshire version, obtained from an old woman known as "The Witch," who lived near the old castle of Balwearie, Fifeshire.

1. Lammakin was as guid a mason
   As ever hewed a stane,
   He biggit Balwearie Castle
   But guerdon he gat nane.

2. It fell upon a day
   When Lord Wearie was frae hame,
   He cam' to seek his siller
   But siller he gat nane.

3. "Whare are the men o' this hoose?"
   Spak' oot the Lammakin;
   "They're in the barns threshing,
   And they canna win in."

4. "Whare are the women o' this hoose?"
   Spak' oot the Lammakin;
   "They're at the waal washing [5]
   And they canna come in."

5. "Whare is the lord o' this hoose?"
   Spak' oot the Lammakin;
   "He's on the saut sea sailing
   And far, far frae hame."

6. "Whare is the leddy o' this hoose?"
   Spak' oot the Lammakin;
   "She's in her chaumer shooing [sewing]
   And she winna come doon."

7. "What wad ye do," quo' Lammakin,
   "To mak' her come doon?"
   "We'll stick [stab] the bairn in the cradle"
   Says the false nourrice to him.

8. Lammakin he stickit it,
   And the fause nourrice she sang,
   Till the bluid sprang oure the cradle
   And frae ilk bar it ran.

9. "O, please the bairn, nourrice,
   And please him wi' the key";
   "He'll no be pleased, my leddy,
   For a' my nourrice fee."

10. "O, please the bairn, nourrice,
    Please him wi' the wand";
    "He'll no' be pleased, my leddy,
    For a' his faither's land."

11. "O, please the bairn, nourrice,
    And please him wi' the bell";
    "He'll no' be pleased, madam
    Till ye come doon yersel'."

12. The firsten step she steppit,
    She steppit on a stane;
    The neisten step she steppit
    It was on Lammakin.

13. "O, mercy, mercy, Lammakin,
    O, mercy ha'e on me:

Altho' ye've killed my young son,
O, let mysel' abee—

14. Ye'll get my auldest dochter,
    Wi' her bonny yellow hair;
    A peck o' the red, red goud,
    And twice as muckle mair!"

15. "O sall I kill her, nourrice,
    Or sall I let her be?"
    "O, kill her, kill her, Lammakin,
    For she's ne'er been guid to me!"

16. "Gae scoor the siller basin,
    Gae scoor it fair and clean,
    To haud yer leddy's life-bluid
    For she's o' noble kin."

17. But ere the siller basin
    Was scoored fair and clean
    The gentle leddy's heart's bluid
    Was drappin' on the stane.

18. Lord Wearie in a month or mair
    Cam' sailin' ower the faem,
    And dowie, dowie was his he'rt
    As he drew near his hame.

19. "There's murder in the kitchen,
    And slauchter in the ha',
    O, Lammakin killed yer young son,
    Yer leddy fair and a'!"

20. "Come here, come here, fause nourrice,
    And I'll gie ye yer fee!"
    The weel-won fee he pey'd her,
    He hanged her on a tree.

21. "Come here, come here, Lammakin,
    And I'll gie ye yer hire!"
    The dear won hire he pey'd him,
    He burnt him in the fire.

From v. 7 this version follows Child's "A" (from Jamieson's *Popular Ballads*, 1806) pretty closely as far as Jamieson's v. 21, but its stark terse conclusion rings much truer than Jamieson's last two verses, which run inconsequently, unless indeed they mean by the tree the one upon which Lambkin was hanged, and the thorns gathered to heap around the nourice's stake.

> O sweetly sang the blackbird
> That sat upon the tree
> But sairer grat Lamkin
> When he was condemned to die.
>
> And bonny sang the mavis
> Out o' the thorny brake,
> But sairer grat the nourice
> When she was tied to the stake.

And this Balwearie version is devoid of the nourice's moral reflection in Jamieson's v. 22 on the lack of difference between the blood of the rich and the poor. It is noteworthy that no daughter appears upon the scene, and the tragic news is evidently told by a servant, on the lord's return.

The word "guerdon" in v. 1 would at first sight seem suspect, as too literary a word, but it is included in Warrack's *Scots Dialect Dictionary*, where its meaning is given as "protection, safeguard." It is an old French word, which might have became current in common speech, like many other instances of such survivals in Scotland of the "Ancient Alliance" with France. Possibly "guerdon" became confused with "gairdin'" (guarding), and one might be tempted to speculate whether guerdon in v. 1 really meant originally that Lammakin had not safeguarded his interests by a proper contract, and hence was more easily cheated of his due by his employer. But enquiries have failed to trace this use of the word outside Warrack's Dictionary, and probably "guerdon" is simply a French importation, like the "jigget" (gigot) of mutton or the "ashet" (assiette) of Scottish vernacular.

The above version was noted by Miss Minnie Kininmonth of Kinghore (Fife), who had heard it "ranted" among the farm folk at Balwearie, where she spent much of her childhood. It first appeared in a manuscript magazine, "Pipers' News," in 1911, and was sent to the Rymour Club by Mrs. Jessie P. Findlay, one of the editors of the manuscript magazine, which circulated in Kirkcaldy. Mrs. Findlay said that Lord Wearie was supposed to be one of the Balwearies of that ilk whose heiress carried the lands by marriage into the Scott family *temp.* Alexander III (1249–86) of Scotland. But as some doubt has been thrown upon the authenticity of this record (in Douglas's Baronetage), it would be idle to speculate whether the murder of an infant heir of the Wearie family in mediaeval times might have created his sister an heiress. What is actually known of Balwearie Castle is that, as Mr. W. Mackay Mackenzie (author of *The Mediaeval Castle in Scotland*) informs me, it is a fifteenth-century tower, a license for its erection being issued to William Scott of Balwearie in February 1464. (The 'bal' of the name denotes a farmstead.) Whether any real connection with Balwearie existed or not, it seems probable that the ballad had a historical foundation; as far as I am aware it has no European counterpart.

FORM II: The Border Ruffian [6]

A

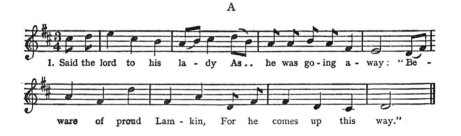

1. Said the lord to his la - dy As.. he was go-ing a - way: "Be - ware of proud Lam - kin, For he comes up this way."

"What do I care for proud Lamkin
Or any of his men? —
When my doors are well bolted
And my windows shut in."

He was scarce gone one hour
When proud Lamkin came by,
He knocked at the hall door
And the nurse let him in.

"O where is your master?
Is he not without?"
"He's gone to old England,"
Cried the false nurse.

"O where is your mistress?
  Is she not within?"
"She's up in her bed-chamber
  With the windows barred in."

"How am I to get at her?"
  Proud Lamkin did cry.
"O here is young Sir Johnson,
  Pierce him and he'll cry."

He took out his bodkin
And pierced young Sir Johnson,
And made the blood trinkle
Right down to his toes.

"O mistress, dear mistress,
  How can you sleep so fast?
Can't you hear your young Sir Johnson
  A-crying his last?

I can't pacify him
On the nurse-milk or pap.
I pray you come down,
Quieten him on your lap."

"How can I come downstairs
  On such a cold winter's night?
No spark of fire burning,
  No candle alight."

"You've got two white holland sheets up there
  As white as the snow,
I pray you come down
  By the light of them so."

As she was coming downstairs,
Not thinking much harm,
Proud Lamkin awaited,
Took her by the arm.

"I have got you, I have got you,"
Proud Lamkin did cry,
"For years I have waited,
 But I have got you as last."

"O spare me my life," she cries,
"For one, two o'clock,
 And I'll give you all the money
 That you will carry on your back."

"If you'll give me the money
 Like the sand on the shore, [? of the sea]
 I'll not keep my bright sword
 From your white skin so free."

"O spare me my life," she cries,
"For one half-an-hour;
 I'll give you my nurse,
 Although she's my flower."

"O where is your nurse?
 Go send her to me;
 She can hold the silver basin
 While your heart's blood runs free."

"False nurse was my friend," she cries
"But now she's my foe;
 She can hold the silver basin
 While my heart's blood do flow."

There was blood in the nursery,
And blood in the hall,
And blood on the stairs,
And her heart's blood was all.

Proud Lamkin was taken
To the gallows to die,
And false nurse she was burned
In a fire near by.

B

1. Said Lord Doug-las to his la - dy In .. walk-ing one day: "Be -
- ware of Lord Lam - kin When he .. comes this way."
"Why need I be - ware of Lord Lam - kin?" she says, "With my
doors .. well bolt - ed And my win - dows barred in."
(No more words).

C

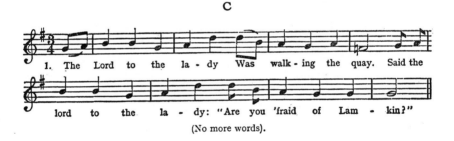

1. The Lord to the la - dy Was walk - ing the quay. Said the
lord to the la - dy: "Are you 'fraid of Lam - kin?"
(No more words).

D

Proud Lam - kin was ta - ken and condemned for to die, And the
false - heart - ed maid - en was burned a - long - side.
(No more words).

To the typical texts above, one may add the fragment of the
"Orange" Northumbrian version (Child's G) perhaps sung as a lullaby,
in Halliwell's *Nursery Rhymes* (Fifth Edition, 1853, p. 212). It is
part of the dialogue between lady and nurse:

"Rock well my cradle
And 'bee-bea [lull to sleep] my son—
You shall have a new gown
When ye [yer?] lord comes home.

Oh, still my child, Orange,[7]
Still him with a bell!"
"I can't still him, ladie,
Till you come down yoursel'."

We may now proceed to consider the early form of the ballad story—best preserved in the Scottish tradition. In the undoubtedly older and completer form, the villain of the piece is a skilled mason who built a "prime castle" and being defrauded of his pay gains access to the castle in the absence of its lord, and from motives of revenge, with the connivance of the false nurse, murders the owner's wife and infant heir. In the secondary form of the ballad the villain is either a lawless ruffian or perhaps another lord at feud with the castle's owner. Without reasonable or adequate explanation of his motive he plans and executes the same crime. He is no ordinary robber, for like the mason it is not booty but revenge which he seeks.

Before the second half of the eighteenth century, in which both forms of the story were almost simultaneously printed by Herd in Scotland and obtained by Percy in England (the respective dates being 1776 and 1775) these two versions must have parted company, and it looks as though the freebooter or Border ruffian version arose from the loss of the first verse, in which half of the mason story is told and the motive for revenge shines clear. The mason ballad would seem to have originated in the south of Scotland, the secondary freebooter form in Northumberland, where border feuds and raids were common in the old days.

Taking first the Scottish tradition, there is no need to suppose with Prof. Child that the name Lambkin was bestowed ironically. Lambkin (dim. of Lambert) is a Flemish name, constant, though sometimes in a corrupt form, such as Longkin or Dunkins or Rankin, in all of the many versions—about forty—of the ballad which I have seen. Bardsley in his *English Surnames* says:

Lambert received a large accession in England through the Flemings, who thus preserved a memorial of the patron of Liege, St. Lambert, who was martyred early in the eighth century. Succumbing to the fashion so prevalent among the Flemings, it is generally found as Lambkin, such entries as Lambekyn fil. Eh or Lambekin Taborer being common.

Lambert and Lambkin, Lampson and Lampkin survive as English surnames to the present day.

Assuming a real event to have been the basis of this tragic and circumstantial story, the "mason guid" might well have been a Flemish craftsman. The Flemings were highly skilled workers, as is patent from the fact that Gresham imported Flemish masons and joiners, under the management of their master Hendryk, to build the Royal Exchange in 1566. Flemish as well as French influence may be seen in the old castles and churches of Fifeshire built or rebuilt in the sixteenth century. Along the east coast of Scotland were colonies of Flemings in the Middle Ages, there being a close connection between Scotch-grown wool and Flemish wool-merchants and weavers. In many old and elaborate descriptions of architecture in England constant reference is made to the Flemings. James IV of Scotland employed Flemish craftsmen to plaster the walls and ceilings of his royal castles—gaunt and comfortless as they were—for the reception of his "English rose," Margaret Tudor. Without elaborating the point further, the reader may be referred to *Flemish Influence in Britain* (1930) by J. Arnold Fleming. Though one cannot prove that Lambkin was a Flemish master-mason, this seems, assuming an historic foundation for the ballad, to be a reasonable possibility. And another is that he was neither called Lambkin because he was like or unlike a lamb but because it was his name. A third point is that if he was a "furriner," it would then as now be considered less of a crime to cheat him.

In Motherwell's text, he is called indifferently Lambert, Linkin and Belinkin (in Motherwell's manuscript, Belankin—a corruption of Bold Lankin?). And it may be noted that Finlay's form Balcanqual seems to have been falsely restored from Beluncan (? Bold Lankin) as he states that Beluncan is sometimes found as a corruption "for the more agreeable sound" of Balcanqual, "an ancient Scottish surname." As Finlay's text is "written over"—as Child remarks—probably Beluncan was really the form he or his old lady corrected, as another name in the ballad was editorially changed.

The strongest Scottish tradition seems to be that which localizes the tragedy at Balwearie, Fife, near former colonies of Flemings; and here the "dule-tree" used to be pointed out on which Lambkin was hanged before the castle gate. Without laying too much stress upon local legend, it may be noted that this Fifeshire version is the only form I have seen in which the castle is named in the text. For the Prime Castle of Motherwell—

> He built up Prime Castle
> But payment gat nane—

seems to me to be wrongly sung or heard for "built a prime castle," that is, a castle of prime importance or strength. "Prime" in this sense is found in Scotland both as a noun meaning the best and an adjective meaning the foremost. It was probably the lilt of the tune which supplied the extra "p" as sung. (On this point—the influence of the tune on the text—I shall have more to say later, apropos the Lambkin tunes.) Another location "Lord Cassilis' [pr. Cassels] house" may be due to a similar confusion of the personal name and the building, as seems to be the case in "Johnny Faa" (the Gypse Laddie) where the "castle-yett" sometimes figures as "Lord Cassilis' yett." By the time the ballad has been recovered in America the castle has sunk to a "cation" or even a "frame-house"!

Who Lord Weir or Wearie (alternatively Erlie or Arran or Earl Robert) was is quite unknown. He does not seem to have belonged to the Scott family. The presumed real event may have had its origin earlier than the date of Balwearie Castle, and Lambkin may be the only real name which, perhaps by very reason of its incongruity to later ears, has survived of the story. Lambkin's accomplice, the "false nurse," has seldom any other name. ("Orange" and "Fortunate" seem to be misconstructions of words in the text.) Her grudge against her mistress—as the ballad sometimes more than hints—is resentment because her lady never bestowed on her any of the fine clothing she had coveted—hence her sarcastic reference to the five golden mantles by the light of which her lady might see to come down. Sometimes the lady appeals to her—as in the B version noted by Gavin Greig (*Last Leaves of Aberdeen Ballads*):

> "Did ye ever want your meat, nursie,
> Did ye ever want your fee,
> Or did ye ever want anything
> A lady had to gie?"

> "I wanted never meat, lady,
> I wanted never my fee,
> But I wanted mony things
> A lady had to gie."

Or when the nurse says her lady was "never guid" to her, her mistress cries out (Macmath manuscript in Child):

> "O haud your tongue, nourrice,
> Sae loud as ye lee,
> Ye'd ne'er a cut finger
> But I pitied thee!"

But always in vain. The nurse's malice is as inexorable as Lambkin's and in all versions of the story she shares his doom, except that in one Irish variant Lambkin murders her after she has served his ends.

We may turn now to the Northumbrian or English tradition, embodied in Percy's "Long Lonkin." This—Child's κ—though obtained in Kent in 1775, was then known to have come from Northumberland.[8] Moreover the words "bairn" and "moss" (peatland or heath) betray its north-country origin. But this is the form which has spread further south in England.

On the north side of the road leading from Heddon on the Wall to Corbridge, which crossed Whittle Dene, through which the Whittle burn flows to the Tyne, stand the ruins of Nafferton Tower, an unfinished fortress begun by Philip de Ulecote, Constable of Chinon and Forester of Northumberland in the time of King John. This Norman baron, presuming on his influence with the Crown, was proceeding with the erection of a castle on his manor here when his neighbour Richard de Umfraville made complaint of the injury and menace involved to his own castle of Prudhoe on the south side (and opposite bank) of the Tyne. Whereupon a Crown writ was issued compelling Philip de Ulecote to stop the work in progress, and the Tower ever after remained at the stage at which it was abandoned by the thirteenth-century workmen. The bearing of this piece of history—which, together with the Northumbrian tradition surrounding the ballad, I take from W. W. Tomlinson's *Comprehensive Guide to Northumberland* (Tenth Edition)—is that in course of time the ruinous hold became known as "Lang Lonkin's Castle"—a gigantic freebooter "Lang Lonkin" ("long" meaning of course "tall") having lived in it—so it was said—to the terror of the countryside. And the Longkin ballad in the "Orange" version (Child's G) as noted from the recitation of an old woman of Ovington, near by, was believed to refer to one of his crimes. The story was told of him that during the absence of its owner and through the treachery of a serving maid called Orange he gained entrance to Welton Hall—close to the Whittle Dene—and murdered the lady and child. (No motive, however, is adduced or even suggested in the local version of the ballad.) He then dragged the lady's body into the dene and threw it into a deep pool still known as Lang Lonkin's Hole. Further it is said that Lonkin hanged himself on or fell from a huge tree overlooking the well. His skull lay about the castle for some time, and, to conclude the story, to the present day his ghost haunts the district, and a mother has but to shake a bunch of keys and call out "There's Lang Lonkin!" to recall her straying children at nightfall. There is another "corroborative detail" of the doings of Lonkin, a second deep pool in the stream, called the Whirl Dub, being pointed out as the place into which Lonkin when hard pressed flung a rich booty sewed up in a bull's hide. At the bottom of this dub it is said still to lie.

It is quite possible that there did exist a notorious Border ruffian known as Long Lonkin, to whom the headless Northumbrian version of "Lambkin" became attached, and that the tradition gathered accretions from time to time. Miss Broadwood has a note in *Journal*, V, 84, that in a deed of May, 1316, relating to lands on the south side of the Tyne (though drawn up in London) one of the witnesses is John Lonkin. (Lonkin seems to be simply a corrupt form of Lambkin.) In any case the villain of the ballad has been in Northumberland identified with this real or legendary outlaw, though Nafferton Tower was neither built by nor for Long Lonkin, as has been seen. But it is often characteristic of ballads to "fly in the face of all history," as Child notes in a letter to his friend "W. W.," Aberdeen.

The most important difference between the Scottish and Northumbrian versions is that in the latter the mason motive has faded out of the story, and the ballad opens with the lord parting from his lady and warning her against the attack which may be made upon the castle or house by Lonkin in his absence.

Soon after the mason vanishes from the story it obviously becomes necessary for the singer to find a new and adequate motive for Lonkin's enmity.[9] Now, in some of what I judge to be later versions of the cheated mason ballad, the lady in desperate terror seeks to gain time (as I read the incident) while hoping for rescue by offering Lambkin more gold than he can carry away if he will but spare her life for twelve hours—one hour—five minutes—and finally offers him her nurse "although she's my flower," or her eldest daughter, or daughter Betsy, to stay his hand.[10] About the same stage in the ballad's Scottish career (as I conceive) a certain Jeanie or Jenny, who appears to be the lady's one faithful bower-maid and who offers to die in her stead, is commanded by Lambkin to scour the silver basin to hold her lady's blood. But false nurse always urges Lambkin on to the murder. It seems to be this same devoted maid who on her master's return breaks the direful news:

> Her maiden looked out from the turret so high
> And she saw her master from London ride by:
> "O master, O master, don't lay the blame on me,
> 'Twas the false nurse and Lankin that killed your fair ladye!

Or thus, in the Fifeshire version:

> There's murder in the kitchen
> And slaughter in the ha',
> O, Lammakin killed yer young son,
> Yer leddy fair and a'.

As the result of the suggestions of the text, the daughter is next actually brought upon the stage (she is sent for from school, in an American variant) to hold the basin, and in the further process of decadence is followed by Lady Nelly and other lady daughters ad libitum and ad absurdum. This (in Percy's version) is a rather interesting petering out of the ballad, because it recalls the list of relatives sent for, one by one, to come to Queen Jane's bedside in the nursery version of "The Death of Queen Jane" (see *Journal*, II, 221). But Betsy having been brought upon the scene is now made to serve another purpose. The singer, one may postulate, casting about for the motive probably—and very properly—demanded by his audience or his own intelligence for Longkin's enmity, interpolates the information that the murderer had wished to marry Lady Betsy, but her parents had frowned upon his suit. Therefore we are now asked to believe that by a strange mental process he plans and carries out the murder of his love's nearest and dearest—scorning the offer of the maiden herself which actually occurs in the text.[11] So we arrive lastly at the flat and lamentable conventionality of the ballad-sheet:

It's of some noble lord, as you shall quickly hear,
He had one only daughter, young Lankon loved her dear;
Her father tried to part them without fear or strife,
But bold Lankon he contrivèd to take away her [sic] life.

A variation upon this proffered elucidation of the workings of Lankon's mind is found in A. K. Davis's fragmentary and confused Virginian version B (see *Traditional Ballads of Virginia*, p. 357). "Ward Lampkin" was sung by an old negro servant who introduced the ballad by explaining that Ward Lampkin had been in love with the "Landlady" before her marriage, and had always sworn to have his revenge. (A similar interpolation occurs in an Irish text.) The lord was going off on a trip and urged his wife to have some protection, to which warning the first verse of the remembered fragment was her reply:

Why should I reward Lampkin,
Why need I reward him?
When my doors are fast bolted
And windows pinned down. [? in]

(Ward Lampkin perhaps derives his name from the first line.)

Probably this verse (which suggests a lost "cheated mason" opening, in which Lampkin "comes craving his money to seek"—as in another version) originally meant that if Lampkin should come craving his pay in the lord's absence, the lady need not fear, the castle being secure against his entry. In this version it is Ward Lampkin who tells the nurse—Fortunate is her curious name—that the baby is crying in the nursery, so as to get her out of the way, this change in the situation being, one guesses, due to the dislike of devoted coloured servants for a story of a trusted nurse's treachery. (The murder of the baby has been lost or excluded from this form.) As the eighteenth-century editor jibbed at the crass selfishness of the mother's appeal:

O mercy, mercy, Lambkin,
Ha'e mercy upon me;
Though you have ta'en my young son's life
Ye may lat mysel' be!

—substituting the more correct maternal sentiment:

O monster, monster, spare my child,
Wha never scaithèd thee!

(the child is already done to death, but that circumstance can also be revised)—so the Virginian negro must absolve "fause nerrice"—changed or corrupted [12] to "Fortunate"—from complicity. She has been got away by a ruse while the murder of the lady is a-doing, and though her fate was admittedly to be burnt, she was an innocent victim. So through a combined process of elimination, selection, and development, the story of the cheated and revengeful mason retains in the end only the murder scene intact, and the motive abundantly clear in the admirable opening "mason" verse—which sets forth half the plot in four short lines—is replaced by feebler and feebler explanations furnished by a later line of singers.

Thus an examination of about forty variants shows, as already stated, that the decay sets in as soon as the mason is lost from the story, the common motive of love or jealousy taking the place of the more unusual and distinctive theme. Moreover, the Betsy of the lady's desperate offer—which I do not regard as a genuine one—becomes (wrongly, I think) fused with the teller of the tragic news; for "O master, master, do not blame me!" in the mouth of the servant who has helplessly witnessed her mistress's murder is surely the original form, rather than a similar appeal on the lips of a young daughter. And it is more humanly credible that even a convinced murderer should ask a servant to scour the silver basin than the lady's own daughter, or the daughter, in a still more decadent form, be invited to hold it for her own gore.

Another point may be noticed. The scouring of the silver basin that the lady's "noble blood may be kept [caught] clean" is evidently connected with the old superstition—whatever its foundation—against shedding noble or innocent blood upon the ground. For the first case see my note on "The Wife wrapt in Wether's Skin" (*Journal*, II, 223–24); for the second, the incident of the spreading of white blankets on the ground at the execution of Illiam Dhone (*Journal*, VII, 326). And again for the respect due to noble birth we have the hanging of Geordie in gold or silver chains, and in the Lambkin ballad itself the stabbing of the baby with a bodkin, skewer, or dagger of silver.

Another interesting point is the evidence "Lambkin" affords of how a confusion between the voices of the dialogue creates new permutations in the situation and the sentiments of the persons supposed to be speaking. Note how the changes are rung in different versions upon the appeal to Lambkin's mercy:

[LADY]: Ye've killed my bairn, Lamkin,
    but lat mysell be,
    Ye'll be as weel payit a mason
    as was ever pay'd a fee.—Child M.

[JENNY, THE MAID]: O no, no, no, Lambkin,
    My heart will be sare, [woe?]
    O take my life, Lambkin,
    Let my lady go.—Child c.

[LADY BETSY]: O rather kill me, Rankin
    And let my mother go.—Child D.

[LADY]: O mercy, mercy, Lamkin,
    O mercy ha'e on me.
    Although ye've killed my young son
    O lat mysel abee.—Rymour Club.

[LORD WEARIE]: Woe be to you, Lambkin,
    Some bad death may ye dee
    Though ye hae killed my lady
    Ye micht hae latten my young son be.
        —Aberdeenshire (*Last Leaves,* etc.)

There seems to have arisen a similar confusion amongst the persons addressed by Lambkin and commanded to hold the basin, figured variously as a faithful maid, the false nurse, and the daughter. Where a ballad consists almost entirely of dialogue such changes of identity are almost certain to occur, e.g., the change of sex in the two chief characters in "The Prickly Bush."

The unsatisfactory state of "Lambkin" in some of the earlier printed Scottish texts—whose spurious verses were thrown out by Child's expert judgment—is largely due, as I believe, to the ballad having been noted from recitation instead of singing—a notable step downwards in a ballad's career. The small irregularities which occur naturally in ballad lines ride lightly and rhythmically upon the current of the tune, whereas when they are written down the literary editor, especially of a hundred to a hundred and fifty years ago, has a great temptation to trim superfluous syllables and fill apparent gaps—not to speak of adding embellishments of his own to make it *read* better.

Sometimes, as in editing "Lambkin," he drops into common iambic ballad-metre in making such emendations and additions, for instance substituting

"O gentle nourice, still my child"

for "O still my bairn, nourice," throwing the verses he disturbs out of gear through ignoring—or actual ignorance of—the tune, combined with an irrepressible love of adjectives, for which the short lines of "Lambkin" leave no room, even had they been needed. (The "fause" nourrice is an almost solitary label.) Only in a late and degraded form of this ballad—probably a broadsheet version—do we find the lines padded out to fit a common ballad-tune, as in the verse quoted above, "It's of some noble lord, as you shall quickly hear." For the rhythm of "Lambkin" is a triple metre, fitting a triple-time tune, constant as such in almost all versions where a tune has been noted at all.

A factor in a ballad's evolution which has often been entirely ignored by our folk-song scholars—either from lack of knowledge or interest, or from lack of realization of its importance—is this relation between the text and the tune. Speaking generally, a new ballad coming into currency would not be sung to a new tune. The singer brings to the new words some tune he already knows and so makes them acquainted. Often the tune brings with it some of the words—perhaps only the refrain—the singer already associates with it, which may have no relation whatever to the new ballad. The contact of tune and words results in the adaptation of the one to the other. Sometimes one, sometimes each, insensibly yields something of its rhythm, or stretches or contracts its line or melody, and before long the pair settle as it were into place, and the old tune may then be halfway towards a new one.

As constant as "Lambkin's" name is its triple-time metre—a metre which can be traced back to the sixteenth century in folk-song, and may be earlier. It is the metre of "The Death of Queen Jane" [Seymour], of "Six Dukes Went A-fishing" [?Death of the Duke of Suffolk], of the old song "The Cuckoo" (Oh, meeting is pleasure and parting is grief), of "The Lost Lady Found," "The Virgin Unspotted," and in Scotland of "Lord Ronald," "Colin's Cattle," and a version of "Gil Morrice," to which tune Herd says "Lammikin" is sung. It is also known in Wales; and "Lambkin" tunes show connections with most of these other tunes, though it is impossible to say how and when borrowings took place. There is an echo of "Queen Jane" in William

Allingham's Irish version of "Lambkin," which may have been sung to the same tune:

> There's blood in the kitchen,
> And blood in the hall,
> And the young Mayor of England
> Lies dead by the wall.

"Mayor" should perhaps be "heir," but even so the "England" must be imported. "Lambkin" tunes are unfortunately very much scarcer than texts. A small number have been noted in America, where both Form I and II are represented in more or less fragmentary or corrupted versions. It may be noted that in the case of Mr. Sharp's Appalachian version of Form I, a pentatonic tune, Scottish in character, adheres to it, whereas a Maine version, Form II, in *British Ballads from Maine*, goes to a tune of English character, as do the Newfoundland Form II versions printed above, particularly "B," which is a blend of "Virgin Unspotted" and "The Cuckoo." The one Scottish tune quite different from any other "Lambkin" is that in the *Scotish Minstrel*, quoted above. As this takes up two verses instead of one it can hardly be in its original state; but as its patter is AABB possibly a simple AB strain has been repeated in each part to form the double verse. The tune is at any rate "folk" in character and its unusual cadences are curiously reminiscent of a Faroese ballad-air "Asmundur Adalsson" in Hjalmar Thuren's *Dans og Kvaddigtning paa Faerøerne*, the last twelve notes of this tune being almost identical. Some oddities in the texts are probably due to mishearing of the words as sung, since words are sometimes run together by the singer. "Prime castle" and "Orange" have already been noticed. "Johnson" as the baby's name was perhaps evolved from "young-son," with the musical accent on "young"—"Can't you hear your little young-son?"—and in

> "Fause nurse was my friend," she cries,
> "But now she's my foe,"—

it is easy to see how "Fause-nurse" might be heard as a Christian name, and "Fortunate" substituted for it at the earliest opportunity.

To sum up, the apparent confinement of the "Lambkin" ballad to the English-speaking race would point to its being based upon a real event in British domestic history, the ballad branching off at an early date into the Northumbrian form, which was the one to spread southwards in England, while the mason motive was retained in Scotland and amongst Scottish settlers in America. Had more tunes been recorded in the States, to match the number of texts, it might have been possible to say with certainty whether a Scottish tune adhered as a rule—as well as in the cases noted—to the mason tradition, and an English tune to the "lawless foe" form of the tragedy.

Finally, "Lambkin," of which so many versions have been discovered, shows the ballad—an exemplar of ballads in general—as a live and growing thing, coloured and shaped in its course through centuries by the many minds through which it has passed—some folk content to "tell the tale as 'twas told to me," sometimes in imperfect phonetics and with lapses of memory, others chafing against the obscure or the inexplicable—often the result of the same bad phonetics or forgetfulness—and so impelled to invent, as in folk-etymologies, a rational explanation for what seems irrational; or rebelling against what for any reason—conscious or sub-conscious—the singer dislikes, and substituting something more pleasing to himself. For the folk mind is not all of one level of taste and intelligence, and it is not only literary editors who have tampered with our old ballads but the folk themselves who leave their individual marks upon them. Particularly in the case of the Scottish ballads, it is difficult to say where, with simpler social habits of life in Scotland in bygone days, the folk end and the gentry begin, especially as the Scottish peasantry of three hundred years ago was less illiterate than the corresponding social class in England. There is certainly little visible gap between the literacy of some of the eighteenth-century old Scottish ladies who wrote down the ballads from memory in any spelling that pleased them and the singers from whom they themselves had learned their store of folk-poetry.

A list of the extant versions of "Lambkin" is appended for reference by students.

Child, *English and Scottish Ballads* (26 texts).
Folk Song Journal, I, 212; II, 111; V, 81–84 (4 texts, 5 tunes).
English Folk Songs from the S. Appalachians, No. 23 (1 text and tune).
Traditional Ballads of Virginia, No. 26 (3 texts and fragment, 1 tune).
British Ballads from Maine, pp. 200–203 (1 text and fragment, 1 tune).
Last Leaves of Aberdeen Ballads, No. XXXIV (2 texts).
R. A. Smith's *Scotish Minstrel*, II, 94 (1 text, 1 tune).
Christie's *Traditional Ballad Airs* (1 text, 1 tune).
Newfoundland versions above (1 text, 3 fragments, 4 tunes).
Recent American Versions from Ohio, Michigan and Tennessee, etc.
(These I have not seen.)

13

＊＊＊＊＊＊＊＊＊＊＊＊＊＊＊＊＊＊＊＊＊

Some Effects
of Scribal and Typographical Error
on Oral Tradition

W. EDSON RICHMOND

THE oral nature of popular literature, of one form of folklore in other words, has been so emphasized in the past few years that frequently the fact that printed folklore also exists is lost sight of. Indeed, though no competent scholar would boldly assert that printed folklore does not exist, such an assumption is not uncommonly implicit in the definitions which may be found for various types of popular literature. The emphasis, for example, which has been placed upon oral transmission as the principal element contributing to the creation of a popular ballad and which may be traced at least as far back as Sir Walter Scott's day,[1] if not, as is probable, considerably further, suggests that all printed ballads except those in the volumes of scholarly collectors are suspect.

If we are to deal at all with contemporary materials of Western European civilization, however, we must realize that today the printed page is nearly as much the property of the "folk" as is oral tradition and that it differs from the latter only in that to it is attributed more authority than is usually given today to the unsupported word.

It is true, of course, that the broadside ballad is easily distinguishable from the so-called popular ballad of tradition and that the broadside ballad cannot in general stand alongside the ballad of tradition if any accepted canons of literary taste be applied—but then, neither can many modern American ballads which appear to be solely the product of oral tradition unsullied by printer's ink. Moreover, it has long been known that broadsides have acted as intermediaries in the transmission of what appears to be purely oral per se.[2] It is the purpose of this paper to point out the effect which typographical and scribal error may have upon subsequent oral transmission of popular ballads and by extension the effect which printing may have upon folklore in general.

Insofar as strict oral transmission of any material is concerned, it is obvious that there are two processes at work at the same time. There is, first of all, that re-creational force which results from the taste of the transmitters and which results in what may be called "good" folklore by those whose standards are primarily literary or aesthetic. There is secondly, however, a force which has nothing whatsoever to do with communal taste and which can best be described as a corrupting rather than a re-creational force, though it may not destroy the worth of the material either as a piece of folklore or as a literary text. This force results from two human failings: poor memory—either individually or as a folk—and the inability to reproduce or interpret accurately that which has been heard or seen. It is this force which in oral transmission distorts the history of the historical ballads, which sometimes changes the locale of a ballad from one place to another, which creates nonsense syllables or meaningless lines, which, in short, distorts without either necessarily improving or destroying the material itself.

Whether the first-mentioned force is effective in the printed transmission (or even the oral transmission) of folk literature or not is a moot point,[3] it is certain, however, that the second force has had a far reaching effect upon folklore both in its printed and its oral traditions, each being at least partly dependent upon the other.

The second force is in reality a composite of many minor forces; a "distortion complex" composed of precisely the same forces as those which operate in the evolution of a language. These forces in turn result from the unfamiliarity of the speaker of a language (or the teller of a tale, or the singer of a song) with the things which he utters and from the lack of any effective conservative force which makes exactness a virtue. Consequently, a tremendous amount of variation in oral literature may be explained in terms of the attempts which the tellers, folk singers, and last—but far from least—editors and collectors of folkloristic materials have made, however unconsciously, to explain what they have heard in terms of what they *think* they have heard or in terms of what they know.

Insofar as purely oral tradition is concerned, the effects of this "distortion complex" have been frequently noted in the pages of ballad scholarship. Not always with the same purpose in view, various scholars and editors have pointed out particular examples of this type of variation.[4] But one need not depend upon other scholars for his exempla; one need only open any ballad collection and compare versions and variants of particular ballads with each other. If one examines the texts of "The Wife of Usher's Well" (79), for example, he finds the perfectly acceptable but archaic word *grammarye,* "black magic," of Child variant 79D [5] corrupted to the nonsensically meaningless, but phonetically analogous *granerlee* in a version from Georgia [6] or the meaningful but equally inaccurate word *grammar* in West Virginia variant.[7] If "The Gypsy Laddie" (200) be examined instead, one will find the word *glamourie*—according to Jamieson in *An Etymological Dictionary of the Scottish Language* (Paisley, 1880), II, 394, *glaumerie,* etc., is to cause deception of sight by means of a charm—in the last line of the usual second stanza:

> She cam tripping down the stair,
>   And all her maids before her;
> As soon as they saw her weel-faurd face
>   They coost their *glamourye* owre her.
>   Child, 200 c

is shifted to create what was perhaps to later or to non-Scotch singers a more understandable albeit foolish stanza:

> The Earl of Castle's lady came down,
>   With the waiting-maid beside her;
> As soon as her fair face they saw,
>   They called their *grandmother* over
>   Child, 200 G

And finally a similar folk-etymology may be seen in the corruption of the word *harped* as it appears in the following stanza of an English version of "The Two Brothers" (49):

> She put the small pipes to her mouth,
>   And she *harped* both far and near,

> Till she *harped* the small birds off the briers,
> And her true love out of the grave.
>
> Child, 49 B

to *hopped* in a variant recorded by Cecil Sharp [8] in the Southern Appalachians:

> She went *hopping* all over her true lover's grave
> A twelve-months and a day.
> She hopped her true love out of his grave
> So he can get no rest.

Here, of course, we cannot be entirely sure that the fault lies with the singer, for the collector, speaking as he did Received Standard British, would be unlikely to recognize in the flurry of collecting the normal southern American substitution of the low-back vowel for the low-central vowel followed by *r*.

Such examples may, of course, be multiplied ad infinitum, but to do so here would be merely to underline the point that the fruit of all oral tradition is subject to the same laws as is language in general, although the nature of a particular folktale or ballad may in itself act as a conservative force, particularly if the material belongs to the genre of saga rather than *Märchen*. There is, however, another large class of variations which result to a considerably lesser degree if at all from oral corruption: the variations which result from scribal and typographical confusion and later pass into tradition or are perpetuated in the pages of scholarly collections in the name of scientific exactitude.

One of the difficulties which always handicaps the collector is the inaccuracy of his tools. Only recently have the various types of recorders been brought to such perfection that they have become both reliable and a necessity for a collector of folk material. But even when a satisfactory recorder is used, the collector's needs are not entirely fulfilled: the collection which he has made on wire, tape, or disc remains a tool, and no matter how desirable it might be to pass the material on to others in this form, it is impracticable to do so if there be any mass of materials. He must, instead, rely upon the printed page, and unfortunately the printed page cannot reproduce what the collector has heard with any more than the merest approach to scientific fidelity. Musical notation is at best a compromise too frequently incomprehensible to a large portion of the audience; but it is, at any rate, accepted as such. Not so with the text itself which is often as much of a compromise as is musical notation but seldom recognized as such even though the English alphabet has long been recognized as an unsatisfactory tool for the symbolization and reproduction of the English language. In short, the modern folklorist is in a scarcely more satisfactory position for passing on his materials than were Percy, Scott, and Ritson even though he may be a more efficient collector. He has the undoubted advantage of having at his constant command a nearly perfect reproduction of all that his informant has given him with, if he desires, the irrelevant edited out, a record which may be played and replayed without ever giving way to tiredness, boredom, or in-explicable variation; but he also has the added disadvantage of know-ing as his predecessors did not that exact reproduction on the printed page is not only desirable but also impossible. This impasse has led to incongruities which have later found their way into oral tradition.

As a consequence, the two major types of corruption which may arise as a result of the attempt to set in print what arises from oral tradition—scribal error and typographical error—are not always easily distinguishable one from another; but in general it may be said that scribal errors result from the attempts of collectors and editors to re-produce as closely as their orthography allows the sounds and words which they have heard, and typographical errors result from some peculiarity either in the forms of letters which allow for confusion or in the arbitrary system of capitalization, punctuation, word division, etc., which is peculiar to any given language.

The most common of these errors is scribal error. It usually takes the form of a phonetic spelling for some word or words with which the collector is unfamiliar, and it may result either in complete confusion or some analogical form. Errors of this type may be found in the earliest ballad collections. Thus it is that perhaps from sheer ignorance, perhaps because of the near-phonetic and certainly unstable spelling of his own day, the anonymous seventeenth-century scribe of *Bishop Percy's Folio Manuscript* corrupted *Terouenne* to *Turwin, Boulogne* to *Bullen, Montreuil* to *Mutrell,* and *Guienne* to *Gynye* in his version of *Fflodden Ffeild*.[9] And indeed, foreign place-names seem particu-larly susceptible to this type of error, sometimes being so changed that they nearly defy recognition. A Breton text of a ballad which if it is not the original of is at least analogous to "Johnie Scot" (99), for example, calls its hero *Les Aubrays*[10] and in Child variant B Johnie Scot is asked whether he is the "king of Aulsberry." There can be little doubt that *Aulsberry* is a corruption of *Les Aubrays* nor that the names *Salgeree* and *Salvary* which are substituted for it in two Maine variants [11] are corruptions in turn of Aulsberry. One might even predicate here a lost variant employing the name *Salisbury* which would act as a missing link. In like manner, Child variant B of "Sir Lionel" (18) has corrupted the name Artois from the romance *Sir Eglamour of Artois*,[12] which may have been the original of the ballad, to the *wood o Tore,* and in this case the corruption was probably aided by analogy with Tore, Morayshire, a place not over fifteen miles distant from Buckie, Bannfshire, the source of this particular variant.

Not only the exotic is corrupted in this manner. The name *Aughrim* (County Roscommon, Ireland) as it appears in Child variant H of "The Lass of Roch Royal" (76) is phonetically spelled *Ocram* in Child variant L* [13] the name *Anstruther* (Fifeshire) as it appears in "Rose the Red and White Lily" (103 B) is spelled *Anster* as it is locally pronounced.[14] In a similar manner, *Edinburgh* has produced *Eddenburrough* in "Johnie Armstrong" (169), *Edinbro* in "The Earl of Errol" (231), *Embro* in "The Laird of Wariston" (194), and many other forms in many other ballads; *London* has produced *Londeen* in "The Gay Goshawk" (96), *Lunan* and *Lunnon* in "The Earl of Aboyne" (235), and *Lonnon* in "Lord Lovel" (75).

Little distortion results, of course, when the words corrupted by phonetic spelling are as well known as *Edinburgh* and *London.* More frequently however, place names which are corrupted in this manner are less well known. The obscure name *Ochiltree Walls, Ayrshire,* appears in Child variant D of "The Broom of Cowdenknows" (217) as *Ochiltree Warwis,* the last element of which represents the usual north-of-England and Scotch phonetic spelling of the word *walls,* and this in turn is corrupted to the phonetically similar but nonexistent *Youghal Tree Wells,* in a modern Aberdeenshire variant of the ballad.[15] Even London, however, undergoes a curious transformation with a peculiar effect in at least one ballad, "Young Allan" (245). In this instance a perfectly normal combination of ship- and place-names has been corrupted to a meaningless ship-name. In the second stanza of variant A "A' the skippers of bonny Lothain" give praise to various of their possessions, and Young Allan ". . . he reesd his comely cog":

> "I hae as good a ship this day
> As ever sailed our seas,
> Except it be the Burges Black,

> But an the small Cordvine,
> The Comely Cog of Dornisdale;
> We's lay that three bye in time."

The ship with which we are here concerned is the *Burges Black* of line three in the stanza above. That name (with the addition of an *-s*) is retained in variant c, but in variant c another ship's name, *The Black Snake of Leve London*, is added, and this name in turn replaces *The Burges Black* in variant B and becomes the *Black Shater o Leve London* in variant E. Precisely why such a name as the *Black Snake of Leve London* should replace the easily understood *Burges Black* of variant A is difficult to say, for in itself it already exhibits the beginnings of a change which in later versions renders it nearly unrecognizable. The *Leve London*, of course, presents little problem: it is simply the Middle English *lef, leef* in its weak adjectival form *leve*, "dear, pleasant," and the phrase *Leve London* is a ballad commonplace which takes its place in literature alongside the "windy Troy" of the *Iliad*. The other elements of the name, though equally explicable, are, however, less obvious. The word *Snake* appears to be Old English *snacc*, Icelandic *snekkja*, "a fast ship," cognate with Danish *smak* and thus with the Modern English word *smack* of similar meaning. Even in the north, however, the word *snacc* was archaic if not obsolete by the beginning of the seventeenth century, and it is scarcely to be wondered at that the scribes who first took down the ballads found in Buchan's mss., in *Buchan's Ballads of the North of Scotland*, and in the Kinloch mss. (in which variants B, c, and E appear respectively) should have trouble with the word. John Hill Burton, who inscribed variant E of "Young Allan" in the Kinloch mss., apparently had no idea at all of what the word was, and his confusion shows in the manuscript itself, for Professor Child points out that "The writer of E had begun the word with something different from *sh*, but with what I cannot make out." [16] In view of the fact, however, that the central vowel in the Old English word *snacc* would normally become [*e*], it is not particularly remarkable that the confused scribes should transcribe it as the phonetically analogous *snake*. Even allowing for the peculiarities of ship-names, however, snakes to the ballad singers and scribes were not ships, and to the unlearned the words *Leve London* had little or no meaning. As a consequence, the names are phonetically but meaninglessly set down as the "snakes o Leveland den" and "snakes o Levelanden," in variant Bb of the ballad and "black snakes o Levelanden" in cb. One might also point out as a partial psychological justification for such corruption that without too great an extension of fact snakes could be said to live in dens!

In the foregoing pages we have paid particular attention to those corruptions which, although they could conceivably have been typographical in origin, were probably scribal; corruptions, that is, which resulted either from the attempts of a collector to put down on paper things which he did not fully understand or from the perpetuation of errors caused by the ignorance of his informants. In the following pages we shall examine a few examples of errors which must be typographical; corruptions which arose from arbitrary rules of typography, from a printer's error, or from the misinterpretation of the printed or written page.

The arbitrary nature of capitalization and word division leads to the most frequent type of typographical error. By these means proper nouns are created from common nouns and common from proper; nonsense phrases are created from misunderstood words or one word from a misunderstood phrase. Such changes result at best in a severe derangement of meaning and at worst in complete incoherence. Three variants —B, C, D— of "The Clerk's Two Sons O Owsenford" (72) localize the scene of the sons' amours in *Bloomsbury*, *Billsbury*, and *Berwick* respectively, but a fourth simply says:

> They hadna been in fair *Parish*
> A twelvemonth an a day,
> Till the clerk's twa sons o Owsenford
> Wi the mayor's twa daughters lay.
> Child, 72 A

Here, although Professor Child (II, 173) suggests *Paris* as the source of *Parish* in the first line of the stanza quoted above, it seems more likely—particularly in view of the English localization of the other variants—that we have simply the name *Parish* created from the common noun *parish*.

One of the most clear cut examples of this type of typographical error—the corruption of the line "They bigget a bower on yon burnbrae" in "Bessie Bell and Mary Gray" (201) to "They built their home on Yonburn Bay" in a West Virginia variant and to "They built 'em a house on Yonders bay" in a Virginia variant—has already been pointed out in an earlier article as an indication of one type of place-name creation in the ballads.[17] But these examples do not stand alone in balladry. Even in Scotland the word *yonder* appears to be ill understood in late tradition, and Buchan prints what was obviously "Thomas o yonder dale" as "Thomas o Yonderdale"[18] in the ballad so entitled in Child (253).

Just a little less arbitrary than capitalization is word division, and this orthographical problem also has had its effect upon folk literature. If "The Outlaw Murray" (305) be examined, the development of a Selkirkshire place-name into a near meaningless phrase can be traced and shown to be the result of typographical error. Located about five miles northwest of Selkirk and central to the area once haunted, at least according to legend, by James Murray, Laird of Traiquair, lies the village of Penmanscore.[19] This name is variously divided in variants of the ballad, being *Penman's core* in Child variant Aa and *Penman Score* in Child variant Ad. Other variants of "The Outlaw Murray," however, show yet another kind of typographical error: the substitution of one letter for another similar in form. Thus it is that Scott creates the name *Permanscore* by substituting *r* for *n* in the variant which he prints in *The Minstrelsy of the Scottish Border*.[20] There can be little doubt that the meaningless but phonetically acceptable "poor man's score" and "poor man's house" found in Glenriddell's mss.[21] are developments of Scott's spelling. In a similar manner, Conscouthart Green, a place in the Bewcastledale of Cumberland, has been corrupted to *Corscowthart Green* by the same typographical substitution of *r* for *n* in "Hobie Noble" (189), the first form appearing Child variant A, the second in Child variant Ab.

It is not always, of course, that corruptions of any type—oral, scribal, or typographical—have significance in folk literature. The typographical substitution of *r* for *n* in the name *Penmanscore* may be necessary as the first step in creating such a phrase as "poor man's house" in "The Outlaw Murray," but it does not necessarily follow that one corruption leads to another and that sense always shifts to nonsense to new sense.[22] When the corrupted word or phrase is a relatively unimportant one it may suffer only one shift in form and have no further effect upon subsequent transmission. Perhaps the best example of this kind of change is found in the only extant version of "The Earl of Westmoreland" (177). Originally printed in *Percy's Folio*,[23] the ballad lists as one of the Earl of Westmoreland's lieutenants in the rebellion of 1569–70 one Iohn of Carnakie, and this name Professor Child (III, 418) amends, no doubt correctly, to Iohn of Carnabie, on the basis that John Carnaby of Langley was in a list of persons indicted for rebellion, noting also that no reason appears why he should be distinguished either in history or in the ballad. It is apparent here either (1) that Professors Hale and Furnivall misread a *k* for a *b* or (2) that the copyist of the manuscript made the error of misreading *k* for *b*.[24] That the latter hypothesis (or yet a third, that the scribe of Bishop Percy's manuscript perpetuated the error of an earlier manuscript or broadside) be true appears more probable in the light of the reputation which Professors Hale and Furnivall bear for careful scholarship and in view of the corrupt nature of the ballad "The Earl of Westmoreland" as a whole.[25]

In at least one other instance the similarity of the letters *k* and *b* seems to have given chroniclers and broadside printers a deal of trouble and to have had some little effect upon a legend if not upon the individual ballads which form a basis for the legend. In this instance one finds both the substitution of the letter *b* for *k* and an example of typographical metathesis.

With the exception of "Robin Hood and the Valiant Knight" (153), practically all [26] of the ballads of the cycle which deal with Robin Hood's death place it at Kirklees, Yorkshire, an identifiable place and the site of an ancient Cistercian nunnery. The superscription to the epitaph which is appended to "Robin Hood and the Valiant Knight," however, reads as follows:

Robin Hood's Epitaph
Set on his tomb
By the Prioress of Birkslay Monastery, in
Yorkshire.

When discussing this epitaph, Professor Child (III, 103; italics added) points out that:

Grafton, in his Chronicle, 1569, citing "an olde and auncient pamphlet," says: For the sayd Robert Hood, beyng afterwardes troubled with sicknesse, came to a certain nonry in Yorkshire, called *Birklies*, where, desirying to be let blood, he was betrayed and bled to death: edition of 1809, p. 221. So the Harleian MS, No. 1233, article 199, of the middle of the seventeenth century, and not worth citing, but cited by Ritson. According to Stanihurst, in Holinshed's Ireland (p. 28

of ed. of 1808), after Robin Hood had been betrayed at a nunnery in Scotland called *Bricklies*, Little John was fain to flee the realm.

It is obvious, particularly in light of the fact that Kirklees is a known place on the banks of the River Calder in the West Riding of Yorkshire and near the heart of the Robin Hood country, that the *Birklies* of Grafton's Chronicle, the *Birkslay* of "Robin Hood and the Valiant Knight," and the *Bricklies* of Holinshed's *Ireland* represent two evolutionary steps: (1) the substitution of *b* for *k* initially and (2) the metathesis of *i* and *r*. After this last step was accomplished it was then possible for the ballad to be relocalized in the south of Scotland as Holinshed has it despite the conservative force of tradition which normally holds Robin Hood to the Barnesdale-Sherwood area.

In the foregoing pages a few widely-scattered examples of the effect of scribal and typographical error upon oral tradition have been examined. These examples, moreover, have been selected from a relatively restricted and conservative body of folk literature: the English and Scottish popular ballads and a few of their American variants. The selection of material has been made, in other words, from a type of folk literature bound by such conservative forces as meter, tune, and in some cases, rhyme. From this study certain definite conclusions may be drawn: (1) despite theories propounded to the contrary, manuscripts and the printed page occupy a definite place in the communication of folk literature among English speaking peoples; and (2) peculiarities of writing and printing may be introduced into what has hitherto frequently been accepted as purely oral. Further, a hypothesis may be predicated that this kind of error may be expected more and more frequently as the incidence of literacy increases among those people still concerned with our folk literature. Such conclusions are helpful because they may be of aid in indicating the effect of literacy upon the folk and because they may help to indicate the relationship of a given piece of folk literature collected from oral tradition to its written and printed versions.

✳✳✳✳✳✳✳✳✳✳✳✳✳✳✳✳✳✳✳

14

The Scottish Ballads

JOHN SPEIRS

AS we have them in the collections, the Scottish ballads are poems chiefly of the eighteenth century. That they are quite different from other poems of that century may at first occasion surprise, but has its explanation. On the other hand it has been denied (by the primitivists) that they are poems of that century at all. It has been argued that there is no reason to suppose they did not come into being centuries earlier than the century in which they were written down. It has also been observed (that is not difficult) that a good deal of the "material" used is "mediaeval." But a poem and the language it is in are one and the same. Translated it either becomes a new poem or ceases to be a poem at all. It is sufficient therefore to point to the language the ballads are in, which in most cases is at the point of development it was in the eighteenth century. (This is not merely a matter of language but of sensibility. The ballads taken down after the beginnings of the nineteenth century show a distinct modification of sensibility.) Certainly the ballads are traditional. But so also is every poem —in its own degree.

I have isolated the Scottish ballads from the other ballads in Child's collection for the purposes of this consideration. Child includes several: "Judas," "St. Stephen and King Herod," which belong with mediaeval verse. "Robyn and Gandelyn" is fifteenth century, and the finer of the Robin Hood ballads also are rather earlier than the Scottish ballads. The broadsheets that fluttered across the English country from the printing presses of "the town" are more nearly contemporaneous with the Scottish ballads. Scotland seems to have suffered less than England from the broadsheet contagion, being at that time less exposed, though nowadays newspapers, in Scotland as in England, have long since superseded ballads and broadsheets both. They are comparatively few Scottish ballads in Percy's *Reliques*. But it was in Scotland that the collectors of the eighteenth century found their finest poems.

The Scottish ballads and the English ballads are not wholly distinct from each other, but both are distinct from "literary" English verse. The simultaneous existence of two distinct types of verse points to the simultaneous existence of two distinct traditions. But that is no reason for supposing, as has been done, that the oral tradition (represented by the ballads of the collections) and the "literary" tradition were distinct to begin with, since an examination of the ballads themselves, their metre,[1] their conventions, shows them to be not Mediaeval verse certainly, but a development, a "popular"[2] development, from Mediaeval verse. They were the verse which entertained the largely unlettered "people," and they possess in themselves a life distinct and apart both from the "literary" verse they were contemporaneous with and from the Mediaeval verse they are a development from.

The Scottish Ballads therefore are, as every poem is, new and at the same time old. They are late (later, I think, than has been held) in that they belong mostly to the eighteenth century, but late also in that they bear on themselves the mark of a long ancestry. They are stiff with a poetic diction. To illustrate this poetic diction with an exhaustive list of phrases—yellow hair, cherry cheeks, lily-white, rose-red, clay-cauld—would be superfluous; the ballads themselves are the composite illustration of it: any analysis of the ballads is necessarily an analysis of it. Its strength is that it is to a considerable extent a stylization of popular speech. It is "simple": it is "sensuous": and it retains something of the vitality of popular speech. Its most evident limitation as an artistic medium is perhaps its intractability to the expression of subtle shades of perception, its ready formation of simple, and at moments brutally effective, contrasts:

> And clear, clear was her yellow hair
> Whereon the red blood dreeps

not only in colour:

> Shool'd the mools on his yellow hair

When therefore the late eighteenth century began looking for a poetry which should be "simple, sensuous, and passionate," it certainly found such in the ballads. What fascinated the late century were these "natural" qualities and not merely that here was a Poetic Diction different from the prevailing Poetic Diction and therefore "fresh." Bishop Percy in his introduction to his *Reliques* (1765) is still apologetic, but he indicates clearly enough what he, and his contemporaries, supposed were the merits of the ballads.

> In a polished age, like the present, I am sensible that many of these reliques of antiquity will require great allowances to be made for them. Yet have they, for the most part, a pleasing simplicity, and many artless graces, which in the opinion of no mean critics [3] have been thought to compensate for the want of higher beauties, and, if they do not dazzle the imagination, are frequently found to interest the heart.

The description is to a certain extent just. We can all of us recall lines in the ballads which affect us suddenly and sharply (to express it more strongly than the Bishop) with an apparent utmost economy of means. Yet once the stylization of the diction, especially in certain of the Scottish ballads, is perceived the impression is more generally one of "artificiality." It will be sufficient to refer the reader to the finer of the "Twa Sisters" (Binnorie) variations. But the precise degree of conventional richness of one couplet from one ballad,

> The bride cam tripping down the stair
> Wi' the scales o' red gowd on her hair,

(Hind Horn) cannot of course be appreciated unless one remembers the recurrences in other ballads of "brides," ladies who "cam tripping down the stair," "red gowd" and adorned "hair."

This poetic diction is built into a rhetoric—partly by means of repetitions.[4] The "Gil Brenton" (Cospatrick), the "Cruel Brother" and the "Babylon" variations come first to my mind as exemplifying it. What it indicates is the adaptation of speech to something outside itself, to declamation or to song. This also imposes upon it a certain rigidity which arrests any development from it, such as there was in Elizabethan dramatic verse from its earlier rhetorical "simplicity" to its later close-down-to-speech complexity. But what in the ballads is lost in simplification is gained in effectiveness of presentation:

> "What news, what news"? said young Hind Horn:
> "No news, no news," said the old beggar man.
> "No news," said the beggar ,"No news at a',
> But there is a wedding in the king's ha'."

What the repetition does is to increase the expectancy. This is resolved into a surprise. A conversation seems to be reproduced in what seems a hard unyielding medium, but with (as also and more especially in "Lamkin") quite astonishingly effective results. The ballad dialogue is both itself stylized and an integral part of the stylization. "All imaginative art," writes Mr. Yeats (in his remarkable essay *Certain Noble Plays of Japan*), "remains at a distance and this distance once chosen must be firmly held against a pushing world . . . The arts which interest me, while seeming to separate from the world and us a group of figures, images, symbols, enable us to pass for a few moments into a deep of the mind that had hitherto been too subtle for our habitation" seem, in fact, "to recede from us into some more powerful life." The ballads are more than the beginnings of such an art.

When the eighteenth century found the ballads artistically rude and unpolished it may have been simply that the variations are for the most part very fragmentary, so that anything like a completely formed poem in the literary sense is rare. The ballads are sets of variations, fragmentary indeed, but in the extremely conventionalized medium I have spoken of. It is in this sense they are "impersonal" apart altogether from their anonymity as to authorship.

Not that this medium itself remains constant. Even the Scottish Ballads, considered as a group by themselves, break up into lesser groups as soon as one looks at them closely enough. "Hughie the Graeme," "Dick o' the Cow," "Jamie Telfer," "Jock o' the Side," "Kinmont Willie," for example, form a group possessing robust characteristics of its own considerably apart from what I have taken to be the central group. But these lesser groups retain a vital relation with each other and with the whole, which evidences a homogeneous community, in vital contact also with its neighbours but not dependent on imported stuff.

The mere existence of this ballad poetry among the largely unlettered Scottish "people" in the eighteenth century is evidence also of the existence then of a popular taste that there is no equivalent of now among the lettered "people" either in Scotland or in England.[5] The contemporary popular taste as represented by the contemporary popular entertainment (popular fiction, popular films, jazz music) is of a very much lower order. There is now such a gap between it and the literary tradition that it is difficult to know how long the literary tradition itself, deprived of sustenance from beneath, can persist.

But more particular evidence of the quality of popular taste a generation or two ago is provided by a comparison between the variations of any one ballad (such as was recently made by Professor Gerould). Between the eight variations of the two opening lines of the "Unquiet Grave" (which Professor Gerould sets down) there is indeed very little to choose. This is the case also with an astonishingly large proportion of the ballad variations. Whether they were always the result of forgetfulness or not (it is very doubtful) they exhibit an astonishingly high degree of artistic competence to have been so widespread. Whoever was responsible for them could substitute lines as good for the lines which were either forgotten or not. They exhibit in practice a popular taste acquired, quite unconsciously, through long familiarity with ballads. My reason for doubting whether the variations arose simply from the necessity for filling up gaps in memory, rather than from some deeper necessity, may become clear from a comparison between two passages from two variations of the "Cruel Mother":

Child B. As she was going to the church,
      She saw a sweet babe in the porch.

      O sweet babe, and thou were mine,
      I wad cleed thee in the silk so fine.

      O mother dear when I was thine,
      You did na prove to me sae kind.

Child C. She has howked a hole baith deep and wide,
      She has put them in baith side by side.

      She has covered them oer wi a marble stane
      Thinking she would gang maiden hame.

      As she was walking by her father's castle wa,
      She saw twa pretty babes playing at the ba.

      O bonnie babes, gin ye were mine,
      I would dress you up in satin fine.

      O cruel mother, we were thine . . .

These variations are in fact two independent poems. There is here a difference of vision.

This suggests also the nature of what, I think, one learns to look for in the Scottish ballads. When the fragments belonging to the group are set together (not that one supposes they were ever anything else than fragmentary) portions of the outlines of a pattern within that of the conventionalized medium become discernible. What these form the very fragmentary revelation of is a folk mythology. It is, I wish tentatively to suggest, the central thing in the Scottish ballads, from which a complete understanding of them must proceed. It is here (Hugh of Lincoln):

> She's gane into the Jew's garden
> Where the grass grew lang and green:
> She powd an apple red and white
> To wyle the young thing in.

It is also here (The Demon Lover—The Carpenter's Wife):

> I'll show you where the white lilies grow
> On the banks of Italie.

And later in the same poem:

> "O what hills are yon, yon pleasant hills,
> That the sun shines sweetly on?"
> "O yon are the hills of heaven" he said
> "Where you will never win."
>
> "O whaten a mountain is yon," she said
> "All so dreary wi frost and snow?"
> "O yon is the mountain of hell" he said
> "Where you and I will go."

and it is, wizened, here (Alison Gross):

> She's turned me into an ugly worm
> And gard me toddle about the tree.

It is a symbolism which is unmistakable wherever it occurs—the green garden, the apple, the braid, braid road across the lily leven (Thomas the Rhymer) or down by yon sunny fell (Queen of Elflan's Nourice), the rose broken from the tree (Tam Lin), the nut broken from the tree (Hind Etin), the place "at the foot of our Lord's knee" "set about wi gilly-flowers" where women go who die in childbirth (Sweet William's Ghost). I find what corresponds with it in Bunyan whose work is the expression of a folk-mythology which is not merely derivative from the

Authorized Version. But I seem to find the same quality of vision, individualized, in Blake.

It is at this point that it becomes necessary to stress the fundamental difference between the Scottish ballads and the romantic poetry of the nineteenth century (with which work Blake is also, I think, wrongly associated). That poetry took over for its own purposes a quantity of what may be described as the external machinery of the ballads. Its poetic diction is derived, through Coleridge and *La Belle Dame Sans Merci*, almost as much from that of the ballads (chiefly because of their apparent picturesque mediaevalism) as from Spenser and Milton. But this poetic diction is cut off from the vigor—

> She stickit him like a swine

—of the popular speech which the poetic diction of the ballads is to a considerable extent a stylization of. Correspondingly there is nothing in common between the vital, if very fragmentary, vision of the Scottish ballads, and the insubstantial dream of nineteenth century poetry.

The ballad art, like other art, seems "to separate from the world and us a group of figures, images, symbols" and thereby "enables us to pass . . . into a deep of the mind." It is difficult to resist the conclusion that nineteenth century "appreciation" subtly externalized (and sentimentalized) the significance of these "figures, images, symbols," even those which most appealed to it:

> And he saw neither sun nor moon
> But he heard the roaring of the sea.

(Thomas the Rhymer) has a definite significance in its context.

> "Get dancers here to dance" she said.
> "And minstrels for to play
> For here's my young son, Florentine,
> Come here wi me to stay . . ."
>
> For naething coud the companie do,
> Nor naething coud they say
> But they saw a flock o' pretty birds
> That took their bride away.
> (Earl of Mar's Daughter)

There is more than a nursery-tale significance in, for example, the birds—that is to say, in "Cow-me-doo" as well as in the "Twa Corbies"; rather, there is the significance there often is, latent, in a nursery tale which has been a folk tale.

If the symbolism of which I have spoken is kept in mind the other images too assume, in varying degrees, a symbolical value in relation to it. The images of finery, for example, particularly of dress, which are so frequent in the Scottish ballads, are then recognized to possess a symbolical value as profound as in Bunyan ("he that is clad in Silk and Velvet"). That finery is associated with folly, pride and death. It is Vanity.

> Fair Margaret was a rich ladye
>   The king's cousin was she;
> Fair Margaret was a rich ladye
>   As vain as vain could be.
>
> She ward her wealth on the gay cleedin
>   That comes frae yont the sea,
> She spent her time frae morning till night
>   Adorning her fair bodye.
>
> Ae night she sate in her stately ha
>   Kaimin her yellow hair . . .
>   (Proud Lady Margaret)

This religious sense is behind the peculiar satiric element (a fierce exultant derision almost) in the lines:

> O our Scots Nobles were richt laith
>   To weet their cork-heild schoone:
> Bot lang, owre a the play wer playd,
>   Thair hats they swam aboone.
>
> O lang, lang may their ladies sit,
>   Wi thair fans into their hand,
> Or ere they se Sir Patrick Spence
>   Cam sailing to the land.
>
> O lang, lang may the ladies stand
>   Wi thair gold kems in their hair,

Waiting for their ain deir lords,
For they'll se thame na mair.
(from Percy's *Reliques*)

and this religious sense is present also, pityingly and wonderingly, in

But she put on the glistering gold
To shine through Edinburgh town

in its "Marie Hamilton" context—a poem which seems to me charged with this religious sense.

The ballads are concerned, it is true, almost entirely with the circle of the life of the body, with birth, instinctive action, death and the decay of the body. Again, they present on the one hand (as W. P. Ker and others noted) images of a princely grandeur erected out of earth, and on the other hand, its counterpart, the earthiness of death and decay. These images are contrasted and associated, if not explicitly, by their mutual presence. The total effect is thus sombre. It has been customary to speak of the "paganism" of the Scottish ballads. I suppose I mean the same thing but I should prefer to describe them (keeping in mind the symbolism I have spoken of) as, in a profound sense, "religious." [6] They embody, in any case, very fragmentarily indeed, but with startling immediacy, a vision of human life which sprang apparently from the imagination of "the folk."

15

✳✳✳✳✳✳✳✳✳✳✳✳✳✳✳✳✳✳✳✳

Mary Hamilton
and the Anglo-American Ballad
as an Art Form

TRISTRAM P. COFFIN

ANGLO-AMERICAN ballad poems are the texts of ballads, printed without music and judged by the literary standards of Anglo-American culture. These texts, comprising the greatest single art form that oral tradition has produced, are seldom discussed as art by the amateurs and anthropologically-trained researchers who work with them. As a result, most teachers and many scholars think of Anglo-American ballad poetry as something a bit unusual in the realm of human endeavor, something a breed apart from "conscious" arts like drama, concert music, poetry in print. Today, it is frequently assumed that such ballad poetry "just happens" or that the folk, working in communion, have mystically borne what we recognize as great literature. Yet we know better. We know things don't "just happen"; and we know the old "communal theory of ballad composition" to be almost completely wrong. It seems long past high time that the whole subject of the Anglo-American ballad text as art were brought up for review.

MacEdward Leach has characterized all ballads as follows:

> A ballad is story. Of the four elements common to all narrative—action, character, setting, and theme—the ballad emphasizes the first. Setting is casual; theme is often implied; characters are usually types and even when more individual are undeveloped, but action carries the interest. The action is usually highly dramatic, often startling and all the more impressive because it is unrelieved. The ballad practices rigid

economy in relating the action; incidents antecedent to the climax are often omitted, as are explanatory and motivating details. The action is usually of a plot sort and the plot often reduced to the moment of climax; that is, of the unstable situation and the resolution which constitutes plot, the ballad often concentrates on the resolution leaving the listener to supply details and antecedent material.

Almost without exception ballads were sung; often they were accompanied by instrumental music. The tunes are traditional and probably as old as the words, but of the two—story and melody—story is basic.[1]

Leach's definition would be disputed by few folklorists. Add to his points the idea that ballads are individually composed, and are most often fed down to the folk from a somewhat more highly educated stratum of society, and one has a good picture of the ballad as modern scholarship sees it. Ballads, thus, are widely considered to be plotted narratives, rising from relatively trained minds, taken over and fostered by the folk until they become the verses and masterpieces that our collectors uncover.

The word "plotted" is of particular significance. It shall be a main purpose of this paper to suggest that plotting is vestigial, rather than vital, in the make-up of Anglo-American ballads. Unified action is a sign of the trained artist from the time of Homer through the Renaissance to the twentieth century.[2] Such organization of narrative tends to distinguish a man with training in the traditions of Western European literature from the ignorant or primitive. Plotting is honored by the tradition in which the Anglo-American ballad is born, but there is little evidence to support a contention that the folk, in whose oral heritage the ballad lives, care very much at all for unified action. Their myths and their tales lack unified action, except as a vestige. Generally, the folk tend to discard plotting in favor of something one might call "impact" or "emotional core."

Leach, as other writers on the ballad, stresses action as the most essential ingredient. I feel, however, that Anglo-American ballads stress impact over action and retain, in the long run, only enough of the original action or plot unity to hold this core of emotion in some sort of focus. In our ballad, details are kept and discarded to fit the core, and little real attention is paid to plot consistency or structure. Plot is present, but in the background. The emotional core, a part of the musical as well as the textual meaning of the song, is emphasized and cherished.

To understand the process by which an Anglo-American ballad becomes a poem, one must go into the problem of "emotional core" in some detail. It is essential that we understand what our folk consider a ballad to be and how it should be sung. Two things are certain: to our folk a ballad is song, not poetry; for us ballads become poems because certain variants (often by sheer chance) measure up to Western European aesthetic standards.

A ballad survives among our folk because it embodies a basic human reaction to a dramatic situation. This reaction is reinterpreted by each person who renders the ballad. As an emotional core it dominates the artistic act, and melody, setting, character, and plot are used only as means by which to get it across. This core is more important to the singer and the listeners than the details of the action themselves. For while a singer is often scrupulous not to change the version of a song as he sings it, he shows little interest in the consistency or meaning of the details he is not changing. Ballads resemble gossip. They are transmitted like gossip, and their variation comes about in much the way gossip variation occurs.

The thesis presented above accounts for a number of the unique qualities of folk art and, through these qualities, designates the pattern of development that our ballads take over a stretch of time.

1. That many singers actually miss the point of the ballad action may well be because they focus attention on the emotional core of the song rather than on the plot detail. For example, about six years ago I published a paper dealing with an Arkansas version of "The Drowsy Sleeper." [3] My informant considered "The Drowsy Sleeper" to be an incest tale, but the woman who had taught the song to him had considered it a suicide-love story. Although the factual detail was the same (actually all the words were the same) in both texts, my informant had changed the emotional core that these details went to make up.

2. Such focus on the emotional core of a song may also account for the fact that the folk tolerate contradictions and preposterous images in their songs. So lines like "he mounted a roan, she a milk-white steed, whilst himself upon a dapple gray" and "up spoke a pretty little parrot exceeding on a willow tree" [4] survive even from generation to generation.

3. Finally, if we accept the thesis of the "emotional core," the difficulties encountered by all scholars who attempt to define the Anglo-American ballad are accounted for. Every text of every ballad is in a different stage of development and derives from a different artistic environment. The details of the action are never precisely conceived. As a result, there is nothing exact enough about a ballad to define.

As an Anglo-American ballad survives in oral tradition, the details become conventionalized so that songs of the same general type (love songs, ghost songs, etc.) tend to grow more and more alike, to use more and more of the same clichés. As Moore said, "In a way the ballad resembles the proverb: there is nothing left in it which is not acceptable to all who preserve it by repetition. The simple ballads which have served a general public are non-technical in diction, whereas the modern songs of special classes . . . are highly technical. The same levelling process destroys whatever individual character the original poem may have." [5] And (p. 400), "After a painstaking study of the subject, I have yet to find a clear case where a ballad can be shown to have improved as a result of oral transmission, except in the way of becoming more lyrical." Moore's words, along with other things, have led me to believe that the life of an Anglo-American ballad can be charted somewhat like this:

STAGE I. A poem, created by an individual, enters or is retained in oral tradition. This poem has three major parts: an emotional core, details of action, frills of a poetic style that are too "sophisticated" for the folk. At this stage the poem is frequently not for singing and may well be closer to literature than to musical expression. The Frazer broadside of "Sally and Billy" or "The Rich Lady from London" (the song so often cited erroneously as Child 295) offers a relatively modern example:

> 'Tis of a young sailor, from Dover he came,
> He courted pretty Sally, pretty Sally was her name,
> But she was so lofty, and her portion was so high,
> That she on a sailor would scarce cast an eye.
>
> .   .   .   .
>
> "So adieu to my daddy, my mammy, and friends,
> And adieu to the young sailor for he will make no amends.
> Likewise this young sailor he will not pity me,
> Ten thousands times now my folly I see." [6]

So, of course, do any number of other newspaper, almanac, and broadside texts.

STAGE 2. This is the "ballad" stage. The frills of subliterary style have been worn away by oral tradition; some of the action details have been lost. Any so-called "traditional" ballad can serve as an illustration of Stage 2, although in the cases of both "Sally and Billy" and "Geordie" the American texts are close enough to print so that the transition from Stage 1 to Stage 2 is not complete. In fact, a majority of American songs lie in the area between the first two stages and were in the process of evolving toward traditional balladry when hindered by print and the urbanization of the folk. Some songs are born at this mid-point, to be sure. Individuals like Booth Campbell or Sir Walter Scott, who are used to singing or working within the conventions of folk tradition, may compose songs that never pass through Stage 1, that are traditional in language and detail at their birth.[7]

STAGE 3. In this final stage the ballad develops in one of two ways. Either unessential details drop off until lyric emerges, or essential details drop off until only a meaningless jumble, centered about a dramatic core, is left. The so-called "degenerate" ballad (and that is a poor term) is either a lyric or a nonsense song. The Scarborough text of "Geordie" beginning,

> Come bridle me up my milk-white steed.
> The brownie ain't so able, O.
> While I ride down to Charlottetown
> To plead for the life of my Georgie, O.[8]

shows the start of a development toward something like the lyrical "Rantin' Laddie" that is given in toto below:

> Aft hae I played at the cards an' dice
> For the love o' a rantin' laddie, O,
> But noo I maun sit in the ingle neuk
> An' by-lo a bastard babbie O.
>
> Sing hush-a-by, an' hush-a-by,
> An' hush-a-by-lo babbie, O,
> O hush-a-by, an' hush-a-by,
> An' hush-a-by, wee babbie, O.
>
> Sing hush-a-by, an' hush-a-by,
> An' hush-a-by-lo babbie, O,
> O had your tongue, ma ain wee wean,
> An A gae a sook o' the pappie, O.[9]

In much the same way the nonsensical Wisconsin "Sally and Billy" that begins with the meaningless lines,

> There was a ship captain
> That sailed on the sea.
> He called on Miss Betsy;
> Pretty Polly did say
> You go to that sea captain
> And grant me love or ruined I'll be.[10]

has its counterparts in "Bessy Bell" nursery rhymes and the amazing Texas version of Child 84, "Boberick Allen." [11] Both lyric and nonsense stages develop, of course, from forgetting. Yet it is significant to note that it is the detail, not the emotional core, that is forgotten. The emotional core may be varied or modified, but it is the essential ingredient of any one song as long as that song exists.[12]

Ballads in Stage 3 and ballads in the process of moving from Stage 2 to Stage 3 are the only Anglo-American ballads that can meet the requirements of Western European poetry.[13] While it is certainly true that collectors are always finding Anglo-American ballads with complete or nearly complete plot unity, the variants that subordinate plot detail and focus on the emotional impact are the variants that are accepted as art. To become great poetry, our ballads must lose so much of their original style, atmosphere, and detail that they must become lyrics as well.

Which of our ballads will meet the requirements of Western European poetry as they move toward lyric is governed by chance. A balance attained in oral tradition between stress on plot unification and stress on emotional impact gives some texts a magnificent half-lyric, half-narrative effect. Individuals, coming in series, often generations apart, change lines, phrases, and situations to fit their personal fancies and to render what they consider to be the song's emotional core before giving the ballad back to oral tradition. Some of these individuals are untrained geniuses, a few may be trained geniuses like Burns or Scott, most are without artistic talent. The geniuses give us the texts, or parts of texts, that measured by Western European standards are art. Their efforts are communal in the sense that there are usually many "authors" working on the tradition of any one song or version of a song. But it must be remembered that often these geniuses live decades apart, handle the song separately, and store it in an ineffectual oral tradition in between. Oral tradition is an aimless thing. It will stumble into art—but not with any sort of consistency.

The widely anthologized Child A version of "Mary Hamilton" is an example of an Anglo-American ballad poem that has gained artistic acceptance. The plot of the song is quite simple. Mary, Queen of Scots, has four maids-in-waiting, each selected for her virginal name and her beauty. One of the maids, Mary Hamilton as she is called in the ballad, not only flaunts the conventions of society by having an affair with the Queen's husband, but is unfortunate enough to bear a child as fruit of this indiscretion. She attempts to destroy the baby, is caught, tried, and hanged for murder. Characterization and real setting are almost nonexistent, but the emotional core of the ballad is given great emphasis. This core, the tragedy of beauty and youth led astray, the lack of sympathy within the law, the girl's resigned indifference to her lot, are driven home with full force.

1. Word's gane to the kitchen,
        And word's gane to the ha,
    That Marie Hamilton gangs wi bairn
        To the hichest Stewart of a'.

2. He's courted her in the kitchen,
        He's courted her in the ha,
    He's courted her in the laigh cellar,
        And that was warst of a'.

3. She's tyed it in her apron
        And she's thrown it in the sea;
    Says, Sink ye, swim ye, bonny wee babe!
        You'l neer get mair o me.

4. Down then cam the auld queen,
        Goud tassels tying her hair:
    "O Marie, where's the bonny wee babe
        That I heard greet sae sair?"

5. "There was never a babe intill my room,
        As little designs to be;
    It was but a touch o my sair side,
        Come oer my fair bodie."

6. "O Marie, put on your robes o black,
    Or else your robes o brown,
    For ye maun gang wi me the night,
    To see fair Edinbro town."

7. "I winna put on my robes o black,
    Nor yet my robes o brown;
    But I'll put on my robes o white,
    To shine through Edinbro town."

8. When she gaed up the Cannogate,
    She laughd loud laughters three;
    But whan she cam down the Cannogate
    The tear blinded her ee.

9. When she gaed up the Parliament stair,
    The heel cam aff her shee;
    And lang or she cam down again
    She was condemnd to dee.

10. When she cam down the Cannogate,
    The Cannogate sae free,
    Many a ladie lookd oer her window,
    Weeping for this ladie.

11. "Ye need nae weep for me," she says,
    "Ye need nae weep for me;
    For had I not slain mine own sweet babe,
    This death I wadna dee.

12. "Bring me a bottle of wine," she says,
    "The best that eer ye hae,
    That I may drink to my weil-wishers,
    And they may drink to me.

13. "Here's a health to the jolly sailors,
    That sail upon the main;
    Let them never let on to my father and mother
    But what I'm coming hame.

14. "There's a health to the jolly sailors,
    That sail upon the sea;

Let them never let on to my father and mother
That I cam here to dee.

15. "Oh little did my mother think,
      The day she cradled me,
      What lands I was to travel through,
      What death I was to dee.

16. "Oh little did my father think,
      The day he held up me,
      What lands I was to travel through,
      What death I was to dee.

17. "Last night I washd the queen's feet,
      And gently laid her down;
      And a' the thanks I've gotten the nicht
      To be hangd in Edinbro town!

18. "Last nicht there was four Maries,
      The nicht there'l be but three;
      There was Marie Seton, and Marie Beton,
      And Marie Carmichael, and me." [14]

Only the first five of the eighteen stanzas that make up Child A are devoted to the rumors of Mary Hamilton's pregnancy, the courtship by Darnley, the murder of the child, and the Queen's discovery that she has been deceived. This juicy copy could not be dispatched more decorously had Mary of Scotland written the lines herself. The next five stanzas are devoted to the trial and conviction of Mary Hamilton, although again no effort is made to capitalize upon dramatic potentialities. Mary Hamilton, somewhat ironically, decides to dress in white, laughs and cries conventionally before and after the trial, and has her misfortune symbolized by losing the heel to her shoe. If the folk as a whole really cared about plot it is doubtful that the narrative possibilities of these events would be so ignored.

Stanzas 11–18, almost half the text, show what really interested the folk who preserved the Child A variant. Stanzas 11–18 deal with material that reflects the girl's feelings as she stands on the gallows waiting to die. The first ten stanzas have remained in the song only because they bring into focus the last eight. The folk recognize that the emotional situation brought on by the seduction and subsequent murder is the artistically vital part of the ballad.

That these stanzas are primarily cliché stanzas is not of importance. They are admirably suited to the emotional situation at hand. Mary tells the sentimentalists that congregate at every hanging not to weep for her, her death is her own doing. She calls for wine in a burst of braggadocio. Her toast mentions her parents, and her mood changes. Mary becomes sentimental herself, and the ballad draws to its end in four heart-rending stanzas. This is the essence of the story: the beauty and youth of a girl snuffed out by law.

It is true that one can turn the page in Child and read the B text to discover that Mary Hamilton would not work "for wantonness and play" and that Darnley came to the gallows to ask Mary Hamilton to "dine with him." But these details, as the ones in Scott's composite version,[15] do nothing to increase the impact of the emotional core. Nor does it matter that Mary Hamilton was really a girl in the Russian court of Peter the Great and that, besides Seaton and Beaton, Livingston and Fleming were the names of Mary of Scotland's other Maries. A girl is a girl, the law is the law, in any age, in any place.

As an Anglo-American ballad survives in oral tradition more and more of the plot material can be expected to vanish, until only a lyric expressing the emotional core is left. Barry's collection from Maine (see n. 9) includes, page 258, the following variant of "Mary Hamilton":

Yestre'en the queen had four Maries,
　　This nicht she'll hae but three;
There was Mary Beaton, an' Mary Seaton,
　　An' Mary Carmichael an' me.

Last nicht I dressed Queen Mary
　　An' pit on her braw silken goon,
An' a' thanks I've gat this nicht
　　Is tae be hanged in Edinboro toon.

O little did my mither ken,
　　The day she cradled me,
The land I was tae travel in,
　　The death I was tae dee.

They've tied a hanky roon me een,
　　An' they'll no let me see tae dee:

An' they've pit on a robe o' black
  Tae hang on the gallows tree.

Yestre'en the queen had four Maries,
  This nicht she'll hae but three:
There was Mary Beaton, an' Mary Seaton,
  An' Mary Carmichael an' me.

Here is a lyric poem with but the merest suggestion of plot. Only the facts that the girl was one of the Queen's favored maidens and is now about to die remain clear. Yet the emotional core, girlhood and its beauty snuffed out by law, is as clear as it was in Child A.

It is certain that the Maine lyric did not evolve from Child A (or some similar text) merely through the miracles of forgetting and fusing alone. A member of the folk, or some learned poet, framed Mary's lament with the "Beaton and Seaton" stanza. Perhaps this poet, or another, purposefully discarded some of the plot detail as well. These points are relatively unimportant. The basic thing is that "Mary Hamilton" as it is found today is almost always a lyric and that the tendency to preserve the core and not the plot of the song is typical.

The tendency is also typical of the American song "Charles Guiteau"—an example of mediocre poetry. Here the murderer of James A. Garfield waits for his death with the "little did my mither ken" cliché on his lips. The lines are just as adequate for a nineteenth century assassin as they are for a medieval flirt, and the folk have sloughed nearly all the plot detail included in the original subliterary text; but "Charles Guiteau," unlike "Mary Hamilton," never passed through the hands of a genius or series of geniuses who could lift it above sentimental verse.

In the hands of A. E. Housman, the "Mary Hamilton" situation was touched by a great poet. "The Culprit," the poem that opens with the lines "The night my father got me / His mind was not on me," [16] tells of the musings of a man about to be hung. It is in reality a restatement of the emotions Mary Hamilton expressed in stanzas 11–18 in the Child A text. Why the youth is on the gallows, how he got there, are too clinical for Housman's poetic purpose. Like the folk singer who shaped "Mary Hamilton" and even "Charles Guiteau," Housman did not clutter his lyric with action detail.

Beyond the observations made on the Child A "Mary Hamilton"

lie similar observations that can be made on the Scott "Twa Corbies," the Percy "Sir Patrick Spens," the Percy "Edward," the Mackie-Macmath "Lord Randal," and the other most widely anthologized of our ballads.[17] All of them are basically lyrics. In each case there is a full plot, now lost forever, that the folk have seen fit to discard. A realization of the importance of the "emotional core" to the folk is essential to a sensitive evaluation of Anglo-American ballad poems. The teacher, the critic, the poet, even the researcher, must know that in certain ballad variants there is to be found a fine blend of plot residue and universal emotion that produced priceless offspring from mediocre stock. An Anglo-American ballad may look like narrative. At its birth it may be narrative. But its whole life proceeds as a denial of its origin.

Notes

1. P. 146.
2. *PMLA*, XIV (1906), 799.
3. *Modern Philology*, I (1903–4), 378.
4. The second edition is unimportant. Four new texts were added to it, "Brave Earl Brand and the King of England's Daughter" which merited only a footnote in the third edition. "St. Stephen and Herod" (22) was retained for the third edition; while "Gifts from over the Sea" and "The Hawthorne Tree" were discarded.
5. These classes are intended to be convenient and suggestive rather than rigid and mutually exclusive since a text might often fall into two or more groups. A text might be lyric and at the same time be the victim of a modern editor. There might easily be debate about the assignment of any ballad to its special group, but the transfer of one or another text to a different group does not affect the general conclusion.
6. *Modern Philology*, I, 378 n.
7. *Johnson's Cyclopedia*, I (1895), 464.
8. *Modern Philology*, I, 378.
9. *PMLA*, XIV, 799.
10. *Poetic Origins and the Ballad* (New York, 1921).
11. *PMLA*, XXIII (1908), 141 f.
12. See above, Professor Child's comments on the Buchan texts. Concerning "Young Ronald" (304) he remarks: "In this and not a few other cases I have suppressed disgust, and admitted an actually worthless and a manifestly . . . at least in part . . . spurious ballad, because of a remote possibility that it might contain relics or be a debased representative of something better. Such was the advice of my lamented friend, Grundtvig, in more instances than those in which I have brought myself to defer to his judgment." Of "Outlaw Murray" (305): "That it was not originally intended to insert 'The Outlaw Murray' in this collection will be apparent from the position it occupies. I am convinced that it did not begin its existence as a popular ballad, and I am not convinced that (as Scott asserts) 'it had been for ages a popular song in Selkirkshire'. But the 'song' gained a place in oral tradition, as we see from b, c, and I prefer to err by including rather than excluding." He also says of it, "I cannot assent to the praise bestowed by Scott on 'The Outlaw Murray'. The story lacks point, and the style is affected—not that of the unconscious poet of the real *traditional* ballad." Of the "Crafty

Farmer" (283): "This very ordinary ballad has enjoyed great popularity, and is given for that reason and as a specimen of its class."

13. For example: "Judas" (23), "Brown Robins' Confession" (57), "Edward" (13), "Earl Brand" (7), "Young Beichan" (53), "Walter Lesley" (296), "The Gray Cock" (248).

14. *PMLA*, XXIII, 141 f.

15. *Poetic Origins and the Ballad*, pp. 27, 41, 88, 107, 171.

16. The fatal attraction of the discussion of origins as a substitute for critical analysis of the problems of definition is illustrated by Mr. Arthur Kyle Davis' introduction to the *Traditional Ballads of Virginia* (Cambridge, Mass., 1929). The editor devotes a scant two pages to the matter of definition and is thereby launched upon a five page discussion of the theory of origins. A still more marked disproportion appears in Hustvedt's *Ballad Books and Ballad Men* (Cambridge, Mass., 1930) which devotes two pages to definition and sixteen to a review of the theories of origins.

17. Mr. Kittredge in 1904 says in the introduction to the one-volume edition (p. xiii): "Professor Child's great collection . . . in five volumes . . . comprises the whole extant mass of this material. . . . A few variants of this or that ballad have come to light since the publication of this admirable work, but no additional ballads have been discovered." Professor Ker in his lecture "On the History of the Ballads" says: "The English [ballads] are all together in Child's five volumes . . ." Professor Reed Smith says (*South Carolina Ballads*, Cambridge, Mass., 1928, p. 65): "The surviving ballads are 305 in number and are known to enthusiasts almost as familiarly by their numbers in Child as by their titles . . . [Child's collection] is the authoritative resting-place of what has survived of the splendid body of English and Scottish ballads." One or two other ballads have made a plea for entrance to the closed ranks, notably "The Bitter Withy," whose cause has been supported by Professor Gerould (*PMLA*, XXIII, 141–67). The same advocate has urged the claims for "A Ballad of the Twelfth Day," *MLR*, VIII (1913), 65 f. and IX (1914), 235–36. But even Professor Gerould prefaces his arguments with: "From the completion of Professor Child's magnificent work up to the present no ballad has been discovered which would merit insertion under a new title in that corpus. Variants of ballads already known continue to be unearthed with gratifying frequency, but so well did the great collector glean the field that it can seldom fall to the lot of any follower to bring to light a new specimen." Greig insists (*Last Leaves of Traditional Ballads and Ballad Airs*, Aberdeen, 1925, p. xxxi): "Child had all of the English and Scottish Traditional Ballads (305) except 'Young Betrice'" which "may possibly be a version of 'Hugh Spencer's Feats in France'."

18. *PMLA*, XLVI (1929), 629.

19. That there may be some contemporary chafing under the restraint imposed in the canon of the Child ballads is attested by the foreword to Barry, Eckstrom and Smyth's *British Ballads from Maine* (New Haven, 1929) wherein the editors point out (p. xviii) that "in some respects it has been impossible to be bound by Professor Child." Professor Davis also says (*Traditional Ballads of Virginia*, p. 11), "The editor is not inclined to draw too hard and fast a distinction between the Child ballads and all other ballads."

THE BALLAD AND COMMUNAL POETRY

1. There is a fine modern ring in the famous article (*Heidelberger Jahrbucher*, 1815, reprinted in Schlegel's *Werke*, XII, 383 ff.), a crisp finality of rejection. "Was man an Zeitaltern und Völkern rühmt, löset sich immer bei näherer Betrachtung in die Eigenschaften und Handlungen einzelner Menschen auf" (p. 385). Then follows the famous allegory of the tower and the architect. Later (pp. 390 ff.) the modern theory of constant borrowing as main factor in the spread of popular tales, and of the love of entertainment as their chief cause, is clearly anticipated. W. Grimm's answer (*Aldeutsche Blätter*, III, 370 f.) denies Schlegel's assertions, but for lack of space gives no argument.

2. To the regret of scholars everywhere, Professor Child has left nothing on the subject of ballad origins which he wished to be quoted or regarded.

3. Mr. Joseph Jacobs, in a cheery paper which he wrote "as a stopgap" for *Folk-Lore*, June, 1893 (IV, 2, 233 ff.), says that there is no such thing as the folk behind what one calls folk tales, folklore, popular ballads. "Artistry is individual. . . . The folk is simply a name for our ignorance," and is not even responsible for custom. He would break down all barriers between folklore and literature, and declares that in the music hall will be found "the *Volkslieder* of today." During the International Folk-Lore Congress of 1891 (see *Proceedings*, p. 64), Mr. Newell pleaded for his theory that folk tales are a degenerate form, amid a low civilization of something which was composed amid a high civilization.

During the same congress Mr. Jacobs solved the particular problem by remarking (p. 86) that Scotch ballads "lack initials at the end." Mr. J. F. Campbell, in his delightful *Popular Tales of the West Highlands* (new ed., IV, 114, 118), understands by the word "ballad . . . a bit of popular history, or a popular tale or romance, turned into verse, which will fit some popular air," and makes the sequence of origins begin with tradition, follow with a tale, and so into a popular ballad. He concedes "the stamp of originality and the traces of many minds." In another place (1, xxxiv) he seems to give precedence to singing, but he is evidently on the artist's side. Mr. Jacobs, again, in a well-known passage (*English Fairy Tales*, p. 240), thinks that verse and prose began together; the *cante-fable* "is probably the protoplasm out of which both ballad and folk-tale have been differentiated." I prefer to think (this is Campbell's unwitting concession) that "the older the narrator is, the less educated, and the farther removed from the rest of the world, the more his stories are garnished with" rhythmic passages, originally "a bardic composition," and while the original raconteur may have been a bit of an artist in verse as well, all this cannot affect the ballad with its communal elements of refrain, dance, and improvisation. Further material on this subject may be found in the Introduction to my *Old English Ballads*, Boston, 1894.

4. "Zur Volksdichtung," in *Zeitschr. f. Völkerpsychologie*, XI, 30.

5. Lachmann's letter to Lehrs, quoted by Friedländer in his *Homerische Kritik von Wolf bis Grote*, Berlin, 1853, p. viii. Steinthal's comments (*Z. f. V.*, VII, 31 ff.) are not at all clear. Lachmann simply opposes this *gemeinsames dichten* to the act of the single poet, while Mr. Jacobs relies on "some bucolic wit"— that is, an individual poet, however humble—for all poetry that has been attributed to "the folk."

6. See a sketch of the new science of poetics as it should be, by Eugen Wolff, "Vorstudien zur Poetik," in *Zeitschr. f. vergleich. Literatur*, VI (1893), 423 ff.

7. See Strong's trans., pp. xxiv, xxxvi ff., xliii ff., and the whole chapter on "Original Creation."

8. The straightforward assertion is slightly damaged later by a concession (p. xlv) that "in all the psychical processes there is very little voluntary effort and consciousness, and very little individuality displays itself."

9. *Grundriss d. germ. Philol.*, i, 73, 231.

10. *Die Sprache als Kunst*, 2. Aufg., i, 246 ff. "Sprache nimmt ihren Ausgangspunkt von den Individuen." So (I, 30) the art of speech comes "aus Einzelbestrebungen"; and see I, 124. It is a dangerous concession, however, when Gerber speaks (I, 131) of "die Entwickelung des Menschen von der Natursprache, in welcher ein Minimum des Ich sich bethätigt, bis zur Sprache der Kunst, welche den Menschen wesentlich ausspricht," and concedes (I, 309) that "die Kunstthätigkeit welche sie [i.e., "Sprachkunstwerke"] schuf, keine bewusste war." Take away individuality and conscious art, and spontaneous or communal art seems no wild hypothesis.

11. *Les Lois de l'Imitation*, Paris, 1890. See pp. 3, 16, 30, 32, 230 ff., 265, for remarks which bear upon the present subject.

12. "Un sauvage de genie . . . a donné lieu, dans une famille unique, aux premières manifestations linguistiques. De cette famille comme d'un centre, l'exemple . . ." (p. 279); and in the same spirit (p. 48): "A l'origine un anthropoïde a imaginé . . . les rudiments d'un langage." All this is in the early eighteenth-century strain; for an antidote, see Renan, *De l'Origine du Langage*, p. 77, and his query (p. 92): "Qui oserait dire que les facultes humaines sont des inventions libres de l'homme? Or, inventer un langage eut été aussi impossible que d'inventer une faculté."

13. Tarde, p. 74, with reference to views of Darwin and Romanes.

14. See *Popular Science Monthly*, May, 1895, pp. 34 ff., for Mr. Spencer's sane account of origins.

15. *Essai Comparatif sur l'Origine et l' Histoire des Rythmes*, Paris, 1889. Another radical in this subject is Dr. Ernst Meurmann, in Wundt's *Philosophische Studien*, X (1894), 249–322, 393–440, whose praiseworthy effort to reorganize the science of rhythms on the basis of psycho-physics is somewhat marred by his contempt for earlier investigators. The future, however, seems to him big with promise.

16. *Faithful Shepherdess*, "To the Reader."

17. *Essai*, pp. 10, 13, 15.

18. *Essai*, p. 25.

19. This merry process of poetizing the world over, without the investment of any home capital, has some resemblance to the device known among brokers as "kiting cheques."

20. *Essai*, pp. 102, 104. I cannot quite understand the praise given to this essay by a reviewer in the *American Journal of Philology*, vol. XI.

21. *Essai*, p. 79. Of course, as every one admits, the artist in dancing was early on the scene; dances were often (and are often now among our own Indians) in-

tricate enough, and had to be taught, explained, conducted. See Bastian, "Masken und Maskereien," in *Zeitschr. f. Völkerpsych.*, XIV, 347. But in spite of M. Kawczynski, we are sure that there was and is spontaneous dancing.

22. "L'absence de toute reflexion, la spontaneite . . . doit etre rappelee toutes les fois qu'il s'agit des oeuvres primitives de l'humanite."—*De l'Origine du Langage*, pp. 21 ff.

23. *Poetics*, trans. S. H. Butcher, London, 1895, pp. 15 ff.

24. "A wild religious excitement," says Butcher in a note, p. 252, "a bacchic ecstasy. This aimless ecstasy was brought under artistic law."

25. An important element in the question. See for evidence my *Old English Ballads*, pp. xc ff.; Bielschowsky, *Geschichte d. deutschen Dorfpoesie im 13ten Jhdt.*, *passim*; J. F. Campbell, *Pop. Tales*, 21, xxxvii and IV, 164 ff., with his reference to the Nialssaga ballad, "composed and sung at a meeting of neighbors."

26. *Besonnenheit; begeisterung.* See *Sprache als Kunst*, I, 32.

27. *Ibid.*, I, 77.

28. Cicero's tribute, *Pro Arch.*, VIII, is distinctly nobler than Gerber's reasoning would allow; but it is communal improvisation, after all, with which we are concerned—the verse which Aristotle rightly denied to art and conceded to "instinct" and nature. Schopenhauer, in his interesting discussion of poetry (*Welt als Wille u. Vorstellung*, I, & 51), treats even artistic lyric as a kind of improvisation, and couples Goethe's best lyric with a folk song from the *Wunderhorn*. All critics, it seems to me, fail to fix their attention on those elements and conditions of the ballad for which evidence is so plentiful. Hence even Steinthal fails in his effort to show the *dichtender Volksgeist* at work, by tracing one of Uhland's ballads in its progress among the people.

29. J. Darmesteter and others have protested against this word, but races are not necessarily connected by common descent. The "historic race" is successfully defined and defended by G. Le Bon, *L'Évolution des Peuples*, Paris, 1894.

30. Defending the *Gasammtgeist*, and entitled "Ueber Ziele und Wege der Völkerpsychologie," *Philosophische Studien*, IV (1888), 1 ff. See particularly pp. 11 ff. and p. 17, where Wundt concedes that "die Volksseele is an sich ein ebenso berechtigter, ja nothwendiger Gegenstand psychologischer Untersuchung wie die individuelle Seele."

31. "All felt, thought, and acted in concert. Everything leads us to believe that at the outset collectivism was at its maximum and individualism at its minimum." —Reclus, *Primitive Folk*, p. 57.

32. See his *Psychologie des Foules*, pp. 12, 15.

33. Material such as I have collected in proof of this assertation—all evidence, in fact, drawn from the customs of savages and inferior races—is too cumbrous to be inserted here, and needs, in addition, so many allowances, balances, comments, as to deserve separate treatment. The reader may turn the pages of Spencer's unfinished *Descriptive Sociology* and find plenty of raw material. See note i, p. 49.

34. Folk poetry was a survival of prehistoric gregarious or communal song, the verse of the horde; ballads are a crossed and disguised survival of folk poetry.

35. Paul, *Principles*, 128.

36. See R. M. Meyer on the Refrain, *Zeitschr. f. vgl. Lit.*, I, 34 ff.

37. Paul's *Grundriss*, II, i, 512 ff., and in ten Brink's *Beowulf* (*Quellen u. Forschungen*, LXII), p. 105 ff.

38. In *Mind*, XVI (1891), 498–506. I have to thank Prof. F. H. Giddings for reference to this article.

39. On the decrease of individual divergences as one retraces history, see Le Bon, *L'Évolution des Peuples*, pp. 37 ff. "Contrairement à nos rêves égalitaires, le résultat de la civilisation moderne n'est pas de rendre les hommes de plus en plus égaux, mais, au contraire, de plus en plus différents." On p. 43 this is proved from physiology (of the skull); see also p. 167. Even Tarde (work quoted, p. 230) admits communal spontaneity—in a faltering fashion, one must confess—and mutters something about "hypnotized" crowds, "suggestion," *electrisation psychologique*, and what not. See also the president's address of Mr. Andrew Lang at the International Folk-lore Congress, 1891. Sir Henry Maine and Mr. Herbert Spencer agree in this matter: see Spencer, *Sociology* (3d ed.), I, 702; II, 289, 311: "organisms which, when adult, appear to have scarcely anything in common, were in their first stages very similar; . . . all organisms start with a common structure." Further, see Giddings, *Sociology*, p. 262. On the special evolution of the artistic dancer, musician, poet, see Spencer, *Pop. Sci. Mo.*, 1895, pp. 364 ff., 433 ff., especially the quotation from Grote, p. 368. But Mr. Spencer fails even here to recognize the importance of the chorus. More satisfactory for our purposes is his "Origin and Function of Music," in *Illustrations of Universal Progress*, New York, 1867, pp. 223 ff. See pp. 224, 232.

40. "Das charakteristische Merkmal der Volkspoesie," *Zeitschr. f. Völkerpsych.*, XIX (1889), 115 ff.

41. *Ibid.*, p. 120.

42. Germs of artistry, assertions of the individual, but without real control of the mass, nobody call in question.

43. There is a very valuable paper by Krohn on "La Chanson Populaire en Finlande," in *Proceedings*, Int. Folk-Lore Cong., 1891, pp. 134 ff. In modern songs of the people Krohn notes this invasion of thought: "La poésie s'est réfugiée dans la pensée, mais elle n'a pu se maintenir intacte de trivialité." Again, "La poésie lyrique est remplacée par la musique lyrique"—communal poetry, in other words, going to pieces.

44. Gerber (L, 50) calls poetry "die Kunst des Gedankens."

45. *Welt als Wille u. Vorst.*, II, 489.

46. *Origin and Function of Music*, p. 232. One is tempted to tamper a little with Goethe's (*Dauer im Wechsel*)

> Danke dass die Gunst der Musen
> Unvergangliches verheisst:
> Den Gehalt in deinem Busen
> Und die Form in deinem Geist

and to search for that muse who once presided over communal emotions and wrote *pandēmos* after her proper name.

BALLAD AND DANCE

1. *Servant*. O master, if you did not but hear the pedler at the door, you would never dance again after a tabor and pipe; no, the bagpipe could not move you; he sings several tunes faster than you'll tell money; he utters them as he had eaten ballads . . .

Winter's Tale, III, sc. 3.

2. F. B. Gummere, *The Popular Ballad* (Boston, 1907), p. 49.

3. See article by Miss Pound (*Mod. Lang. Notes*, XXXIV, 162–65) in which the validity of this instance is brought into question.

4. A. Olrik, *Danske Folkeviser i Udvalg* (3d ed., Copenhagen, 1913), p. 20.

5. *Ibid.*, p. 88.

6. Hjalmar Thuren, *Folkesangen paa Foerøerne* (København, 1908), p. 226.

7. Hulda Garborg, *Songdansen i Nordlandi* (Christiania, 1913).

8. Chambers, quoted by Gummere, *Popular Ballad*, p. 107.

9. *Ibid.*, p. 166.

10. *Ibid.*, p. 164.

11. *Lied und Epos* (Dortmund, 1905), p. 4.

12. *Danmark's Heltedigtning* (Copenhagen, 1903), pp. 85–86.

INTERDEPENDENCE OF TUNES AND TEXTS

1. For the tune in question and further discussion of it, see *California Folklore Quarterly*, I (1942), 188–90.

2. Raine, *Land of Saddle Bags* (1924), p. 118.

3. Archer Taylor, *"Edward" and "Sven i Rosengård"* (1931), especially pp. 26 and 38. See also my independent argument to the same effect in *Southern Folklore Quarterly*, IV (1940), 1–13, 159–61.

4. L. C. Wimberly, *Folklore in English and Scottish Popular Ballads* (1928), p. 192.

5. A. Williams, *Folk Songs of the Upper Thames* (1923), p. 118.

6. Durfey, *Pills to Purge Melancholy* (1719), III, 293–94. A third form of the tune, with other titles, is in Playford, *The Dancing Master*, 1650 (reprint, 1933), p. 421; this was reprinted, with grossly unjustifiable majorization of a Dorian tune, by William Chappel (n.d.), I, 274.

THE PRINCIPAL MELODIC FAMILIES

1. In the *Journal of the Folk Song Society* (hereinafter called *JFSS*), II (1906), 261, Miss Anne G. Gilchrist notes that Neil Gow and Sons, in publishing the second part of their *Repository of Original Scotch Tunes*, stated that they had never heard *"Two Professional Musicians* who play the same notes of *any* tune"—hence, they propose a "standard" setting of each tune in their publication. Miss Gilchrist remarks that the statement "points to a large number of then existent variants of the best known tunes, in actual performance."

2. This is implied throughout the preface to his rare *A Collection of Highland Vocal Airs* (c. 1784), and definitely stated on page 4 of that valuable dissertation.

3. Throughout his well-known *Popular Music of the Olden Time* (1855–59), Chappell discusses his material as composed of individual airs, and points out occasionally the occurrences of what look like variant forms of some of them.

4. See, for instance, the notes at the foot of page 92 of the second volume of his *Albyn's Anthology* (1818); and again, the note, p. 96 of the same volume, where he speaks of variant manifestations as striking examples of "the commutability of our National Melodies, without any violence to their original beauty."

5. See his *Airs and Melodies Peculiar to the Highlands of Scotland and the Isles* (1815), p. 3, where he falls afoul of McDonald for what he thinks is bad notation of certain widespread tunes; also pp. 105, 106 (where he again accuses McDonald of "murdering" tunes), note to No. 7; p. 107, note to No. 31; etc. Fraser is apparently obsessed by the idea of the need for a "standard" version, as were the Gows: cf. his note to No. 19 (p. 107), and to Nos. 70 (p. 110), 85 (p. 111), and 150 (p. 115), where Fraser gives an air which he has treated traditionally himself. He says that this air was "very imperfect, but constantly dwelt upon his mind until modelled into its present shape." Other notes testify to his recognition of variant forms of certain tunes.

6. See his introduction to *The Popular Songs and Melodies of Scotland*, Balmoral Edition (London & Glasgow, 1908), p. viii; and *passim* in his notes to the several melodies throughout the work.

7. Of course, the whole of John Glen's *Early Scottish Melodies* (Edinburgh, 1900) is written from the point of view that distinct individual airs are found in several variant forms; the writer gives a number of comparative tables of these forms in the course of his valuable notes on the earliest Scots melodies and those in the *Scots Musical Museum.*

8. Petrie gives the most explicit statement of his view that tunes may often be found in quite diverse forms in the introduction to his *Ancient Music of Ireland;* see this introduction reprinted in C. V. Stanford's *Complete Petrie Collection of Ancient Irish Music* (London: Boosey & Co., cop. 1902), p. x.

9. Dr. Joyce has made particularly valuable observations (supported by examples) of how tunes vary in tradition in his *Ancient Irish Music* (Dublin: M. H. Gill; London: Longmans, Green & Co., 1872, or re-issue of 1912). See especially his notes to No. 21 in that volume. Joyce's *Old Irish Folk Music and Songs* (London: Longmans, Green & Co., 1909) contains notices of the same sort.

10. According to Alexander Keith, his editor, in *Last Leaves of Traditional Ballads and Ballad Airs* (Aberdeen: The Buchan Club, 1925), pp. xli–xliii, Greig thought that the total number of folk-song airs in the northeast of Scotland was under 300. Keith concurs, and in the pages just cited, mentions the frequent occurrence of an air to different pieces and in many variant forms.

11. See his *Handbook of Irish Music* (posthumous; London: Longmans, Green & Co., 1928), pp. 190, 191, especially. On page 192 Father Henebry makes what looks like an exceedingly daring statement. Commenting on the "ballad" airs, he says "They are all four-strain, or ABBA tunes . . . and appear to have . . . a common ground scheme . . . which is always recognizable through an infinity of

changes. The early prototype from which they are all undoubtedly descended has been the most prolific tune in Irish music." In the course of the present article I shall try to show why these words cannot be accepted in their entirety for British folk-tune versions.

12. See especially his *English Folk-Song: Some Conclusions* (London: Novello & Co., 1907), p. 122.

13. See P. W. Joyce, *Old Irish Folk Music and Songs,* pp. ix, x.

14. Bunting's assertions regarding tune-variation are quoted at length, and criticized, by J. F. Graham and by Petrie, in the introductions referred to in notes 6 and 8.

15. So also says Petrie, in effect, on page x of the introduction referred to in note 8.

16. Nothing could exceed the justice of Keith's remarks in the work cited in note 10, above. Barry's penetrating study of many tune-versions is apparent in all his works, and shows with particular clearness in his *British Ballads from Maine,* with F. H. Eckstorm and M. Smyth (New Haven: Yale University Press, 1929) and in the volumes of the *Bulletin of the Folk-Song Society of the Northeast* (Cambridge, Mass.: Powell Printing Co., 1930–37), to which he was the major contributor of critical and historical notes.

17. Keith, *op. cit.,* p. xlii, criticizes C. J. Sharp's statement that the singer is "more or less unconscious of his melody" and cites instances of singers' using tunes as aids to recalling words, and singing more than one tune to a single song. Sharp, however, speaks of finding singers in the American Appalachian area who could "mentally separate the tune from the text." See C. J. Sharp, *English Folk Songs from the Southern Appalachians,* ed. Maud Karpeles (London: Oxford University Press, 1932), I, xxvii. My own observation of folk singers' practices is expressed exactly in the words to which this note appends.

18. Sharp (*English Folk-Songs: Some Conclusions,* pp. 112–14) regards the early notations of folk tunes as worthless. They were doubtless inaccurate as regards correct notation of modal features; but that defect is not necessarily a hindrance to melodic identification, since, as Barry justly observes, "Nothing in folk music is more evanescent than modality . . ." (*Southern Folklore Quarterly,* I, 1937, p. 39).

19. For other short discussions of these manifestations of tunes in oral tradition see my brief papers "Aspects of Melodic Kinship and Variation in British-American Folk-Tunes," *Papers Read at the International Congress of Musicology,* 1939 (New York: Music Educators' National Conference, for the American Musicological Society, cop. 1944), pp. 122–29; and "Ballad Tunes and the Hustvedt Indexing Method," *JAF,* LV (1942), 248–54.

20. W. J. Entwistle, *European Balladry* (Oxford: Clarendon Press, 1939), p. 27. Motherwell speaks of textual formulae as "certain common-places which seem an integrant portion of the original mechanism of all our ancient ballads." See his *Minstrelsy Ancient and Modern,* New Edition (Paisley, 1873), p. v. In like manner, the musical formulae may be regarded as "integrant portions of the mechanism" of our tunes—but whether of these tunes' *original* mechanism or not is impossible to tell.

21. In this way alone can I account for the strange observations on page 58 of J. W. Hendren's otherwise valuable *Study of Ballad Rhythm with Special Reference to Ballad Music* (Princeton: Princeton University Press, 1936). The remarks in question are: "Tunes, we may summarize, do not generally survive long distances. We find locally related groups, but no truly *national* tunes. Very few melodies are recorded in this country which have also been recorded in England or Scotland." It is safe to say that the truth is better expressed by statements precisely the opposite of these; except, of course, that we do, also, find locally related groups.

22. See the editorial notes in *JFSS, passim.* I may perhaps be excused from giving specific examples from that journal for the reason that the editors' references are to items of collectanea under local titles, and would be incomprehensible without long and detailed explanation. However, a thoroughly representative example of the sort of editorial note under discussion may be drawn from the pages of the *Journal of the Welsh Folk Song Society*, in which the same vagueness may be found. In that journal, Vol. I, Pt. ii (1910), pp. 85, 86 are notes about tune No. 13, to "White Rose of Summer." Miss Broadwood, on page 85, says "This and No. 15 are very Danish in type." On page 86, however, Frank Kidson asserts that the same tune "strongly suggests the Gaelic type of melody"—as if there were actually known to be only one type so called. The tune in question (along with Nos. 14 and 15 following it) is in reality a rhythmically recast version of the (?Irish) air of "The Boyne Water," which is certainly one of the best-known tunes in Anglo-American tradition.

23. Professor Thelma James demonstrates the truth of this latter statement in her article "The English and Scottish Ballads of Francis James Child," *JAF*, XLVI (1933), 51–68. See especially pp. 56–59.

24. Béla Bartók, *Hungarian Folk Music*, transl. M. D. Calvocoressi (London: Oxford University Press, 1931), pp. 8, 36. Compare Bartók's statements with those of Fr. Henebry, quoted in note 11.

25. The title of Wilhelm Tappert's curious book *Wandernde Melodien* (2nd ed.; Leipzig, 1890) is a misnomer. The work should rather be called "Wandernde Motive" or "Wandernde melodische Bruchstücke," for nearly all its entries are mere fragments; there are few complete melodies or organized tunes in it. Tappert's original contention, in attempting to show the "allmählige Entwicklung" of the folk tunes (a sort of evolutionary theory attaching to the development of popular melody), was correct: that the tunes were not spontaneous creations of a people, starting from nothing, independent of outside influence, and forming under the stimulus of moving circumstances or the fire of genius—but were groupings and re-groupings of melodic formulae common to a widespread musical culture over perhaps a long period time. Where his theory falls down, however, is in his contention that these formulae, since they are found in the works of the "masters" as well as in folk airs, were all taken directly by the folk from the works of these masters. His lists of variant strains (which are simply strains or motifs, not "melodies") are sometimes partly from anonymous art-compositions. And it must be pointed out that the tracing of such a motif through many pieces of music over perhaps several centuries of time is not discovering the origin of any piece of music containing

that motif; nor is it indicating the source of that motif itself—in the works of the "masters" or anywhere else. These strains are, in fact, just what Tappert himself calls one of them: "herrenloses Gut" (p. 62). And in his earnest contentions that "the folk cannot compose—it merely selects," Tappert goes to some pains to show that members of the folk can *recompose* ("Die Umbildung hat keine Ende," etc., p. 6); that they can use, choose, vary, annex, accommodate, the musical material (p. 38). The distinction between melodic selection and rearrangement on the part of the folk singer and melodic selection and rearrangement on the part of the artistic (or formally trained) composer seems to be clear to him; but it is not so to me. I prefer to believe with Joseph Bédier that "recréer et créer sont termes exactement synonymes" (*Les Légendes Épiques* [3rd ed.; Paris: Champion, 1929], III, 447).

26. Some tentative listings of formulae in an effort to indicate features of national melodic style may be seen in C. J. Sharp's *English Folk-Song: Some Conclusions*, pp. 83–86. Compare also Chappell, *Popular Music of the Olden Time*, II, 792–94, and Chappell, *National English Airs* (1840), II, 185, 186.

27. See the modal table provided by Miss Gilchrist to classify her Highland Gaelic tunes, *JFSS*, IV (1910), facing page 152; and the modification of it used by C. J. Sharp in his *English Folk Songs from the Southern Appalachians*, I, xxxii.

28. *English Folk-Song: Some Conclusions*, p. 26.

29. For a discussion, see Annabel Morris Buchanan, "Modal and Melodic Structure in Anglo-American Folk Music. A Neutral Mode," in *Papers Read on the International Congress of Musicology*, 1939, pp. 84–111.

30. What Barry calls the "law of anticipatory iteration" seems to be an aspect of this type of variation (see *Bulletin of the Folk-Song Society of the Northeast*, No. 12 [1937], p. 3, col. 1). However, it seems that the repetition is not always anticipatory—it could sometimes even be called "reminiscent"; hence my attempt at coining a term to indicate the phenomenon.

31. See, for discussion of the phenomenon, *British Ballads from Maine*, pp. 193, 194, where Barry examines a group of tunes sung to Child No. 81.

32. See W. Christie, *Traditional Ballad Airs* (Edinburgh, 1876–81), I, 8, 9. Christie's representation is that he has joined strains which properly belong together, yet which were found apart in the memories of different traditional singers. It is only just to remark, however, that some of his second strains are set to airs which never appear elsewhere with them or any other additional matter; and that these added strains appear nowhere else outside the Christie edition.

33. See Greig-Keith, *Last Leaves of Traditional Ballads and Ballad Airs*, p. xliii.

34. This is a feature especially characteristic of Irish folk music; where the strains of the same air may sometimes be found written out in six bars of ¾ time, or in only two bars of ⁹⁄₈ time. Irish airs—and Irish versions of internationally current melodies—also show tune-lines of five bars' length; hence strains of ten bars each.

35. My language here may be considered strange; but it is unavoidable when considering the character of the musical settings to folk song words. Since (as implied in note 34) the melodies are adaptable to songs in varied meters, and

appear in forms so adapted, metrical considerations do not necessarily fix the form and rhythm of a folk tune permanently. Hence, they do not apply to studies directed toward melodic identification.

36. See, for example, the late ballad "Walter Lesly" (Child No. 296), with its recurrent stanza-ending line about going "to Conland, this winter-time to lye." The practice was a favorite one with broadside ballad writers.

37. *Journal of the English Folk Dance and Song Society*, V (1946), 22. The air which called forth this note was correctly characterized as being obviously only half a tune.

38. Just how uncertain these matters can be, a number of variant forms of tunes might illustrate. For instance, the old melody called "Cupid's Garden" is printed by Chappell (*Popular Music of the Olden Time*, II, 728) with two strains. The phrase-design is AB / A'B', which may further be resolved into abcd / ebcfx: the first strain shows tonic-dominant modulation at the end, and the second is furnished with an extension passage (x). Chappell notes (*ibid.*, p. 727) how singers sometimes "cut" the f-phrase. This version of Chappell's is rare in recorded sets of the tune. A much more widespread version, without either modulation or extension, may be diagrammed thus: AA' / BA, or abac / ebac. It is known in England, Lowland Scotland, Ireland, North America, and even (in one isolated variant) in Flanders—where it was no doubt imported from the British Isles. Forms of the second half only of this more common set are likewise found in tradition. Also, I have recovered, in Pennsylvania and West Virginia, sets that may be rendered in diagrams thus: cfcx and cfcx / eb'cx. Now the question is: Which of these variant forms actually corresponds most to the original? Since we cannot determine this satisfactorily, we cannot actually tell which sets may have been worn down first and then rebuilt—or, indeed, whether there has been any wearing down at all in the full-length sets. In the shorter sets (cfcx, etc.) we may indeed plausibly guess at a wearing-down; but we can feel no certainty about the others. When one is confronted with versions varying in this manner, the difficulty in making a decision about their development-relations becomes very real indeed.

39. It is of course obvious that a number of ballads and songs which we customarily record in the regular, or common, ballad-stanza are set to airs showing the phrase-pattern in question.

40. For example, the tune so often found joined with the ballad of "The Golden Glove" as, e.g., in Sharp-Karpeles, *English Folk Songs from the Southern Appalachians*, I, 377 f., and in many other collections. Yet this is one of the tunes uniquely set in Christie's *Traditional Ballad Airs* (II, 114) to a second strain (made up out of material from the first), and thus there appearing in a form double the length of the otherwise universally known version.

41. Phillips Barry once expressed the opinion that "folk melodies are of simple structure, for the most part, with a constant tendency toward greater simplicity." Barry's utterances about folk music are nearly always of an unshakable justice and correctness; yet in this case I wonder if he was not a little hasty? Is it not possible that the relative degree of simplicity or elaboration (both rather uncertain and debatable quantities) in a folk tune may depend to some extent on the type of song to which any version of the tune is set? At any rate it seems plain that

recomposition is not always in the direction of greater simplification or abbreviation (cf. note 38). Barry's remark quoted above is in his "Some Aspects of Folk-Song," *JAF*, XXV (1912), 274–83, reprinted in *Folk Music in America*, ed. G. Herzog and H. Halpert (National Service Bureau, Federal Theatre Project, Works Progress Administration, 1939); see p. 43 of this reprint.

42. Reference may be made to S. Baring-Gould, H. F. Sheppard, F. W. Bussell, *Songs of the West*, 2d ed., C. J. Sharp (London, 1905), p. 108; C. J. Sharp, ed., *English Folk Songs* (London: Novello, 1919), I, i, ff.; this same set also in Sharp's *Folk Songs from Somerset* (2d series; London, 1905), p. 6; *JFSS*, I, No. 2 (1900), p. 44, No. 4 (1902), p. 162; IV, No. 2 (1910), p. 92, No. 4 (1913), pp. 301–3. The striking variety and different ramifications of these sets, however, come out even more clearly in the numerous versions scattered through C. J. Sharp's MS collection, as also is plainly apparent their interconnection one with another.

43. Representative members of this tune-group may be seen in Sharp-Karpeles, *English Folk Songs from the Southern Appalachians*, I, 410; Barry, *British Ballads from Maine*, p. xxx; *Songs of the West*, p. 8; Sharp, *English Folk Songs* (1919), II, 20; *JFSS*, I, 214; II, 44, 46, 95, 96, 206, 274, 275; V, 190, 192.

44. Similarly puzzling are the interrelations of a group of tunes set to English texts of many love songs belonging to the "Turtle Dove–Truelover's Farewell" complex, itself a song-family consisting of texts that are highly complicated in their relations.

45. Bartók, in *Hungarian Folk Music*, p. 8, notes that Hungarian tunes are "extraordinarily rich in different endings to tune-lines." I am not certain, however, that the phenomenon he refers to is the same as that discussed in the present article.

46. Perhaps one example may illustrate sufficiently for the moment: the strikingly variant ending to the second line of a Cornish singer's tune to the "Outlandish Knight" ballad (Child No. 4), *JFSS*, IV, Pt. 2 (1910), 116. One of these cadential closes represents an ordinary one for the tune, which is widely known; the other is unusual.

47. See Jackson's *White and Negro Spirituals* (New York: J. J. Augustin, cop. 1943), p. 329, note to No. 24; p. 333, note to No. 62, and the airs they refer to; also see page 266 for a brief characterization of this "general melodizing," or "simple repetitive melodizing," as he also calls it.

48. Or, if it does not grow larger, perhaps, then, it gradually alters in such a way that the repertory itself changes little by little from one to another stock of tunes (?). The statement that oral re-creation is a cause of gradual growth in our tune-repertory, however, was made by Barry shortly before his lamented death— see *Bulletin of the Folk-Song Society of the Northeast*, No. 12 (1937), p. 11, col. 2—and since there Barry expressed in one sentence the idea that my own studies have, I think, amply evidenced, and are intended to demonstrate, I naturally consider his suggestion the correct one.

49. Some words of an experienced Irish student and collector may indicate that this postulate is not a mere fancy of my own. In *A Handbook of Irish Music*, p. 190, Fr. Richard Henebry remarks that "it may be useful to explain that whenever a mu-

sician heard a note or an ascent passage in a tune that he considered an improvement, he straightway incorporated it in his own version. I particularly remember,
in my own case, as a boy, how . . . I used to listen . . . to . . . tramp pipers
or fiddlers . . . especially if their style was good . . . in order to assimilate for
myself such changes of version or interpretation as I considered suitable. And I
never knew an Irish musician who did not do the same." Fr. Henebry is here speaking more especially of folk instrumentalists; I, following the internal evidence of
our folk song tunes, am assuming that folk vocalists have done the very thing he
outlines in the words just quoted.

50. This variety is commented on by Werner Danckert, *Das Europäische
Volkslied* (Berlin: Hanhefeld, 1939), pp. 101–4, who considers it the result of
much mixture of musical influences from differing cultures.

51. See, for instance, Marjory Kennedy-Fraser, *Songs of the Hebrides* (London: Boosey & Co.), Vol. II (cop. 1917), p. xiii.

52. I hope that I have not unduly slighted Welsh folk music in treating its
style, by implication as part of the English. What I have just said about the style
of the English tunes and versions, however, also applies to the Welsh; and it is a
matter of record that, despite the presence of a real national Welsh repertory of
traditional airs, some of the very popular Welsh tunes are also common to England
and other British nationalities. Furthermore, it looks as though the Welsh harpers
have been adopting—and adapting—English tunes for a long while. See the list
given by Chappell, *Popular Music of the Olden Time*, I, 64, note *a*—a list by no
means exhaustive.

However, Welsh tunes have themselves some distinctive stylistic features—the
most prominent among them being tonic-dominant modulation, and a tendency to
indulge in melodic sequence, which I take to be elements of instrumental, not
vocal, technique in British traditional music. And Welsh tunes have, like the
others, travelled about among other British peoples. An instance of how sensitive
an earlier collector of folk music could be to national or regional style may be
drawn from Simon Fraser's *Airs . . . Peculiar to the Highlands of Scotland*. In
commenting upon tune No. 146, p. 69, Fraser says (p. 114), "This air the Editor
supposed to be Welsh." He goes on to say that it has not appeared among the
Welsh melodies. Fraser was right in the first instance and wrong in the second.
The tune is indeed Welsh, being a version of the old harpers' melody "Merch
Megan" (Megan's Daughter); and it has certainly appeared more than once in
Welsh collections. Versions may be seen, for example, in *British Harmony* (1781)
—one of the famous "Blind John" Parry's publications—No. 36, p. 35; and in
Edward Jones, *Musical and Poetical Relicks of the Welsh Bards* (London, 1794),
p. 149. A version is printed, with commentary, in Alfred Moffatt's *Minstrelsy of
Wales*; but I cannot furnish exact reference, since the volume is unavailable to
me at the moment.

53. Examples are the song-airs from Co. Waterford in *JFSS*, III (1907–9),
6–38.

54. See Padraic Colum, *Anthology of Irish Verse* (New York: Boni and
Liveright, 1922), p. 8.

55. Examples are P. W. Joyce, *Old Irish Folk Music and Songs* (London: Longmans, Green & Co., 1909), No. 614, p. 316, "The Cuckoo"; and the second part of "Molly St. George" in Bunting's 1796 collection, ed. D. J. O'Sullivan: *Journal of the Irish Folk Song Society*, Vols. 22–23, 1925–26 (1927), p. 43.

56. Compare the air to "A Óganaigh Óig" in D. J. O'Sullivan's edition of the 1796 Bunting collection, *Journal of the Irish Folk Song Society*, Vol. 25, 1928 (1930), p. 12.

57. A few three-phrase tunes have turned up in the American repertory of British folk tunes—all of them being shortened from the normal four-phrase form of one of our most widely known airs. These special versions are curiously restricted in their diffusion, being mostly from Kentucky, with occasional scattered examples elsewhere. See, for example, Sharp-Karpeles, *English Folk Songs from the Southern Appalachians*, I, 317–27, to "The Cruel Ship's Carpenter," versions F (Ky.), G (Ky.), L (Ky.), N (Ky.), T (Va.).—The three-phrase organization so popular among American Negroes generally affects a set of tunes entirely different from those in our Anglo-American repertory.

58. In *JFSS*, IV, Pt. 3 (1911), x.

59. For which see Lucy Broadwood and A. J. Fuller-Maitland, *English County Songs* (London, 1893), p. 36, and *JFSS*, VII, Pt. 2 (1924), 124. The tune called "The Sheep under the Snow" (*English County Songs*, pp. 38–39, *JFSS*, VII, pp. 117, 118) would seem, if not an exclusively Manx air, to have taken a very distinctive shape in the Isle. It is not impossible that it is of island origin. See Miss Gilchrist's note, *JFSS*, *loc. cit.*

60. The record is not assembled in one place; but the influence of Scots and Gaelic dance music on the tunes to English country dances can be observed by anyone who cares to examine the published collectanea.

61. A lone example of a really Scottish-Highland-style tune occurs in the J. S. James edition of the *Original Sacred Harp* (1911; reprinted Atlanta, Georgia, 1929), p. 326, entitled "Weary Pilgrim." The air is there attributed to one L. P. Breedlove, a singing-leader and "composer," one of the revisers of the 1850 *Sacred Harp.*

62. See the camp-meeting spirituals in George Pullen Jackson's *White Spirituals in the Southern Uplands* (Chapel Hill: University of North Carolina Press, 1933); *Spiritual Folk-Songs of Early America* (New York: J. J. Augustin, cop. 1937); *Down East Spirituals and Others* (New York: Augustin, 1943); L. L. McDowell, *Songs of the Old Camp Ground* (Ann Arbor, Mich.: Edwards Bros., Inc., 1937).

63. See Edward Deming Andrews, "Shaker Songs," *The Musical Quarterly* (New York: G. Schirmer), XXIII, No. 4 (Oct., 1937), 491–508; same author, *The Gift to be Simple* (New York: J. J. Augustin, cop. 1940).

64. This view, or its practical equivalent, has recently been developed at length for folklore in general by Carlos Vega, *Panorama de la Musica Popular Argentina* (Buenos Aires: Editorial Losada, S. A., cop. 1944), pp. 19–108. Vega's theories are reminiscent of Hans Naumann's concept of *gesunkenes Kulturgut* and of similar notions dating back to Hoffmann-Krayer and John Meier (Volkstümlichkeit).

65. Cf., for folk traditions in general, W. R. Halliday, *Folklore Studies, Ancient and Modern* (London: Methuen & Co., Ltd., 1942), p. 146. Cf. also Rodney Gallop, *Portugal, A Book of Folk-Ways* (Cambridge: at the University Press, 1936), xiv, 198, 199, for pronouncements on folk-music in general, as well as on Portuguese popular airs. Statements such as the last cited show a complete misunderstanding of the so-called "distortion" (i.e., re-creation) of music by folk musicians; of its conventional, traditional, and essentially cultured and *artistic* nature; and above all, of its cumulative potentialities in moulding and forming the traditional music of a group.

66. Characteristic versions may be seen in C. J. Sharp, *Folk Songs from Somerset*, 2d Series, pp. 10, 11; E. B. Greenleaf and G. Y. Mansfield, *Ballads and Sea Songs of Newfoundland* (Cambridge: Harvard University Press, 1933), pp. 61, 62.

67. For this tune see the edition of Robert Jones' *First Booke of Songes and Ayres*, 1600, by E. H. Fellowes (The English School of Lutenist Song Writers, 2d Series, No. 4; London: Stainer & Bell, Ltd., cop. 1925), pp. 36–39. With the Jones air compare especially the "Sovay" tunes in Greenleaf and Mansfield, *pp. cit.*, p. 63; *JFSS*, III, No. 2 (1907), pp. 127–28 (all three tunes); *JFSS*, VIII, No. 4 (1930), pp. 225, 227, second version; *Oxford History of Music*, Introductory Volume, ed. Percy C. Buck (Oxford University Press, 1929), p. 178.

68. *JAF*, LXI (1948), 210.

69. What may be thought an exception to this rule is furnished by sets of the tune to which is generally sung "General Wolfe," or "The Taking of Quebec." See *JFSS*, VI, No. 1 (1918), 8–10 and accompanying notes; also *JFSS*, VIII, No. 4 (1930), 179, 180. This air, however, may be called "thinly scattered" in tradition, and is not related to any of the dominant or widespread tune-families at all. Its versions are few, and its distribution apparently confined to England and Ireland (one recorded version, *v. JFSS*, VI, the notes cited). What is more significant yet, the recorded versions differ among themselves in a curious way, indicating the progress of folk re-creation of the tune into a shape more congenial to traditional taste than the presumed original, cited *JFSS*, VI, 10. On the failure of investigators to find the originals of the great bulk of our folk airs in older art music, see Sabine Baring-Gould, *A Garland of Country Song* (London, 1895), p. x; R. Vaughan Williams, *National Music* (London: Oxford University Press, 1934), p. 30.

70. E.g., once more, the melodies of American Shakers and the other white religious groups that produced folk spirituals.

71. Some words of Bartók are especially to the point here: "Village art can only be a spontaneous manifestation; the last hour has struck for village art at the moment one interferes and attempts to guide it artistically. Precisely for this reason it would be completely futile to wish, as people have recently tried time and again, to develop village music in this or that direction, to revive old melodies in the village, and similar efforts. If the people of the village do not themselves produce their art from themselves, or choose it, their art is ended." *Die Volksmusik der Magyaren und der benachbarten Völker*, Ausdruck: Ungarische Jahrbücher, Bd. XV, Heft. 2, 3; Ungarische Bibliothek, Reihe I, No. 20 (Berlin: Walter de Gruyter, 1935), p. 19.

THE METER OF THE POPULAR BALLAD

1. For typographical convenience the septenary is frequently broken at the cæsura, and printed as two lines. Child usually followed this practice. The manner of printing, of course, makes no real difference, and I know of no metrist who has failed to recognize the full line as the real unit. In quotation I have not attempted any consistency in this matter, but in metrical notation have always represented the line as a whole.

2. See "A Method toward the Study of Dipodic Verse," by the present writer, *PMLA*, XXXIX, 979–89.

3. Briefly, the Dipodic Index (D) is obtained by the formula:

$$\text{D} = \text{A} + \text{B}$$

A is the figure obtained by subtracting the percentage of syllables of weak stress in the primary position from the percentage of the same class of syllables in the secondary position. B is a corresponding figure, i.e., the result of subtracting the percentage of heavily stressed syllables in the secondary position from the percentage of the same class of syllables in the primary position. A negative value is thus possible, but need not be considered as having any other value than zero. This index gives a rough-and-ready mathematical expression of the strength of the dipodic tendency. If anything, it is conservative, underestimating rather than exaggerating. To be really appreciated the dipodic movement of the verse must be felt in reading.

4. It is difficult to select what could be a really representative list of ballads. In the above I have tried to offer a wide range of type, and the result may accordingly seem to be a rather haphazard collection. It is, however, the full product of my counting (see below for *James Harris*, and *The King's Disguise*); no ballad has been suppressed because its evidence tended to disprove the thesis. Moreover, if the reader misses from the list certain characteristic ballads, he must remember that for the present only one type of meter is being considered (the "septenary" without frequent trisyllabic substitution); *Lord Lovel, Lord Randal*, and *Hind Horn*, as examples, represent types of ballad structure which will be considered later.

5. For the longer ballads the first twenty-five lines have been counted. In such lines as:

Sir Patrick Spence is the best sailor

the last stress has been counted as falling upon the unaccented syllable of the last word. This of course aids in raising the dipodic index, but I believe that is at least in spirit the proper interpretation (see below). In *Fair Annie* (A) the suspected stanzas (8, 9, 10) have been omitted from the counting.

6. Dipodic structure appears also in literary verse, as the result of conscious desire for that effect (see e.g. much of the work of Kipling and Masefield). The poems counted show, however, that it is not a part of the ordinary septenarius technique in modern English verse.

7. As sources of airs I have used mainly the appendices to the Child collection

and to Motherwell's *Minstrelsy*, together with Campbell and Sharp's *English Folk Songs from the Southern Appalachians*. As examples of the way in which the ballads are transcribed into the less common times, with maintenance of the dipodic analogy, see: (1) two-four time: Child 281, 299D, Motherwell XXII; (2) three-four: Child 99A, 169C, Motherwell VIII, XI, XIX; (3) six-eight: Child 163, Motherwell XXIV, Campbell 2A; (4) two-two: Campbell 20C, 15A; (5) three-two and two-two mingled: Campbell 2D, 3A; (6) six-four: Campbell 11C. Even in five-four time four notes can be kept to the measure and four measures to the line (see Campbell, 16C). Different tunes to the same ballad are frequently in different times (see Child 169, and Campbell *passim*).

8. For examples see "Bonny Lizie Baillie," "Judas," "Captain Wedderburn's Courtship," "Lord Thomas and Fair Annet," "Walter Lesly," *et al*. A better interpretation of this situation, especially in connection with music, would perhaps be

$$|\,\acute{\smile}\,\smile\,\acute{\smile}\,\smile\,|\,\acute{\smile}\,\acute{\smile}$$

i.e. a secondary stress falls upon the second syllable of the second dipod. This practice is on the whole more typical of the song and the nursery rhyme than of the ballad, e.g.,

> Sing a song of sixpence . . . .
> Taffy came to my house.

By either interpretation the evidence for dipodic structure is equally strong, so that there is no need to decide here which is preferable.

9. This usage is so general as scarcely to demand references. For other good examples, however, see "Fair Annie," and "The Lass of Roch Royal."

10. See e.g. "Lamkin" (A) 8, 9, 10, 11.

11. The foot might rather be said to be $|-\!-\smile\smile$. The intervention of the cæsura with its extra-metrical pause, however, breaks the metrical time sufficiently to produce the effect of a trisyllabic dipod with an anacrusis at the opening of the second half-line.

12. This situation is a rather complex one. Professor R. W. Gordon of the University of California, who is closely in touch with modern usage in singing and reciting ballads, believes that both methods are used. He reads, for instance, "the bést sailór," but "a braid létter." Since both make good rhythm and are in harmony with the dipodic structure, a positive decision is not necessary for present purposes. Except perhaps in a few words which have conventionally a shifting accent, as, *lady* (*ladye*), and *country* (*countree*), I should personally prefer the second interpretation. Usage of this sort is not uncommon in modern poetry, e.g. in Hilaire Belloc's "South Country":

> The men who live in west England . . .
> The great hills of the south country.

Masefield's "West Wind" shows the usage with a vocative:

> So will you not come home, brother, and rest your tired feet?

These later occurrences may be reminiscent of the ballads, but they show nevertheless, that the rhythm appeals to the modern poetic ear.

13. For some of the very rare exceptions see "Child Maurice," e.g., in the A version:

> 'Here is a glove, a glove,' he says
> 'Lined with the silver grey.'

14. An interesting detail of similar import is to be seen in the use of trisyllabic proper names which occur frequently repeated in certain ballads. Thus "Carterhaugh" would naturally call for a primary accent upon the first and a secondary accent upon the third syllable, and in the nine versions of "Tam Lin" published by Child this word (or some analogue) occurs fifty-three times, *always* so placed as to have its natural accentuation correspond with the dipodic structure of the verse. The usage for "Patrick Spens" ($\acute{~}\smile\acute{~}$), and "Gregory" (in "The Lass of Roch Royal") is nearly as consistent, while "Roch Royal" itself is used twenty-five times, and like "Carterhaugh" carries always the same accentuation.

15. See e.g. Campbell No. 2, 7.

16. This can be illustrated. On the one hand we have:

> 'Come riddle my riddle, dear mother,' he said,
> 'And riddle us both as one.'
> (Lord Thomas and Fair Annet-D)

Here the line is largely trisyllabic, but the nature of the unaccented syllables in so unemphatic that the dipodic swing can still be felt. The situation is different, however, in

> What made the bells of the high chapel ring,
> The ladys make all their moan.
> (Lord Lovel-A)

Here such important words as a noun and a verb are used in the trisyllable substitutions, the necessity of logical stress as a result destroys the simplicity of the dipodic structure.

17. This same distinction may be seen in different versions of the same ballad. Although the broadside version of "James Harris" has no appreciable dipodic tendency, a popular version (F) reaches the quite marked dipodic index of 21. This might be developed into a corroborative test to aid in distinguishing the truly popular ballad from broadsides and imitations.

18. Note that the cæsura remains in the same position.

19. This same tendency may also appear in texts of frequent trisyllabic substitution, e.g. "Alison Gross."

20. For this "carry-through" type of ballad set to times other than four-four, see e.g. Motherwell II, IX.

21. This depends somewhat upon whether we consider *bairn* as of one or two syllables. With the Scottish trilled *r* it is usually more nearly the latter.

22. The attempt to read "Lamkin" and similar texts as lines of four simple feet would necessitate often four and sometimes five syllables in one foot. Only a dipodic foot can stand such expansion.

23. The tabulation below shows the surprising way in which the different ballad texts display the transition from the four-syllable to the three-syllable dipod: (1) No three-syllable—"Lamkin"-P. (2) Three-syllable rare—"Lord Randal"-K, J, L, M, O; "Baron of Braickley"-D; "Lord Saltoun and Auchanachie"-B; "Lamkin"-A *et al.*; "Cherry-Tree Carol"-D. (3) Three-syllable and four-syllable approximately balanced—"Cherry-Tree"-C; "Lamkin"-B *et al.*; "Lord Delamere"-A, C, D. (4) Three-syllable predominating—"Lamkin"-C, G; "Death of Queen Jane"-B; "Delamere"-B; "Glenlogie"-I. (5) Three-syllable except for a few instances—"Lord Randal"-A, C, D, F, I; "Bonnie Annie"-A; "Lamin"-R, T; "Queen Jane"-A, C; "Braickley"-A, B, C; "Charlie Macpherson"-B; "Glenlogie"-A, B, C, D, E, G, H; "Saltoun"-A. (6) Three-syllable exclusively, or at least no absolutely certain case of a four-syllable foot—"Randal"-B, E, G, H; "Bonnie Annie"-B, "Queen Jane"-D, E, F, G; "James Campbell" all versions; "Macpherson"-A; "Glenlogie"-F.

24. Another possible reading of this line would be:

$$\smile-|-\smile-|-\smile\wedge\wedge|-\smile-|-$$

25. Note should be made of the use of the dissyllabic (as well as trisyllabic) dipod in refrains. Since these are often meaningless, they can hardly be said to have metrical significance. By analogy, however, they are important in giving a firmer basis for the practice. Examples are:

> Eh vow bonnie (Babylon-A)
> Hey nien nanny (Sir Lionel-B)
> Fa la lilly (King Edelbrode, fragment)

26. Such lines as:

> He's ben and ben and ben to his bed

naturally suggest the inquiry as to whether ballads ever occur in "octosyllabic" lines. This might easily be the case by development from the analogy of such lines as the above, or by development of a prevailingly dissyllabic dipodic structure with the subsequent decay of the dipodic basis as the text worked away from the music. Some of the trisyllabic texts (e.g. those of "Lord Randal") really display some such result, but, in spite of the fact that I should welcome it for its analogies, I do not believe that we have any ballads which are octosyllabic even by the broadest interpretation. Apparent octosyllabic texts really have refrains which fill out the line. In some cases these have not been preserved in all the versions, but it is usually true (see e.g. "Hind Horn") that the texts which lack refrains are those which have been recorded from recitation. Ballads transcribed from actual singing generally show that the octosyllabic line is in reality expanded by the refrain. Only two ballads have octosyllabic texts without refrains in any version. Of these "Willie's Lady" exists only in one version going back to two sources neither of which apparently was transcribed from singing; "The

Suffolk Miracle" on the other hand is a broadside text, and cannot be considered as evidence of true ballad technique.

27. Other such ballads are: "Sir Patrick Spens" (E), "The Broomfield Hill" (D), "The Two Brothers" (B), "Sir Hugh" (M, N), "The Duke of Athole's Nurse" (C, D, F), "The Earl of Aboyne" (D, et al.), "The Rantin Laddie" (A, D), "The Farmer's Curst Wife." See also below.

28. Another possible reading is:

$$|--\cup|--|\wedge\cup-\cup|--|\wedge-\cup|--|-\cup-|-$$

This does not appeal to my own ear, but I have heard others use it. Note that it omits syllables of primary stress—not an ordinary ballad practice.

29. This development of internal rhyme with the resulting formation of a stanza here displayed is analogous to the same practice in the other more complex forms of ballad meter. Whenever the line becomes very long, it tends to reinforce its structure by additional rhymes. See e.g. "Broomfield Hill" (D), "Mussel-burth Field," "The Broom of Cowdenknowes," "The Grey Cock," *et al.*

30. The airs for this ballad in Motherwell, and Campbell and Sharp are of no aid in this connection. They represent simpler versions of the text.

BALLAD SOURCE STUDY: CHILD BALLAD NO. 4

1. J. W. Walker, *The True History of Robin Hood* (Wakefield, 1952).

2. Cited in F. J. Child, *English and Scottish Popular Ballads*, I (Boston, 1882–98), 24.

3. Svend Grundtvig, *Danmarks gamle Folkeviser*, IV (Copenhagen, 1853 f.), 29.

4. See Léon Pineau, *Les Vieux Chants Populaires Scandinaves*, I (Paris, 1898), 264.

5. Ludwig Erk and Franz Böhme, *Deutscher Liederhort*, I (Leipzig, 1893–94), 150.

6. Child, *English and Scottish Ballads*, I, 195.

7. Erk and Böhme, *Deutscher Liederhort*, I, 148–49.

8. Paul Kretschmer, "Das Märchen von Blaubart," *Mitteilungen der Anthropologischen Gesellschaft in Wien*, XXXI (1901), 62–70.

9. Friedrich Holz, *Das Mädchenräuberballade* (Heidelberg, 1929), pp. 86–102.

10. Holz, *Das Mädchenräuberballade*, p. 94.

11. Pineau, *Les Vieux Chants*, I.

12. Andreas Heusler, "Über die Balladendichtung des Spätmittelalters namentlich im skandinavischen Norden," *Germanisch-Romanische Monatsschrift*, X (1922), 19.

13. Paul de Keyser, "Het Lied van Halewijn. Een psycho-analytisch Onderzoek," *Nederlandsch Tijdschrift voor Volkskunde*, XXVII (1922), 165–74.

14. Sophus Bugge, "Bidrag til Nordiske balladedigtnings Historie," *Det Philologisk-historiske Samfunds Mindeskrift, 1854–1879* (Copenhagen, 1879), pp. 75–92.

15. In his own words: "Efter disse Bemaerkninger skal jeg gjennemgaa Balladen, som den foreligger i de mangfoldige skriftende Former, for at paavise Forbindelser med Fortaellingen om Judith og Holofernes" (p. 81).

16. Karl Müllenhoff and W. Scherer, *Denkmäler deutscher Poesie und Prosa aus dem VIII–XII Jahrhundert* (Berlin, 1892), p. 141.

17. Bugge's emendation does not agree with any suggested by various editors of the poem. See Müllenhoff and Scherer, *Denkmäler deutscher Poesie und Prosa*, p. 141.

18. Hoffman von Fallersleben, *Horae Belgicae II. Niederländische Volkslieder*, 2nd ed. (Hannover, 1856), pp. 43–46.

19. In his Headnote, he describes Bugge's argument as an "entirely novel and somewhat startling hypothesis" (Child, *English and Scottish Popular Ballads*, I, 51).

20. Letter dated 21 March 1880, cited in S. B. Hustvedt, *Ballad Books and Ballad Men* (Cambridge, Mass., 1930, Appendix A, "The Grundtvig-Child Correspondence," p. 286.

21. Pineau, *Les Vieux Chants*, I, 263.

LAMBKIN: A STUDY IN EVOLUTION

1. Christie's *Traditional Ballad Airs*, I, 60. A second strain follows which may be ignored.

2. The earliest printed tune for "Lammikin," from R. A. Smith's *Scotish Ministrel*, 1821–24 ed., II, 94.

3. *Caledonian Musical Repository*, 1806; Herd directs "Lammikin" to be sung to "Gil Morrice."

4. Rymour Club *Miscellanea*, II, pt. iii, p. 136.

5. There is a ballad of "The Water o' Wearie's Well."

6. All of the lettered versions were noted by Maud Karpeles in Newfoundland; "A" and "B" at Conception Bay, "C" at Placentia Bay, and "D" at Fortune Bay.

7. The name "Orange" has probably been evolved from the line "O still my bairn, norice." At the same time, Orange occurs as a girl's name in *Journal*, II, 295, "The Story of Orange"—another version being called "Orange and Lemon."

8. Child's E (from Kinloch's manuscript) bridges the versions north and south of the Border.

9. Even in Percy's copy the singer had interpolated explanations, and said that Longkin and the nurse were engaged in plundering the house when the lord came home.

10. In most of the Scottish versions Betsy does not figure, and she seems to have been a later addition.

11. In one English version he retorts:

> "That for your daughter Betsy!
> She may do me some good,
> She may hold the silver basin
> To catch your heart's blood."

In another:

> "I don't want your daughter Betsy, nor none of the rest,
> I should rather see my naked sword through your milk-white breast."

12. Perhaps influenced by "Fortune"—a woman's name current in England in the seventeenth and eighteenth centuries and carried to New England.

SCRIBAL AND TYPOGRAPHICAL ERROR

1. Even the un- or semi-sophisticated ballad singer of Sir Walter Scott's day saw fit to deplore and condemn printed tradition. The mother of James Hogg, whence came no few of Scott's best texts, has this comment to make about the collecting and printing of ballads: "An ye hae spoilt them a' thegither. They were made for singing, an' no for readin; an they are nouther right spelled nor right setten doun." Of the effect of this incorrect spelling I shall have more to say below.

2. See, for example, H. Tolman's and O. Eddy's discussion of the transmission of "James Harris" (The Daemon Lover), Child No. 243, in "Ballad Texts and Tunes," *JAF*, XXXV, 347, in which the De Marsan Broadside is shown to be the probable source for most of the American variants of this ballad. As I have pointed out in my own article, "Ballad Place Names," *JAF*, LIX, 263–67, however, there appear to be two distinct traditions for this ballad in America, one stemming from the printed De Marsan Broadside and one purely oral in tradition, the two eventually coalescing to produce yet a third version, a not improbable process for many other ballads as well.

3. The attitudes of folklorists and literary scholars differ considerably on this point even when both are applying canons of taste. Cecil Sharp wrote in 1907 in *English Folk-Song: Some Conclusions* (London: Simpkin & Co., p. 10) that "The method of oral transmission is not merely one by which the folksong lives; it is a process by which it grows and by which it is created," a point of view which Don Ramón Menéndez Pidal emphasized in his *Poesia popular y Poesia tradicional en la Literatura Española* (Oxford: Oxford University Press, 1922, p. 22) when he insisted that variants were not accidents but rather essential elements of communal poetizing. Professor John Robert Moore—"The Influence of Transmission on the English Ballads," *MLR*, XI (Oct. 1916), 387—says however: "After a painstaking study of the subject, I have yet to find a clear case where a ballad can be shown to have improved as a result of oral transmission, except in the way of becoming more lyrical. As far as the narrative element is concerned, tradition works nothing but corruption in the ballad . . ." This dichotomy of opinion is still current, but I suggest that the argument rests upon the canons of taste applied, upon the fact that ballads are looked upon as a group rather than as individual pieces of literature which must be studied separately, and upon the fact which appears obvious at least to me that re-creation is found wherever the group is homogeneous, corruption where it is not.

4. See, for examples of the more lengthy treatment of the subject, such landmarks in ballad scholarship as John Meier's *Kunstlieder im Volksmunde* (Halle, 1906, pp. xix ff.), F. B. Gummere's *The Popular Ballad* (Boston, 1907, pp. 61–

66), Phillips Barry's two articles, "William Carter, the Bensontown Homer"— *JAF*, XXVI (April–June, 1912), 156–68—and "The Transmission of Folk-Song" *JAF*, XXVII (January–March, 1914), 67–76—the article by Professor John Robert Moore quoted above, and Professor Gordon Hall Gerould's *The Ballad of Tradition* (Oxford: Oxford University Press, 1932, pp. 163–88, *et passim*) to mention only a few.

5. Francis James Child, *The English and Scottish Popular Ballads* (Boston, 1892–98), V, 294–95. Hereafter the number in parentheses will serve as sufficient documentation for ballads appearing in the Child collection unless there is some textual peculiarity or unless the variant referred to appears out of numerical order in the collection.

6. *JAF*, XLIV (1931), 63–64.

7. John Harrington Cox, *Folksongs of the South* (Cambridge, Mass.: Harvard University Press, 1925), p. 93.

8. *Folk Songs from the Southern Appalachians* (London: Oxford University Press, 1932), I, 17.

9. John W. Hales and Frederick J. Furnivall, *Bishop Percy's Folio Manuscript* (London, 1867), I, 313–40.

10. Child, *English and Scottish Popular Ballads*, II, 378–79.

11. Phillips Barry, Fannie Hardy Eckstorm, and Mary Winslow Smyth, *British Ballads from Maine* (New Haven: Yale University Press, 1929), pp. 216, 219.

12. Hales and Furnivall, *Percy's Folio MSS*, II, 338–89.

13. In support of my contention that such corruptions are primarily scribal, note that variant H comes from a sophisticated Irish woman living in the United States while variant L* derives from a penny broadside originating in England.

14. James Brown Johnston, *Place-Names of Scotland* (3rd ed.; London: J. Murray, 1934).

15. Gavin Greig, *Last Leaves of Traditional Ballads and Ballad Airs*, ed. by Alexander Keith (Aberdeen: The Buchan Club, 1925), p. 269.

16. Child, IV, 383.

17. *JAF*, LIX, 267.

18. Peter Buchan, *Ancient Ballads and Songs of the North of Scotland* (Edinburgh, 1828), I, 221.

19. The name derives from W *Pen-mæn*, "head of the stone," and English *score*, ME *scor*, ON *skor*, "notch, tally." The reference is to a nick or hollow on top of a ridge of hills.

20. 3 vols. (Edinburgh, 1812), I, 95.

21. Child, V, 194–97, variant B.

22. For an excellent analysis of the creation of new sense by oral transmission of one ballad, see Edwin Shepeard Miller, "Nonsense and New Sense in 'Lord Thomas,'" *SFQ*, I, No. 4 (December 1937), 25–37.

23. Hales and Furnivall, I, 292–312.

24. In further support of this hypothesis it might be pointed out that the town of Carnabie is an identifiable place in the East Riding of Yorkshire, an area central to the revolt in the north.

25. For further examples of corruptions in this ballad and emendations which

have contributed to confusion, see my article in *JAF*, LIX, 263–64 and notes 1–2 on those pages.

26. This epitaph in this exact form except for the arrangement of the printed lines is also appended to "Robin Hood's Death and Burial." See Thomas Evans, *Old Ballads* (London, 1810), II, 266.

THE SCOTTISH BALLADS

1. Since metre of this sort was not introduced into English verse (from the French) until the fourteenth century, the ballads must have undergone surprising structural, as well as linguistic, changes, if one adopts the "primitivist" view.

2. "Most of these ballads," says Bishop Percy of his *Reliques*, "are of great simplicity, and seem to have been merely written [sic] for the people."

3. He names "Mr. Addison, Mr. Dryden and the witty Lord Dorset" in a footnote.

4. But the importance of the refrain to the ballads as we have them has been over-emphasized, I think.

5. Mr. Robert Graves is interested in the "ballads" that came into existence among the British troops during the war, but these are the merest drivel as he would agree.

6. The beautiful English specifically religious folkpoems (*St. Stephen and King Herod*, *The Cherry-Tree Carol*, for example) require to be appreciated separately and along with the Miracle Play.

THE BALLAD AS AN ART FORM

1. Maria Leach (ed.), *The Standard Dictionary of Folklore, Mythology, and Legend* (New York, 1949–50), I, 106.

2. Even the revolt against plotting that has taken place in much twentieth-century literature shows a definite consciousness of plotting.

3. "The Problem of Ballad Story Variation and Eugene Haun's 'Drowsy Sleeper,'" *Southern Folklore Quarterly*, XIV (1950), 87–96.

4. See, respectively, Arthur K. Davis, *Traditional Ballads of Virginia* (Cambridge, Mass., 1929), p. 188, and J. Harrington Cox, *Folk Songs of the South* (Cambridge, Mass., 1925), p. 18.

5. *Modern Language Review*, XI (1916), 404–5.

6. Broadside in the Yale University Library. See the Claude L. Frazer Collection, 2:5.

7. Narrative accretion may occur during Stage 2 also. But the addition of narrative detail in Stage 2, even when two whole ballads fuse, offers only a temporary setback to the steady movement toward Stage 3—lyric or nonsense.

8. Dorothy Scarborough, *A Songcatcher in the Southern Mountains* (New York, 1937), p. 213.

9. Phillips Barry (with Fannie H. Eckstorm and Mary W. Smyth), *British Ballads from Maine* (New Haven, 1929), pp. 303–4.

10. *JAF*, XLV (1932), p. 54.

11. *Publications of the Texas Folklore Society*, VII, p. 111, or X, p. 149.

12. It should be noted that a composition can move back up these stages at any time that an individual inserts morals, sentiment, and other poetic frills. Parodists, broadside writers, and the like, frequently made such changes, particularly in the eighteenth century. The Civil War parodies of "Lord Lovel" as printed in many Southern collections, and the moral version of "The Three Ravens" printed in *JAF*, XX (1907), 154, serve as examples. It is also true that a song may be composed at any one of the three stages, even at the lyric or nonsense stage; (see many of the minstrel tunes).

13. American ballads, which, as stated above, are usually in the process of moving from Stage 1 to Stage 2, are generally thought of as inferior to Child ballads when measured by Western European poetic standards.

14. See Child's *The English and Scottish Popular Ballads*, III, 384.

15. Sir Walter Scott, *Minstrelsy of the Scottish Border* (Edinburgh, 1833), II, 294 (Child I).

16. A. E. Housman, *Collected Poems* (New York, 1940), p. 114.

17. See Child for the texts of "The Twa Corbies," "Sir Patrick Spens," "Edward," and "Lord Randal" mentioned.